Making the Most of Small Groups

Differentiation for All

Debbie Diller

Stenhouse Publishers
Portland, Maine

Pembroke Publishers Limited
Markham, Ontario

KH

Stenhouse Publishers
www.stenhouse.com

Pembroke Publishers Limited
www.pembrokepublishers.com

Library of Congress Cataloging-in-Publication Data
Diller, Debbie, 1954–
    Making the most of small groups : differentiation for all / Debbie Diller.
    p. cm.
    Includes bibliographical references.
    ISBN-13: 978-1-57110-431-1 (pbk. : alk. paper)
    ISBN-10: 1-57110-431-3 (pbk. : alk. paper)
    1. Education, Primary—United States. 2. Small groups—Study and teaching (Primary)—United States. I. Title.

LB1507.D55 2006
372.41'62—dc22   2006031884

Published in Canada by
Pembroke Publishers Limited
538 Hood Road
Markham, Ontario L3R 3K9

Cover and interior design by Martha Drury
Cover photographs by Debbie Diller

Manufactured in the United States of America on acid-free paper
13 12 11 10 09 08 07   9 8 7 6 5 4

8/25/08

To my friends and colleagues at Augusta Elementary School, in Hampshire County, West Virginia

Contents

Acknowledgments

This book began as a dream . . . literally. I had just gotten home after spending a week (of many) consulting out of state, and I'd been thinking about small-group instruction on the plane. There had been so many questions and so much confusion about what to do in these groups. Was there a way I could clarify and simplify the small-group teaching process? I went to sleep, exhausted.

The next morning I awoke with a start. Overnight I'd dreamt the table of contents for this book. I bounded out of bed and quickly jotted it down, so I wouldn't forget the ideas. Several days later, I called Philippa Stratton, whom I thank from the bottom of my heart for her incredible support, and told her about my dream. We met for breakfast several weeks later, and she read my table of contents and offered me a contract on the spot.

I have been privileged to work with great numbers of teachers over the past dozen years, learning *with* them how to teach effectively in small groups. Dianne Frasier, thank you for being my first teacher of small groups. As I've told you many times, through your wise and thoughtful modeling, you taught me how to save Jessica as a reader. Thanks to so many teachers in so many places, including those in my adopted hometown, Houston, Texas— my colleagues who worked beside me at Hearne Elementary in Alief ISD, those who attended training in Aldine ISD, Alvin ISD, Clear Creek ISD, Cy-Fair ISD, Deer Park ISD, Houston ISD, Humble ISD, Katy ISD, Pearland ISD, Spring Branch ISD, and Tomball ISD. You allowed me to teach and coach in your classrooms, analyze the lessons, ask and answer tough questions, and problem-solve with you over and over again. Your administrative teams, including principals, assistant principals, curriculum directors, and other administrators, are visionary. Judy Wallis, thanks for teaching me to not be orthodox in my teaching of small groups and to remember that *fair is not equal*.

I'm grateful to the thousands of teachers across the United States and Canada who attended numerous trainings and conferences where I presented and who asked me how to best teach in small groups. I've listened to your questions and have used them to craft this book. I want to list every teacher and every school who has helped me, but there would be no pages left for this book. So, know who you are and use the ideas printed on these pages to help you dig further in your quest to better reach the needs of *all* students in your classrooms and school systems. Some of you are pictured in this book: Maria Bailey, Carol Baker, Kim Czubara, Camella Hardinger, Brenda Hogue, Tracy Hott, Tony Louden, Emily Milleson, Stacey Raley, and Annie Tennis.

Deep appreciation to Brenda Power, whose wisdom, insight, and encouragement made this book what it is. To the Stenhouse folks, both past and present, you are the best. Thanks to your creative team, who make these words appear in the book in front of you, and to your dedicated sales reps, who both sell the books *and* know them.

As always, a big thank-you hug to my friend and colleague Patty Terry, first-grade teacher extraordinaire, who continues to open her classroom to me any time I want to walk through the door. Your help is invaluable. Also, I am grateful to Gretchen Childs, my wonderful associate who eagerly read every page of this book as I wrote it so she could help me deliver this message to others when I physically couldn't get everywhere I wanted to go. Likewise, I'm indebted to my friend Tangye Stephney, who always reminds me that this is spiritual work. Thank you to Sanita Alrey-DeBose, my assistant, for helping me get on the right plane on the right day. And to my family—Tom, Jon, and Jess—who understand the passion behind my work and honor it.

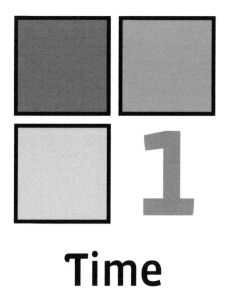

Time

It's back-to-school time, and we're seated around a table—a group of us thinking together about scheduling in our kindergarten-through-third-grade classrooms. "How can we fit it all in? How many small groups a day do you see? How many kids do you usually have in your groups? How do I get started?"

We grab some chart paper and colored sticky notes and get to work, creating a sample daily schedule. First, we brainstorm what to include in a day, listing each routine on a pink sticky note . . . *read-aloud, spelling, language, reading groups, math, science*, and so on. I ask the teachers to think about their "big rocks"—the most important parts of the day that are nonnegotiable, and we jot those on yellow sticky notes: *whole-group reading, small-group reading, independent reading, writing workshop, word study, math, science*, and *social studies*.

Next, we start juggling them around on a piece of chart paper, thinking together about our purposes for each routine and why we think it should be included. We arrange the yellow "big rock" notes down the left-hand side of the chart, thinking

about a good daily sequence. Then we match up the pink sticky notes, deciding which fits where. We put *read-aloud, shared reading*, and *core program* to the right of *whole-group reading*. The pink *reading groups* and *literacy work stations* notes go beside the yellow *small-group reading*. *Spelling, language*, and *handwriting* fit with writing time.

Our next task is to think about how many minutes to spend on each part of the day, so we assign numbers of minutes to each sticky note. Since these teachers must devote ninety minutes to reading instruction daily (according to their school's plan), we look at routines for reading first. We want a balance of some whole-group and some small-group instruction, so we plan for thirty to forty-five minutes of whole-group reading, about forty minutes for small-group reading (two groups daily with twenty minutes for each group), and five minutes for reflection at the end of the reading block. Throughout this discussion, we remind each other to be flexible from day to day and from grade level to grade level.

Someone asks about specials and lunch, which we include in our generic schedule. Following our

Figure 1.1 A chart made with teachers divides the day into manageable chunks.

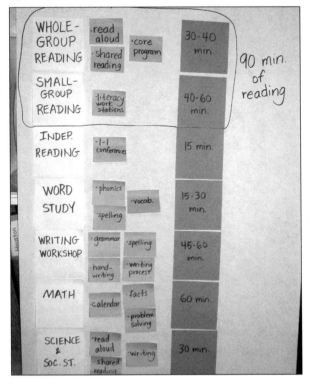

Figure 1.2 Sample schedule including 120 minutes for language arts instruction (ninety minutes for reading checked in boxes)—kindergarten.

Note: Core program may include read-aloud, shared reading, phonemic awareness, phonics, comprehension strategies, etc.

Kindergarten Start of Year
- ☑ 15 min. whole group—core program (with active movement between each segment)
- ☑ 15 min. whole group—core program
- ☑ 15 min. whole group—core program
- ☑ 10 min. independent reading
- ☑ 30 min. writing—related to core program
- ☐ 30 min. centers/working with individuals in centers
- ☑ 5 min. transitions

Kindergarten by Nov./Dec.
- ☑ 15 min. whole group—core program (with active movement between each segment)
- ☑ 15 min. whole group—core program
- ☑ 15 min. whole group—core program
- ☑ 15 min. independent reading (includes sharing time)
- ☐ 30 min. writing—related to core program
- ☑ 30 min. literacy work stations/small-group instruction (2 groups per day)

Figure 1.3 Sample schedule including 120 minutes for language arts instruction (ninety minutes for reading highlighted)—first through third grade.

8:00–8:15	Classroom jobs/independent reading from book bag/poetry notebooks
8:15–8:30	Calendar
8:30–9:00	Read-aloud/shared reading/core program
9:00–9:45	Small group for reading/literacy work stations 9:00–9:20 meet with first reading group 9:25–9:45 meet with second reading group
9:45–9:50	Sharing time for literacy work stations/guided reading
9:50–10:00	Word study/spelling—including word wall, making words lessons, phonics
10:15–10:40	Writer's workshop begins 10:00–10:15 mini-lesson—modeled or shared writing 10:15–10:45 writing time—teacher conferences with small groups/individuals
10:45–11:45	Lunch/recess
11:45–12:00	Sharing time for writing
12:00–1:00	Math
1:00–1:45	Music, art, P.E.
1:45–2:45	Social studies/science
2:45–2:55	Daily News/Afternoon Message—shared writing of what we learned today

meeting, each teacher will make his or her own schedule, using sticky notes like I've modeled. The teachers can insert their own ancillary times in their daily schedules.

We continue through the process of arranging all the other pieces of the day on the chart paper, remembering that this is the schedule we're heading toward. The first few weeks of school will probably look a bit different. We'll be spending more time in whole group, teaching expectations and establishing routines, during these first four to six weeks of school. (See our finished generic chart in Figure 1.1 and sample teacher schedules in Figures 1.2 and 1.3.)

At the end of our morning, we agree on the following:

- There is no such thing as a "perfect" schedule.
- The schedule will have to be flexible, allowing for balance between considering kids' needs *and* the curriculum.
- The first six weeks' schedule will morph somewhat over time into a daily schedule for the rest of the year that includes some whole-group, some small-group, and some one-on-one instruction for reading (as well as time for teaching writing, math, science, and social studies).

Planning for Reading Instruction

The focus of this book is small-group instruction, but I think it's important to see where this fits in the context of *all* reading instruction, as pictured in Figure 1.4. I like to consider each part—whole-group, small-group, and one-on-one instruction—and how they all fit together. The bottom line is to meet the needs of *all* children in our classrooms. Most likely, you'll have to *plan* to fit small-group instruction in your daily schedule, just as you must

Figure 1.4 During read-aloud, as part of whole-group instruction, the teacher models how to think about the book she is reading.

plan to fit exercise into your personal schedule. It's so easy to let whole-group teaching take over and leave little to no time for small-group instruction—just as our workday can extend way beyond school hours into our evenings and weekends if we allow it.

Many teachers, including myself, struggle with how to make the "perfect" schedule—just like in the opening of this chapter. I always created a flexible schedule for my own students when I taught full-time in the classroom, making room for kids' needs along the way. I refer to this as "considering kids and curriculum." I'd look at my state's content standards, *and* the kids' needs based on assessments. (For more information on forming small groups using assessments, see Chapter 3.)

Here are some specifics you might consider as you think about whole-group, small-group, and one-on-one teaching in reading:

Whole Group

Every day each child is involved in some *whole-group instruction*. The purpose of this type of instruction is to *model* reading and writing strategies; I spend most of this time showing students *how* to read and write, using explicit language so kids know exactly what to do. During this time teachers expose all students to on-grade-level reading materials and standards. In whole-group teaching, such as read-aloud and shared reading, we show the class how to read with fluency and expression. We use picture books or chapter books, as well as Big Books and poems, to think aloud about how to pay attention to new vocabulary words or how to make connections with what we're reading. A core reading program has many offerings for whole-group instruction, too. As teachers, we must choose wisely to provide modeling opportunities through mini-lessons that *teach* children *how* to read and think.

Small Group

Every week each child is included in some *small-group instruction*. I don't recommend trying to meet

Figure 1.5 In small group the teacher guides students' reading and thinking and provides support.

with every group every day unless you have additional adult support in your classroom, such as a paraprofessional or a Title I teacher. If you have another adult, that person may also work with a small group so that, in essence, you are seeing every group every day between the two of you.

The purpose of small-group instruction is to meet the needs of all students in your classroom in a powerful way that will accelerate their learning. Work with your students at their *instructional* reading level in small groups. This means that you find a text that can be read at 90 to 94 percent accuracy with good comprehension and some fluency. If the text is harder than this, the child has to work too hard (and often, so do you). If the text is much easier than this, there's not enough work for the child to do. You don't want to work with a small group on a text that is too easy for them; it's too much work to carve out the time to work with that small group.

Our teaching role changes during small-group time. Here, we support and scaffold the reader and help the child read as independently as possible.

We want each student to problem-solve and apply the strategies we have modeled in whole-group instruction skillfully. The focus in small-group teaching is on having the child do more of the work than you are. The key is to know your students and find out what they *can* do during small-group time.

One-on-One

In one-on-one instruction, the teacher confers with individual students during independent reading. In some classrooms, you may choose to do this after lunch or at a time separate from your reading block, which is okay. You'll probably plan to meet with every child briefly sometime over a week or two. If you have twenty-five students in your class, that's four to five conferences per day, each averaging from two to five minutes. I like to listen in to the child's reading, discuss book choices with him, and make suggestions about his reading. I often jot down notes on sticky notes to help me remember what we discussed.

Figure 1.6 By conferring with students one-on-one, the teacher gets to know each child's reading habits and preferences.

Figure 1.7 Reading Framework

Teaching Structure	What?	Who and When?	Why?
Whole-group instruction	■ Read-aloud ■ Shared reading ■ Can be through core program/grade-level standards	■ All students participate every day of the week for about thirty to forty-five min. daily.	■ To expose all students to on-grade-level material ■ To model reading strategies and skills ■ To build oral language/vocabulary
Small-group instruction	■ Small-group reading for comprehension, fluency, phonics, phonemic awareness, vocabulary, etc. ■ May include literature circles and/or guided reading	■ Two small groups of students meet daily for about twenty min. each. ■ Flexible groups meet based on student need. ■ Every group meets with the teacher every week. ■ Low-progress readers meet with the teacher more often.	■ To give students the opportunity to read text at an instructional level ■ To scaffold students' reading so they can practice with support and be successful ■ To focus on specific strategies and skills based upon student need
One-on-one instruction	■ Reading conferences during independent reading time ■ Listening to individual readers ■ Could be a running record	■ Every student meets with the teacher sometime each week for about three to five min.	■ To meet individually with each student to discuss his or her reading and make recommendations ■ To assess individual reading progress

Planning Lessons for Small Group

Now that you have some ideas about planning for time to work with small groups, you're probably thinking about finding time for planning your small-group lessons. As a classroom teacher, I often worked on my small-group lesson plans either before or after school. I planned these lessons daily, so I could use what I noticed the last time I met with a group to help me choose wisely for the next focused lesson.

When I first began learning how to work with small groups, I used to decide which kids I'd meet with and choose a book, thinking that was enough of a plan. We'd sit and read the book together during small group. But several years later, when I had more experience and was working with struggling readers, I found that when I actually took a few minutes to *plan* my instruction for the lesson, my

students' reading really improved. Thoughtful teaching in small groups is a lot different than sitting with a group of kids and listening to them read.

You'll notice that the lessons in this book include a *before*, *during*, and *after* reading segment. That's because I want kids reading or writing each time I meet with them in small group. You'll see this lesson plan format used in Chapters 4 through 8. There are a variety of lesson-plan templates included for you to choose from in the appendixes. You can use these lesson-plan forms or create your own. Chapters 4 through 8 each focus on an essential component of reading instruction—phonemic awareness, phonics, vocabulary, comprehension, or fluency—and give you lots to think about when planning for small group. Here is the basic process I use when planning a small-group reading lesson:

Choose a Lesson-Plan Form

Look in the appendix pages and find the planning form that matches what you want to focus on teaching in your small-group lesson. Choose a focus based on your assessments and what you see that your group needs. Use the chart titled How to Choose a Lesson Focus in Appendix A and shown in Figure 1.8. The lesson plans included in this book make this easy by giving you choices you can simply highlight on the planning sheet. For example, if your students need work on fluency, go to the matching appendix and use the reproducible lesson-plan template for fluency. If you're concentrat-ing on having children read in phrases, highlight that beside Focus at the top of the lesson-plan form. Or use the general lesson-plan form in Appendix A if the other forms seem like too much to manage.

Before Reading

Familiar Rereading

I often choose to have a short warm-up segment to start my lesson, so I preselect one student to listen to while the others read familiar books for a few minutes. These books may be stored in browsing bags or boxes. See Chapter 2 on ideas for organizing materials such as these for small groups.

Figure 1.8 How to Choose a Lesson Focus

If You See This	Choose This Focus
■ low phonemic awareness scores ■ lack of response in whole-group lessons on phonemic awareness ■ inconsistency in phonemic awareness tasks ■ difficulty with segmenting sounds (oral task or when writing) ■ difficulty with blending sounds (oral task or when reading)	■ phonemic awareness
■ low letter-sound knowledge ■ decoding difficulties and reading miscues (pay attention to patterns of errors and focus on those phonics elements in small group) ■ spelling difficulties and writing miscues (pay attention to patterns of errors and focus on those phonics elements in small group)	■ phonics
■ low comprehension scores ■ good decoding but poor comprehension ■ basic understanding but could go deeper with comprehension ■ making errors and no self-correction with regard to meaning ■ difficulty with connecting to the text, visualizing, summarizing, or inferring	■ comprehension
■ low fluency scores ■ choppy or word-by-word reading ■ struggling over words ■ reading in a monotone voice with no intonation or expression ■ reading too quickly and not pausing for punctuation	■ fluency
■ low vocabulary scores ■ limited oral vocabulary (even if native English speaker) ■ little or no attention paid to new words while reading (or writing) ■ use of basic words and could use vocabulary expansion ■ lack of content-area word knowledge	■ vocabulary
Note: You may choose a focus and spend several lessons on the same focus. Work with it until you start to see students improving in this area. Then switch the focus to another area that will improve the reading of children in that group. Plan your lessons day by day, basing tomorrow's lesson on what you saw happening today. Small groups need to be flexible.	

I have found it very helpful to do a running record or take a few notes on one child per group each time I meet with a small reading group. This allows me to systematically check in individually with all students in a group across the span of a week or two. I always end this quick assessment by telling the child something I noticed that he did well and something else he might want to try as a reader today. This "jump-starts" that one child for the lesson, and he is often the shining star that time. By doing this systematically, one child per group each day, I can give a lot in a little time. For ideas on how to organize these notes, see Chapter 3. For samples of these notes, see the section in Chapters 4 through 8 called "What to Look for and How to Take Notes on (Fluency, Phonics, etc.)."

Book Intro

I also plan a short book introduction to help students be successful in their reading. I always read the title with them and have them share what they think the book will be about, using their background knowledge. I give them a brief summary of the book (rather like the back cover or inside flap of a book you might read as an adult), and I tell them anything they need to know about how the book works. For example, if it's nonfiction, we'll look briefly at the headings, captions, and diagrams, and I'll remind them to read these, too.

I set a specific purpose for reading to help them home in and comprehend deeply. In fiction, I might say, "As you start this new book, pay attention to the characters as they're introduced. See what you can learn about them—what they are like and how they act." In nonfiction, my intro might include, "Be thinking about new facts about growing plants. You probably already know something about this topic. Be on the lookout for new information, too." This takes only seconds to do and helps children focus on thinking as they read.

Finally, I remind kids what I expect to see them try as readers today. This should link to my focus. If I want kindergarten readers to use their finger to

point to each word to help them pay attention to print, I show them what this should look like and say, "I'll be watching to see if you use your finger to point under each word and make it match. This will help you pay attention to the words and get them right." If my focus is fluency and I want students to read with intonation and expression, I might say, "Make it sound like the characters are talking, just like I did when I was reading aloud today. I'll be listening to see how you sound." Again, I do this briefly.

I plan ahead for early finishers and tell kids what I want them to do *before* they start to read. Not everyone will finish reading at the same time. I often tell them they can go back and reread. Or with kids who can write well enough to read what they've written, I might have them jot down something in particular on sticky notes . . . new words they found, their connections, questions they had while reading, and so forth.

I recommend keeping book introductions short and focused. *Less is more.* Let the kids talk more than you in the intro. Have them share their ideas about the book, but don't let the time get away from you. If they start trying to tell you a long story, you could gently ask them to write about that dur-

Figure 1.9 A timer helps the teacher stay focused and finish a small-group lesson on time. The stop sign helps minimize student interruptions.

ing writing workshop today, and move on with the lesson. You might want to use a timer and set it for twenty minutes for your small-group lesson. If ten minutes have passed and you're still introducing the book, it's probably time to give it up and move into the during-reading portion. Make sure kids have enough time to do some actual reading during your lesson.

During Reading

You'll want your students to read as independently as possible. They should *not* be doing round-robin reading. This is not considered a best practice. When round-robin reading, students don't get enough reading practice; they are not developing reading comprehension (it's just listening comprehension since they're taking turns and listening to each other); and it's boring . . . for you and them. Instead, have them read it at their own pace, not chorally but independently of each other. If they start to choral read, you can stagger their starting time by a few seconds, you can have every other child turn his chair facing away from the table, or you can simply stand between two choral readers to break them up by asking one to reread to you.

Figure 1.10 When one child depends on the other to figure out the hard words, the teacher sandwiches herself between them, which reminds them to read on their own in small group.

Kids who are reading at the second-grade reading level or higher can learn how to read silently during this time. I simply tap them on the shoulder and ask them to very quietly read to me, so I can hear how their reading sounds. This allows me to check on their decoding and fluency. After listening to a child read a bit, I ask him to tell me about what he's read so far. This is a great way to check for comprehension.

While listening to each individual read a little (not more than a minute or so), I am sure to have a short conversation with her. If a child gets stuck, you may be tempted to give her the word, but don't. Instead, prompt the child—say something to try to get her to solve the problem or do the work. Chapters 4 through 8 have a section called "Some Prompts for (Comprehension, Fluency, Phonics, etc.)." The ideas there can suggest what to say to help the reader. I think you'll find it useful to jot down a few of these prompts you think you might use in the During Reading box on the lesson-plan form you're filling out before the lesson. There's also a bit of space to record the name of a student you'd like more information on that day so you'll remember to keep a note on that student's reading.

During reading, you may want to write a short note about something you noticed that a child did today.

After Reading

When planning a lesson, I jot down a few questions I want to ask after kids finish reading. One question is always connected to the purpose I set before the kids read. For example, if I told them to think about the characters as they read, the first thing I'll ask about is what they learned about the characters. I question deeply to get more thinking from them. If they tell me that Mudge is a big dog, I ask for more. I want them to tell me that he is an enormous dog who drools and has curly hair and is lovable. They need to tell me Mudge is going to make a good companion for Henry.

I'm often asked how to get kids to think when they're reading. My answer is, "Expect it, and ask good questions." I don't ask yes-or-no questions. No deeper comprehension required there. Instead, I use Bloom's taxonomy and ask higher-level-thinking questions. You can easily find lists of questions like these on the Internet. You might keep a set posted at your small-group teaching table. (More on this is in Chapters 2 and 4.) See Figures 1.11 and 1.12 for sample comprehension questions that require deeper thinking.

After students discuss what they read, I end the lesson by referring to my focus. I point out (or have them share) what they did as good readers today, such as rereading or thinking about the blends they've been studying to figure out new words.

Then I remind them to keep doing this the next time they read.

I like to take a minute to jot down a quick reflection of how the lesson went as they leave my small-group table (so I won't forget by the end of the next lesson . . . or the day). I use any notes I took to help me plan for the next lesson. Odds are I'll repeat the focus of my lesson several times in a row. Practice makes permanent.

Links Between Small Group and the Rest of the Day

To maximize time spent in small groups for reading, I think it's important to make links between what students do there and the rest of the day. Chapters

Figure 1.11 Moving to questions that promote deeper thinking in fiction.

Basic Comprehension Questions	Questions That Promote Deeper Comprehension
Who are the characters?	What do you think about the way _____ acted? Who did this character remind you of? Why?
Where and when did the story take place?	If the story had a different setting, how would that change what happened?
What was the problem?	Name the problem. How would you have solved it if you'd been in the story?
What happened in the story?	What can you predict or infer from the story?
What was your favorite part?	What is the most important thing you took away from this story?

Figure 1.12 Moving to questions that promote deeper thinking in nonfiction.

Basic Comprehension Questions	Questions That Promote Deeper Comprehension
What are some facts you learned?	How does _____ compare with _____?
What are some new words you found?	What ideas can you add to? Can you think of another example? A _____ is like _____. A nonexample? A _____ is nothing like _____.
What is the topic?	What is the most important _____?
How many . . . ?	What are the parts or features of _____?
Where or when do . . . ?	Why do you think _____?
What was your favorite part?	What do you think about _____?

4 through 8 also have a section called "Links to Whole-Group Instruction" and another entitled "Links to Literacy Work Stations Practice." When you can make a child's day connected, he learns more. I always strive to connect a child's known information to new information I want him to learn.

During whole-group reading instruction, I watch for what I might need to reinforce in small group. If several students have trouble grasping a strategy or skill, I focus on that task with them in an ad hoc group for a while using materials that are *just right* for them so they can be successful. I make links between what I'm teaching in whole group and small group by reminding kids of whole-group lessons I've taught where I've modeled that strategy I want them to use. Here's where explicit language becomes important. I try to say it the same way in both whole *and* small group. For example, I might tell kids, "move your eyes quickly across the page" as I teach them how to read fluently in shared reading. In small group, I remind them to move their eyes quickly across the page before they read on their own and then I look for evidence of them doing that as they read and reinforce this behavior.

Likewise, I reinforce strategies and skills being practiced in small group during whole-group lessons. If I notice emergent readers who have trouble paying attention to print in small group, I seat those kids close to me during shared reading of a Big Book. Then I let them take turns holding the pointer with me while I point to the words.

There are sample whole-group lesson plans for each reading focus (comprehension, fluency, phonemic awareness, phonics, and vocabulary) in the appendix pages. They will be helpful to you while making links, since they include explicit language for you to use, as well as links to small group.

Also, there are suggestions for literacy work stations—designated areas in the classroom where students can go for the focused practice listed in each chapter. For more ideas on literacy work stations, see my books on this topic, *Literacy Work Stations*

(2003) for K–2 and *Practice with Purpose* (2005) for grades three to six.

Guided Reading

"Where does guided reading fit in?" I'm often asked. If you have been trained in guided reading, you will probably be familiar with many of the suggestions mentioned thus far. But what I write about in this book is not just guided reading. It is more than guided reading—it is focused small-group instruction. As a literacy coach and consultant, I was often frustrated when asked to do guided reading training by teachers' confusion about what to teach in a lesson and their preoccupation with doing it the "right" way. In my mind, there is not really a "right" or "wrong" way to work with kids in small group. I have certainly found some practices that are more effective than others, and that's the focus of this book. I chose not to write a book on guided reading, because there are already books on this topic. If you'd like information on guided reading, you might see Fountas and Pinnell's *Guided Reading* (1996) or Schulman and Payne's *Guided Reading: Making It Work* (2000).

Guided reading requires that you use books leveled from A to Z in a continuum. In my work as a national consultant, I have found that not every school has access to these kinds of books. So I've created small-group lesson ideas that you can use with leveled books, or texts from a basal reading series, or whatever you've got. I have included references to the A through Z levels, but I've also noted grade-level equivalents, such as *early first grade*, to help all teachers have the opportunity to use the methods described in this book.

Benefits of Small-Group Instruction

I believe in small-group reading instruction. I've seen it change countless children's lives over the years, including that of my own daughter, who was a struggling first-grade reader. The ideas in this book should be used flexibly, not in an orthodox fashion. Pay attention to your students, be open, and have fun. Small-group reading is a delight. It enables you to get to know your students better than you've ever known them before. They'll beg to meet with you.

Remember that focus is key in small-group teaching. Choose a focus that zeroes in on something a group of your students needs to learn or practice next. Stick with your focus, but be flexible, too. Know that you shouldn't be exhausted by the end of a lesson. The work should be on the cutting edge of the children's development, so they're doing more of the work than you. Each child in your group should feel successful, and so should you. Likewise, the tasks in small-group instruction shouldn't be things that the kids in your group can do independently. You work hard to carve out time for small groups. Make every minute count.

Reflection Questions for Professional Conversations

1. Meet with a few colleagues, perhaps your grade-level team. Use the sticky-note process from the chapter opening to create a generic daily schedule.

2. Or look at your daily schedule with another teacher. Have you planned for large-group, small-group, and one-on-one instruction in reading? What changes do you need to make, if any, to include these in your day and still have time left for the other "big rocks" that need to fit?

3. What are your "big rocks"—the most important parts of your day? Are they nonnegotiable? How do you handle interruptions, like field trips, testing, and assemblies?

4. How are you currently planning lessons for small-group instruction? What ideas might you try from this chapter?

5. How do you link what you're teaching in small group to the rest of the day? What else might you try?

For Further Information on Small Groups

Cappellini. M. 2005. *Balancing Reading and Language Learning: A Resource for Teaching English Language Learners, K–5*. Portland, ME: Stenhouse.

Mere, C. 2005. *More Than Guided Reading: Finding the Right Instruction Mix, K–3*. Portland, ME: Stenhouse.

Tyner, B. 2003. *Small-Group Reading Instruction—a Differentiated Teaching Model for Beginning and Struggling Readers*. Newark, DE: International Reading Association.

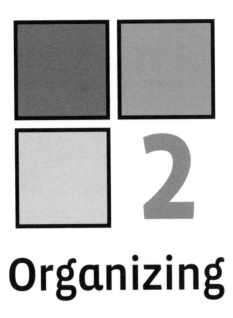

Organizing

Patty, a primary-grade teacher, sits at her small-group reading table with all the materials she needs at her fingertips. This helps to maximize her time with the children and makes her planning and teaching easier. She has dedicated this classroom space to small-group instruction. Although it is tempting to stack things on this table, she resists. Keeping this area organized is a priority, just as teaching in small groups is for her.

Patty begins her lesson by pulling today's new book for the yellow group from the plastic stacking drawers behind her table. She has a drawer labeled with colors to match each of her four reading groups (red, blue, yellow, and green). These colors help her stay organized and easily find materials needed. While calling her "yellow group" folks to the table, she flips a little green stuffed frog with writing on each side to the side that says, "Do Not Disturb" as a reminder to the rest of the class that she is not to be interrupted during small-group time.

She consults her lesson plan for the yellow group in her three-ring binder on the table. After

Figure 2.1 This teacher has everything needed at her fingertips, so her lessons go more smoothly.

she asks the children to begin rereading a familiar book to warm up, she listens in to one child and takes notes about that student's decoding, fluency, and comprehension. She jots the notes on a running-record sheet (they are stacked neatly behind her table) and files it in her notebook behind the child's name to help her remember what that student did as a reader today. She'll consult the notes later to plan further for this student. After school, she'll use her calculator (placed on top of the stacking drawers behind her table) to determine the child's accuracy rate, so she can be sure she has him in the right level of reading difficulty. She'll look at his miscues to determine what to help him with in phonics.

Today this group will focus on practicing using their skills to decode long-vowel patterns. Patty has posted an anchor chart on a bulletin board right behind her small-group table. This chart was developed over the past few weeks in whole-group instruction. Patty reviews the chart with her group. She reminds them to use the chart, if needed, as they read to help them with tricky sounds. She introduces their new book. Before they begin reading on their own, she gives them sticky notes and tells them to write down any words they get stuck on. They'll review these after reading. Her sticky notes and pencils are stored in caddies at her fingertips, so she's able to hand them out quickly. This maximizes her children's reading time.

Figure 2.2 All materials students need are on the small-group table, and are labeled to help with quick and easy storage and retrieval.

As the children read, Martin gets stuck on the word *right*. Patty asks him to name the vowel, and they quickly glance at the anchor chart for the letter *i*. He sees *igh* listed there and applies the sound easily. Patty makes a note on his anecdotal note card, lying on the table in front of him, and tells him she wrote down that he used the chart to help him remember the sound. He needs to remember that pattern and read it quickly next time he sees it in a word.

After reading the book, Patty and the children talk about what they read and clarify understandings to be sure they have comprehended. Then she asks them about their tricky words and they look at their sticky notes together. They match their words to the anchor chart, paying attention to the vowel pattern it represents. She notices they still need help with some of the patterns. They'll continue to work on this skill. She jots a note about this on the Reflection section of her lesson plan.

Next time they meet, they'll build some words with these long-vowel patterns on the small magnetic dry erase board on her table. She has a labeled tackle box with six sets of magnetic letters in it stored in a clear plastic stacking drawer behind her table, so she'll be ready. Tomorrow, she might have them write difficult words on individual dry erase boards. These materials are also kept in her stacking drawers.

Patty has set up her small-group area in a spot where she can view the entire classroom. It's important that she be able to see every nook and cranny, so she can keep an eye on things while the rest of the class is working independently at literacy work stations. Her children work well independently. They know she is mindful of their work, and they are considerate of hers.

Choosing a Small-Group Space

I've found that it's wise to plan ahead for your small-group space. Just like Patty, you might think about the following when finding an area to set up your small-group teaching table:

Figure 2.3 Labeled containers store materials for small group and are stored behind the teacher table for easy access. There are drawers for leveled books, dry erase supplies, phonics materials, magnetic letters, highlighter tape, sticky notes, paper, and pencils.

- Will I be able to see every child from where I'll be working with my small group?
- Where will I store my materials? (You'll want them handy. Consider placing your space by a set of built-in shelves. Or use clear stacking drawers, as pictured in Figure 2.3.)
- Is there a nearby space to display charts and materials I'm teaching with to help kids make

Figure 2.4 A bulletin board behind the small-group teaching area holds phonics charts the teacher refers to during small group to help children make connections and apply what was taught previously.

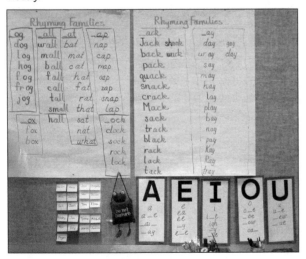

connections? (I like to put the small-group area by a bulletin board. Or use a portable tri-fold project board.)
- What kind of table do I have? Want? (You can use virtually any kind of table—rectangular, square, round, kidney-shaped. Or you might need to use a bank of student desks if you don't have room for a table.)

Materials Needed

You'll want to be sure you have everything you need at your fingertips. Here's a list of essentials for your small-group area:

- small table (kidney-shaped, round, trapezoidal, or rectangular) or a group of student desks (if you don't have room for a table)
- six lap-size dry erase, magnetic boards
- dry erase markers with built-in erasers
- six sets of lowercase magnetic letters (stored in a labeled plastic tackle box; see Figure 7.3)
- tabletop easel (with a dry erase, magnetic surface)
- small-group notebook for lesson plans and anecdotal notes
- paper, pencils, colored markers, index cards, scissors, sticky notes, highlighter tape
- preselected books for each group to read (might be stored in individual containers with one for each group)

Additional Tools

Listed above are materials you should have to get started with effective small-group instruction, but there are a few other things you might want to have handy as well. You'll notice that this book is organized into chapters highlighting reading components from which to choose a focus for each small-group lesson. Here are some additional tools you might want to have available for each:

Comprehension Tools (see Chapter 4)

- question cards, with each card listing questions related to an aspect of Bloom's taxonomy (to help you plan for and ask higher-level questions)
- class-made charts about how to read fiction versus nonfiction (see Figure 4.21)

Fluency Tools (see Chapter 5)

- whisper-phone, commercially made or made from PVC pipe (for students to use to hear themselves read) (see Figure 5.16)
- fluency rubric for student self-assessment (see Appendix D)
- tape recorder (for kids to record and then listen to themselves read fluently)

Phonemic Awareness Tools (see Chapter 6)

- picture sorting cards (see Figure 6.3)
- Elkonin box stamps or Elkonin boxes preprinted on paper (see Figure 6.16)
- counters for pushing sounds (see Figures 6.11 and 6.20)

Phonics Tools (see Chapter 7)

- sound charts (consonants, vowels, blends, rimes)
- individual letter cards (for making words and blending sounds; see Figure 7.14)
- word-sorting cards (see Figure 7.9)

Vocabulary Tools (see Chapter 8)

- dictionary and/or thesaurus
- reference book of idioms
- class-made chart of "Wow Words" (see Figure 8.13)

Writing Tools (see Chapters 4 and 7)

- white painter's masking tape or three-line correction tape (for covering up writing errors)
- thin sentence strips, glue sticks, and envelopes for cut-up sentences
- large sheets of white paper (twelve-by-eighteen-inch for kindergarten)

Minimizing Student Interruptions During Small Group

I'm frequently asked how to keep kids from interrupting the teacher when she is working with a small group. I think that organizing and planning for this ahead of time is one place to begin. Here are some tips for minimizing student interruptions:

- Have a physical object that reminds kids to not interrupt you, like Patty's little stuffed frog with a sign that says, "Do Not Disturb." Pam, a second-grade teacher, displays a red stop sign during her small-group time. My friend Vicky wears a tiara.

Figure 2.5 The teacher calls small groups using a chart made of colored construction paper and sticky notes. A stuffed frog saying "Do Not Disturb" helps minimize interruptions by kids.

- Teach routines well (including bathrooming, Kleenex use, sharpening pencils, etc.) during the first four to six weeks of school so the children know your expectations and know what to do during independent work time. Don't begin small-group instruction until you know your students can work independently. Assign a student to be your materials manager and take care of materials other kids might need (so they don't have to interrupt your lesson).

- If a child misbehaves (or constantly interrupts you), you might have an extra chair or two by your small-group table. Tell the student to have a seat; then simply continue teaching your small group. The interrupting student is no longer interrupting, and may be content paying attention to your group for the remainder of the time.

How to Get and Stay Organized

I have found that the best way to get organized is to establish a space where you'll keep each material, and then keep it there all the time. Don't just throw everything onto a shelf or stack it on your table. Inevitably, you won't be able to find it when you need it. Some teachers I've worked with find it helpful to label their storage containers and always return the materials there right away.

You might want to set a goal of cleaning off your small-group table at the end of your small-group sessions (while children clean up at literacy work stations). Get the kids in your last group to help you put all the materials away. If you do this, you'll be modeling how to stay organized and have the added benefit of a neat, uncluttered space that will make your teaching life easier.

Setting Up a Small-Group Planning Notebook

Many teachers I've worked with have liked having a small-group planning notebook to keep track of

their groups and the lessons they've taught. Here are some things you might want to try when setting up a planning notebook.

Patty uses a three-ring binder labeled Small-Group Planning Notebook. The notebook is divided into four or five sections, one for each group she might work with in her class. She organizes her groups by color and has a chart on her bulletin board with four colored squares on it—red, blue, yellow, and green (and orange if she has five groups). Each square has small sticky notes stuck on it with a name for each child in that group. (See Figure 3.8.) Likewise, Patty has used four or five different-colored plastic dividers (red, blue, yellow, and green—and orange, if needed) with pockets in them in her notebook. These are very handy, since she can put the little books her group will read in each pocket. She can also keep index cards for taking anecdotal notes for each child in that group in the pocket. See pictures of this in Figure 2.8.

In the front of her notebook, she keeps sheets that help her with general planning. (See Appendix A.) For example, she has a list of steps to think

Figure 2.6 Cover for a small-group lesson-planning notebook.

Figure 2.7 A pocket on the inside of a small-group lesson-planning notebook holds a small-group folder.

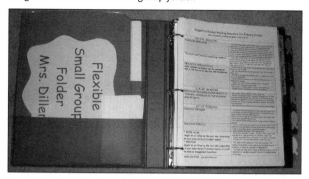

about while planning a small-group lesson, a suggested small-group reading lesson sequence, sheets describing what she might choose for a focus depending on the reading level of her students, and extra lesson-planning sheets. These pages can be found in Appendix A.

Behind the red divider, she includes several recent lesson plans for the red group. Behind her lesson plans for the red group, she has a tabbed section for each student currently meeting with her in that group. Each tab has a child's name written on it, and behind the tab are a few sheets of notebook paper. Patty uses this paper for keeping running records and miscue analysis. She has found it easiest to take running records on the notebook paper by dating the entry and writing the book title before doing the running record.

Figure 2.8 Colored plastic pocket dividers mark sections for lesson plans for each small group. Lesson plans are kept behind each divider for easy access. Note cards for anecdotal notes for each group are stored in the pockets.

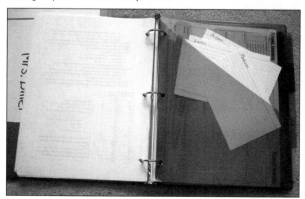

Each colored divider is set up in a similar way. There are recent lesson plans for that group, followed by a tabbed section for each child in the group currently. When she moves a student to a different group (which she does), she simply removes that tab and the following notebook pages for that child, and moves them to a different-colored section (the new group the child will be joining). See the accompanying photos of Patty's notebook in Figures 2.6 through 2.8 for ideas on how you might set up a similar notebook.

When planning her lessons, Patty uses the lesson-plan templates found in the appendixes and uses the process described in Chapter 1. In her regular lesson plans (kept online, as required by her school system), she simply lists which groups she will meet with daily throughout the week and what she thinks her focus for each lesson will be. She writes her detailed, more focused lesson plans on the templates and keeps these in her notebook. These are the plans she uses when teaching thoughtfully in small groups.

Once a month, Patty cleans out the notebook so it doesn't get too thick and bulky. She removes old lesson plans and keeps them in a labeled folder in her file cabinet. Likewise, she takes out old anecdotal notes for each child and stores these in an index-card box. That way, if she needs to document progress (or lack of it), she can pull out these valuable tools to share with parents and administrators.

Special Considerations for Itinerant Small-Group Teachers

Some classrooms have itinerant teachers helping during small-group instruction. These are usually special education or Title I teachers who "push in" to classrooms to work with small groups. This is a great way to maximize your teaching minutes, since the children don't have to waste time walking down the hall to work with another teacher. By coming into your classroom, these teachers can share their techniques for working in small groups

Figure 2.9 Itinerant teachers, as well as the classroom teacher, work with small groups in the classroom. They use student desks as small-group teaching areas.

with you and vice versa. You can complement each child's instruction rather than create confusion by having the student hear different messages from different teachers.

Sometimes it's tricky to figure out how to find room for these "visiting" teachers. I've seen different ways of working this out. In some classrooms, the teacher has an extra table so they can both work at different tables and have two groups going on simultaneously. In others (usually smaller rooms), the classroom teacher works at a small-group table and the itinerant teacher sits with a group at a bank of student desks. This isn't a problem, since the students are working on a variety of tasks all around the room at their literacy work stations. These traveling teachers usually bring their small-group reading materials with them on a cart. They keep the same items on their carts that the teacher has at her small-group table. (See the Materials Needed list on page 14.) These materials can be used from classroom to classroom.

No matter if you are working by yourself during small-group time and trying to manage reading with all your children sometime across the week or

if you have the support of a helping teacher during this time, getting and staying organized will make your life easier. You'll enjoy working in small groups more if you can quickly and easily locate the materials you'll need. Having routines in place to minimize interruptions will help. And knowing what you'll be teaching through the use of focused lesson plans will make this one of the best and most productive times of your day.

Figure 2.10 Having her teaching materials organized helps this teacher get more power out of her small-group lessons.

Reflection Questions for Professional Conversations

1. Where is your small-group teaching space located? How's it working for you? What have you learned in this chapter that might improve this space?

2. What materials have you found essential for teaching in small groups? How do you store and keep up with these? What new things might you add or try?

3. How are you currently organizing for small-group instruction? Do you use a notebook or folder? Share what you're using for keeping notes and plans with a colleague. Discuss ideas you got from reading this chapter that you might try to implement to improve your record keeping. Then decide what you'll try, give it a go, and share back in a week or two.

4. If you have students who meet with a special education or Title I reading teacher, think about the possibility of having them meet in your classroom during your small-group reading time. You'll need to talk with your administrators about scheduling, but this is very doable—especially if you start it at the beginning of the year.

5. If you are a special education or Title I reading teacher, think about "pushing in" to the regular classroom. Use the ideas in this chapter to create a traveling cart for small-group instruction.

For Further Information on Organizing Materials

Morgenstern, J. 2004. *Organizing from the Inside Out.* New York: Henry Holt.

Clayton, M. K., and M. B. Forton. 2001. *Classroom Spaces That Work.* Greenfield, MA: Northeast Foundation for Children.

3

Grouping

School started three weeks ago. Mrs. Luna has started to introduce literacy work stations, one at a time, to her class (a multiage room with both first and second graders) so her students will learn to work independently. They are also learning routines for independent reading. Mrs. Luna is not yet ready to start working with small groups. But she is ready to think about which students she will work with in which group.

About the second week of school, Mrs. Luna began collecting anecdotal notes on individual students. She observes them during whole-group instruction as well as while they are working independently. As she introduces literacy work stations and independent reading, she's watching for literacy behaviors students already have in place. For example, she notes that Aiden self-corrects while reading and Kaitlyn reads with wonderful expression and intonation. Every day she jots down these kinds of notes on her clipboard assessment tool. (See Figure 3.1.) She takes notes on just a few students a day.

Figure 3.1 Clipboard holds a four-by-six-inch card for each student to be used by the teacher during independent reading, literacy work stations, or whole-group instruction for taking notes about students' literacy behaviors.

Mrs. Luna also writes notes about the kinds of books her students are reading independently. Destiny is reading on grade level and enjoys a variety of books. Hannah is struggling and needs to read books about six months below grade level. Mrs. Luna will use these notes to look for evidence of phonemic awareness, phonics understanding, comprehension, fluency, vocabulary development, and their reading levels to help her decide how to group her students.

In addition to this informal assessment, her school uses DIBELS (Dynamic Indicators of Basic Early Literacy Skills), a formal assessment system. She is required to test students on several elements of literacy several times throughout the year, reporting the results on a PalmPilot. This formal measure gives her research-based data that can also help her form groups. Through live chats online, Mrs. Luna often "talks" with other teachers across the nation about testing, so she knows that other school systems are using DRA (Developmental Reading Assessment), Rigby Benchmark, and TPRI (Texas Primary Reading Inventory) as formal assessment tools.

In the past, Mrs. Luna was sometimes overwhelmed with all the data collection, but she reminds herself that DIBELS (and other formal assessments) are tools to help her form and work with kids in small groups. This data is just one piece of information. She is just beginning testing this week. She will meet with individual students and listen to them read word lists and short pieces of text, and perform other tasks as directed by this assessment. While she tests, her students will do independent tasks at their seats as suggested in the section titled "Managing Formal Testing" in this chapter. She won't have children go to work stations during testing, because they aren't yet trained to work independently enough. She plans to spend another couple of weeks working with them on stations (while she monitors) before she begins small-group instruction and they work totally independent of her.

After Mrs. Luna has completed testing, she will use this information to help her form small groups. However, these groups are flexible, so she uses her observations about the students in class as well. She will use her assessment data, anecdotal notes, and knowledge of reading development to form her initial groups. She plans to start meeting with groups in about two to three weeks, after she's completed all testing and has trained her children to work independently of her during work stations time.

Using Formal and Informal Assessments

As noted in the example above, teachers may use a combination of both formal and informal assessments to make decisions about small-group instruction. Most schools require certain formal assessments, such as TPRI, DIBELS, DRA, and/or QRI (Qualitative Reading Inventory). Because these are required and are so time-consuming, I've found that many teachers feel that the data collected from these tests are the only tools they have to form small groups.

However, I believe that using these measures in tandem with what you're noticing about your kids is even smarter. Think about what a doctor does when making a diagnosis. Your doctor may perform some standard tests, such as taking your temperature, doing a blood test, or listening to your heart. In addition, your doctor asks you about your symptoms and how long you've had them. Then the physician combines these formal tests along with informal data to decide on the best treatment. Your doctor relies on test results combined with observations. Think of how you would feel if the doctor had an assistant run tests on you, but never talked with you about your symptoms.

I believe it's wise to invest the time to listen to individuals read in formal as well as informal settings. Many teachers ask if it's okay for someone else to do the testing for them to save time. I recommend that you test your own students so you can get to know them as readers and writers and individuals. You might notice something that will help a child immediately and that isn't recorded on the test. For example, as I listen to Madison, I notice that she keeps reading the wrong short vowel. On the test her school uses, I am only supposed to record if it's right or wrong. But I notice this pattern of error and jot down a quick note about it. This will help me get more specific as I work with Madison in both whole- and small-group settings in the coming weeks.

Likewise, as I listen to Ethan, I am required to time how fast he can read an on-grade-level passage. I notice that he reads fast, but he doesn't stop at the punctuation and uses a monotone voice. Again, my combination of the formal measure *and* the informal anecdotal note will help me better plan instruction for him. See Figure 3.2 for a summary of using formal and informal assessments.

Figure 3.2 Formal and Informal Assessments in Small Groups

Examples of Formal Assessments for Forming and Working in Small Groups	Examples of Informal Assessments for Forming and Working in Small Groups
■ Standardized tests, like those used in most states	■ Anecdotal notes taken during independent work time or small-group instruction
■ DIBELS or TPRI, used for determining skill needs	■ Observations made during whole-group instruction or testing
■ DRA or Rigby Benchmark, used for determining instructional reading level, strategy use, and phonics miscues	■ Informal reading inventories, such as Jerry Johns and Flynt Cooter, used for determining instructional reading level, strategy use, and phonics miscues
■ Observation Survey, for determining emergent students' knowledge about print	■ Student or parent questionnaires and surveys, used for determining student interests

Managing Formal Testing

I'm often asked how to manage formal testing, especially at the start of the school year. One suggestion I give is to try to wait a few weeks to begin testing if possible. Some students need the time to get to know you and their new setting in order to feel comfortable and show you what they really know. Others may not have read much during the summer and need a few weeks of instruction to get back in the groove of reading. I've found that it's usually worth waiting a couple of weeks, because your test results will reflect more closely where your students are really working as readers and writers. Some teachers have told me that by the time they finish testing, the kids' reading levels have already changed and they feel it has been a waste of their time. Be sure to remember that formal testing has a place, and its purpose is to show where kids began and how they grew until the end of the year.

Another tip is to do some of your "easy" testing first. Most assessments have multiple parts, so you might want to get the simple bits out of the way. If you know that some children already know their letters and sounds, do the assessment with those kids first. I've found that if you practice working with an assessment on kids who know the material, it actually makes it easier for you to administer that assessment over time. Likewise, if you realize that some students will most likely struggle with the first part of a two-part assessment (in which they have to pass Part A to move to Part B), give them Part A and be finished with it. As you do this, you can begin to think about groups and focus on your neediest students, finding out what they know and what they need.

At the beginning of the school year, it's hard for young students to work very independently. So what can you have them do while you're testing individuals? Think of easy things that *all* kids can be successful with. Try to minimize "busywork" and give students things that are fun and that help them get to know each other and learn to work with others. Of course, it would be best for students to engage in deep, meaningful encounters with text. But let's be real. It's the beginning of the year. You haven't trained students to engage in deep, meaningful independent practice yet, especially in kindergarten and first grade. You'll probably want to avoid small-group activities while you're testing, since these usually require teacher supervision. Here are some ideas shared by teachers:

- Have kids write about or draw their favorite things to do, their families and pets, what they did during the summer, etc.
- Let kids work with play dough on individual mats to create objects and spell names and other words. Older students might write about their creations on paper.
- Give students stencils or patterns to make their own creations.
- Use "scrap boxes" filled with scrap paper, toilet paper rolls, little doodads, etc., along with scissors and glue sticks. Kids can create their own works of art with the materials. Be sure to include things that are easy to glue together, so kids don't have to mess with adhesive tape, staples, or white glue.
- Give kids back-to-school "packets" with easy and fun-to-do sheets that review things learned in the previous grade level.
- Let kids work with partners to do puzzles or word sorts.
- Have kids read independently, browse books at their tables, or read easy books with buddies.
- Use guest readers, such as parents, grandparents, community volunteers, administrators, or teachers who don't yet have classroom teaching responsibilities (speech therapist, literacy coaches, Title I reading teachers, etc.).

Have all your testing materials at your fingertips, and cluster parts that can be done quickly. Know as much as possible about the child before starting.

For example, if administering the DRA, use the level where the child finished the previous year to begin. If doing TPRI, do the same segment with one child after another, rather than doing all the tests with that student at once. Post kids' names, so they'll know the order in which they'll come to your table for testing to minimize time. They can look up and see when their turn will be. Do the testing in bits, so kids don't tire out too quickly.

Managing Anecdotal Notes

Anecdotal notes seem like a good idea but are sometimes difficult to keep up with. One idea is to use a clipboard assessment tool (pictured in Figure 3.1) on which to take notes during independent reading and literacy work stations. You might even jot down notes while doing your formal testing. (Chapters 4 through 8 will show you examples of the kinds of notes you might take and how to use them in the section called "What to Look for and How to Take Notes.")

But once small group begins, it's hard to use this clipboard tool because of time constraints and flipping from card to card. Some teachers take notes on sticky notes or address labels during small group, but these often get misplaced. Others write notes on notepads or directly on their lesson plans, but it's hard to transfer these observations to individual students' folders.

One possibility is to keep an index-card file with ABC dividers, and file a card for each student behind the first letter of that child's first name. (See Figure 3.3.) Then pull the cards needed for that small group. Put each child's card at his or her place at the table so it's ready for you to write notes on it while listening in to individuals. As described in Chapter 2, you might keep a small-group planning notebook with double-pocket insertable plastic dividers (available from Avery in five different colors). The index cards for each small group can then be kept in the pocket for that group. When the card gets filled up, place it in the index-card file box for

Figure 3.3 This four-by-six-inch card file contains index cards for each student in alphabetical order. These cards are used for anecdotal notes during small-group instruction. Also, when cards on the clipboard tool get filled, they are stored in this file.

I use a colored file folder (so I can easily find it) that will stay at the small-group reading table. I title the front Flexible Small Groups Folder and on the back I place information that summarizes where students should be reading at that grade level to help me stay on track. See Figures 3.5, 3.6, and 3.7.

Figure 3.5 Front of a flexible small-groups folder.

storage. Use these cards and notes both for planning lessons and for parent conferences.

Forming Small Groups

After you've done your testing and collected some anecdotal notes, you're ready to form groups. I like to create a *flexible* flexible groups folder for thinking about small groups. It can be used to help plan whole-group instruction, too.

Figure 3.4 Small-group table ready for kids. Each place has a student's book bag, new book, and index card ready for notes to be written on it.

Figure 3.6 Inside of a flexible small-groups folder.

Figure 3.7 Back of a flexible small-groups folder.

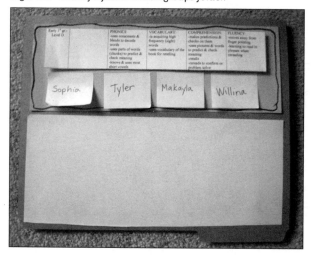

Figure 3.8 Small groups are noted on the bulletin board by the teacher's table. Each colored square has sticky notes with the names of the children in that group on it.

Inside, I divide the folder into four or five sections, depending on the number of small groups I will form. I recommend starting with four groups if possible. Don't try to have more than five groups, because it will be too difficult to keep up with.

Then I write each student's name on a small sticky note and place the kids into groups according to their reading levels and what they need to practice. Because the names are on sticky notes, I have the flexibility to move them around until I'm pleased with how the groups look based on my formal and informal data. At the top of each section, I attach a label with Velcro dots to help me remember what to focus on (see Appendix B, "Reading Levels and What to Focus on in Lessons"). They correspond to reading levels and the needs related to the components of reading—phonemic awareness, phonics, comprehension, vocabulary, and fluency.

You might also post a sticky note list of which kids are in which group, as shown in Figure 3.8. Simply cut colored construction paper into 4½-by-6 inch pieces, one for each colored group, and staple them to a board near your small-group teaching area.

If possible, I recommend working with another teacher to help you form your groups. It is helpful to have a colleague's perspective as you decide

which students to group together for particular needs. This is especially true if you have a Title I or special education teacher working with some of your children. If you have a literacy coach on your campus, this person can also provide support in helping you use assessment data to form (and reconfigure) your groups.

An Example Using TPRI to Form Small Groups in a First-Grade Classroom

During the third week of school, I meet with Mrs. Rex, a first-grade teacher. She teaches in a large suburban school whose population is rapidly changing. This year almost half of her students are learning English as a second language. The school is in an affluent neighborhood, and many professionals from around the world are moving to the area. Mrs.

Figure 3.9 A class summary sheet using the Texas Primary Reading Inventory.

Student Name	Screening Status	Task 1 Blending Word Parts	Task 2 Blending Phonemes	Task 3 Deleting Initial Sounds	Task 4 Deleting Final Sounds	Task 5 Initial Consonants	Task 6 Final Consonants	Task 7 Middle Vowels	Task 8 Initial Blends	Task 9 Final Blends	Task 11 Final Story Read	Accuracy Level	Fluency Rate WCPM	Explicit Questions 0-3	Implicit Questions 0-3	Vocabulary Questions 0-2	Total Reading Comprehension 0-8
Iker	SD	5	5	3	1	5	5	5	3	4	K	Lis	0	1	1	2	4
Ritika	D										5	Ind	59	3	3	2	8
Danny	SD	5	5	4	4	5	5	4	5	5	5	Inst	52	3	2	0	5
Ishahi	SD	5	5	5	5	5	5	4	5	5	5	Ind	96	3	2	0	5
Jane	SD	4	4	3	4	5	5	4	5	5	1	Ind	33	3	2	2	7
Peter	SD	5	4	4	5	5	5	5	5	5	1	Ind	46	3	1	2	6
Will	SD	5	5	4	1	5	5	5	5	5	1	Ind	57	1	2	2	5
Waqas	SD	4	5	1	5	5	5	5	5	4	1	Ind	67	0	1	0	1
Samantha	D										5	Ind	38	3	0	0	3
Haeleigh	D										5	Ind	93	3	3	1	7
Christina	D										5	Inst	67	2	1	1	4
Benjamin	D										5	Ind	95	3	2	1	6
Meghana	D										5	Ind	132	3	2	2	7
Anthony	SD	3	1	0	0	4	5	5	4	2	K	List	0	3	2	0	5
Aimen	D										5	Ind	56	3	1	0	4
Kelvin	D										5	Ind	87	3	1	0	4
Griffin	D										2	Inst	27	2	3	2	7
Amy	D										5	Ind	115	3	3	2	8
Cande	SD	0	0	0	0	0	0	0	0	0	0	0	0	0	0	0	0
Marian	SD	5	3	3	2	5	5	5	3	4	1	Ind	29	3	3	2	8

TPRI Class Summary Sheet — Grade 1
Beginning-of-Year
Teacher: ___
Date: September
Campus: ___

*Fluency (WCPM) is measured on Instructional or Independent Level text. If an alternative story was selected (due to initial placement in Frustrational Level text), only the final fluency measure is reported here.
**Does not include Listening Accuracy Level.

© 2006 The University of Texas System and Texas Education Agency

Rex already knows that vocabulary must be a major focus of her daily teaching.

She has just finished administering the TPRI (Texas Primary Reading Inventory) to each child individually; we look at her data to form groups. See Mrs. Rex's class summary sheet of data in Figure 3.9. This assessment, required by her school district and state department, consists of tasks measuring phonemic awareness, graphophonemic knowledge, reading accuracy, fluency, and comprehension/vocabulary.

We begin by setting up her flexible groups folder, dividing the inside of a manila folder into four sections for the four groups Mrs. Rex plans to have. She likes to use color to help her organize her groups, so we glue colored construction paper in four different colors to the inside of the folder to represent each of her groups. Then we write the name of each child on a 1½-by-2 inch sticky note. (See Mrs. Rex's flexible groups folder in Figures 3.10 and 3.11.)

As we use her assessments to form groups, we look first at students' reading levels; these range from K (kindergarten) to Story 5 (end of first grade). According to the TPRI, most of Mrs. Rex's students read either on Story 1 (beginning of first grade) or Story 5 (end of first grade). We notice that some can decode Story 5 with limited comprehension, and others read Story 5 with excellent comprehension. This is where we start to form groups. We place the sticky notes naming students who read Story 5 with excellent comprehension in one reading group. As

Figure 3.10 Mrs. Rex's flexible small-groups folder as we work on assigning groups.

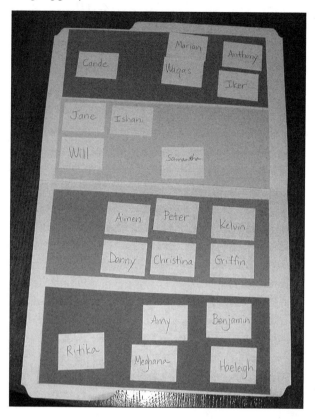

Figure 3.11 Mrs. Rex's finished flexible small-groups folder.

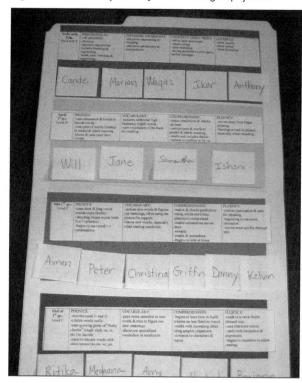

we add each name, we also consider each child's level of English language proficiency. Those with more developed language will be in this group for now. Mrs. Rex will choose books from the end of first grade to use with these students and focus on deeper comprehension. She'll also have them write in response to what they're reading to strengthen both reading and writing skills.

Next, we form a group of students who were decoding Story 5 but had limited comprehension. They will meet together to work with Mrs. Rex on vocabulary and comprehension and will read mid-first-grade level; the text is easier than their decoding level. Mrs. Rex will work with them to help them better understand what they read. She'll also model comprehension and vocabulary strategies in whole-group instruction, which will help her entire class.

We notice that the rest of the class is reading on either K (kindergarten) or Story 1 (beginning of first grade) level. We divide these students into two small groups according to several factors, including their phonemic awareness needs. Most of Mrs. Rex's class has strong graphophonemic (or phonics) knowledge, including initial and final consonants, middle vowels, and initial and final blends. There are only a few children needing work on beginning phonics, so we group them together. They are reading on an early-first-grade level, so Mrs. Rex will focus on phonics and comprehension with them.

In further analyzing Mrs. Rex's data, we discover that Waqas, a very reluctant child and a second language learner, is doing little to no work in class but scored well on phonemic awareness, phonics, and fluently decoding early-first-grade-level text. However, he has virtually no comprehension. We decide to initially group him with students needing the most support to help him gain confidence and show what he knows. Most likely, he will move into another group quickly as he becomes more secure with English.

Also in this group will be Cande, a recent arrival to the country who is not yet speaking English. Mrs. Rex is concerned about this child, and so will work with her one-on-one for short times during the day. Mrs. Rex has labeled common objects around the classroom and has asked a student to guide Cande around the room several times a day, naming objects together. In addition, Mrs. Rex helps Cande match her classmates' names to photos and talks about each as they do so.

Anthony and Iker, two beginning second language learners, will also be in this group. They need some support in phonemic awareness and phonics. Mrs. Rex will meet with this group daily, since they need the most help. They will work on phonemic awareness and oral language development to start. Mrs. Rex may also do shared reading of familiar poems and books with this group to help them feel like readers. In addition, Mrs. Rex will make books containing pictures of familiar objects and classmates, which the group can read with her. These will include high-frequency words like *I*, *see*, *the*, *and*, *a*, *with*, and *my*.

Using Velcro, Mrs. Rex attaches a laminated strip at the top of each colored section in her folder to help her know which skills to focus on at each level. (See Figure 3.11 and Appendix B.) Mrs. Rex highlights what she'll focus on in each group with a colored marker.

Mrs. Rex will begin meeting regularly with her groups as soon as she has her students trained to work independently in literacy work stations. She may start to work with her most struggling four students in one group daily next week. For now, she'll plan to work with them for about ten minutes at a time while the rest of her class is writing independently or working on projects at their seats.

An Example Using DIBELS to Form Small Groups in a Third-Grade Classroom

In this example, the teacher, Mrs. Holt, has been working with students in small groups throughout the school year. She teaches in a small rural school in the Appalachian Mountains. It is now spring, and she is meeting with Ms. Riley, a Title I reading teacher who also works with some of her students, to look at her assessment data from DIBELS (Dynamic Indicators of Basic Early Literacy Skills), an assessment tool required by her school and the state department. This test is given to low-progress students every few weeks to monitor their growth (as well as to all students in the beginning, middle, and end of the year).

These teachers are looking at three students in particular—Jessie, Elizabeth, and Thomas—who are being progress monitored (or tested every several weeks) with DIBELS. Two more children in her classroom read at an early-first-grade level and receive special education services. They are also progress monitored, and are showing very small gains. A resource teacher meets with them in Mrs. Holt's room daily during her small-group instruction time. The rest of the class is making adequate progress and is reading on or above grade level. The majority of Mrs. Holt's class is divided into three different groups, based upon their reading level. One group reads above grade level, and the other two read on grade level. Depending on their skill needs, Mrs. Holt periodically changes children from one group to another.

Today she and Ms. Riley are looking at the most recent assessment data for Thomas, Elizabeth, and Jessie. Thomas began the year with a low score on reading rate, so he needs to improve on fluency. His ORF (Oral Reading Fluency) score was 59 words per minute. This was well below the benchmark target, so Thomas was considered "Intensive," meaning his progress is monitored every two weeks with DIBELS. When giving this assessment, Mrs. Holt listens to him read a short passage while she times him. Besides determining his reading rate, she also listens to his phrasing and intonation. Her goal is to help his fluency improve. Throughout the year, his scores moved from the initial 59 to 71 words per minute in January. His most recent fluency score is 73 words per minute.

Elizabeth also is being monitored for fluency. At the beginning of the year, her ORF was 73 words per minute and her most current score is 88. Her DIBELS status, based upon assessment data, was "Strategic" at the start of the year, which means she has been monitored once a month for fluency.

Jessie also was shown to be "Intensive" on fluency and was tested every other week. Her September score was 60 words per minute. Currently, she is considered "Strategic" and is monitored monthly. According to her most recent check, she is now reading at 90 words per minute.

Besides DIBELS, Mrs. Holt uses another assessment tool, the QPS (Quick Phonics Screener) to determine students' phonics knowledge. It directs children to read words in isolation as well as sentences using that same phonics pattern. The QPS ranges from letter/sound knowledge to a continuum including short vowels, digraphs, blends, long-vowel patterns with silent *e*, *r*-controlled vowels, vowel teams, two-to-four-syllable words, and prefixes/suffixes. Mrs. Holt has found this assessment to be especially useful with her students who need to improve their fluency, since she sees a direct connection between their phonics difficulties and their reading rate. By finding their instructional level of phonics (the phonics patterns that are difficult for them), she is better able to meet students' needs and choose books where they can be successful. She chooses text at their instructional reading level (where they can read with 90 to 94 percent accuracy and some comprehension) that includes phonics patterns they need to practice.

Mrs. Holt and Ms. Riley look at the scores from the QPS for the three students they're considering. Thomas is now on decoding two- and three-syllable words, having mastered the prior phonics skills. Elizabeth is at the same place. Jessie, however, still needs to focus on short vowels. For now, Mrs. Holt will move her into the small group with the two special education students who need support with this same skill. She'll work with Jessie's group on short-vowel patterns and have them practice reading little books with many short-vowel words in them.

She'll meet with Thomas and Elizabeth as a group for now, also focusing on phonics (decoding two- and three-syllable words) and fluency while having them read interesting text at their level (mid–second grade). For now, she'll plan to do focused phonics lessons with a brief phonics warm-up reviewing the skill needed (breaking a word into parts and reading each part, then blending the parts together); they'll then read text that is slightly below third-grade level and contains many two- and three-syllable words, which they'll be able to decode with a bit of help. Mrs. Holt will also teach them how to read in phrases to improve their fluency. She knows that comprehension is equally important, so she'll be sure to talk with students about what they're reading (to ensure they don't just learn to decode without comprehension).

Mrs. Holt and Ms. Riley have discussed how fluency is a bridge between phonics and comprehension. So for now in small group, Mrs. Holt will have Thomas and Elizabeth read books with dialogue to help them read with expression and improve their comprehension. She'll look for books that these two can read with about 95 to 99 percent accuracy for a few sessions, so they can get the *feel* of reading fluently.

Using Running Records and Miscue Analysis

I'm often asked about running records or informal reading inventories and their place in grouping and regrouping decisions. Personally, I find them very valuable because they give me clues about what students are using and what they're confusing. In the grouping examples above, Mrs. Rex used running records as part of TPRI. These helped her determine children's instructional reading level, or which story they could read with 90 to 94 percent accuracy. Mrs. Holt's assessments focused on fluency and phonics. She didn't use running records. Rather, she used a word list and a sentence-reading task. She did make note of errors, but her assessment did not include *running* or connected text. Even though Mrs. Holt didn't use running records as her required assessment, she could still incorporate them into her small-group teaching. By making notes about the miscues students make while reading in small group, she could analyze the types of phonics errors children are making on a daily basis, which could help inform her teaching.

Running records (see Figure 3.12 for a sample) are a way for a teacher to record a child's reading behaviors in a kind of shorthand, making it easy to go back later and analyze miscues the child made. I use running records in two ways. One is to determine a benchmark, or the reading level where the child should be placed for optimum small-group instruction—like Mrs. Rex did. This is usually done at the beginning and end of the year and, sometimes, midyear. In this case, the text is *unfamiliar*, brand-new, or never seen before. You read a brief standard introduction and have the student read.

Figure 3.12 Sample of a running record.

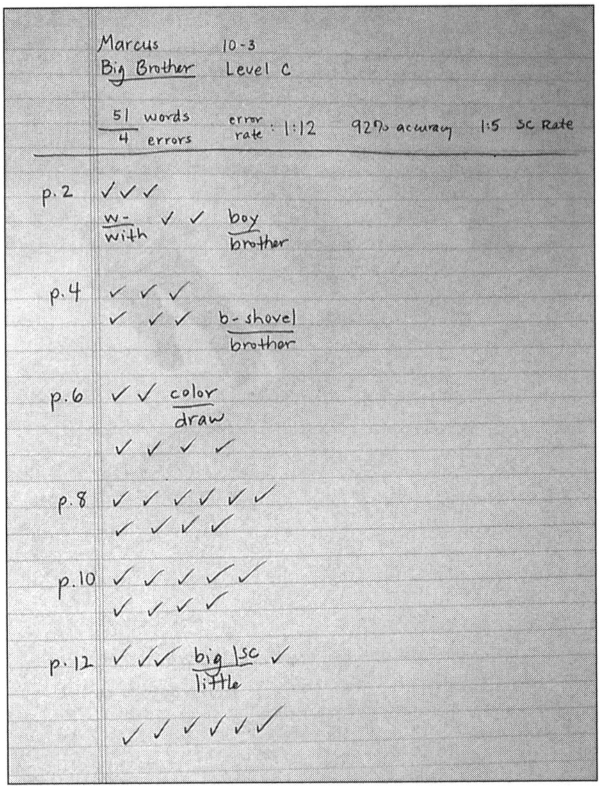

You listen in and do the running record, then have the child retell. For more detailed information about running records, see Marie Clay's *Running Records for Classroom Teachers* (2000). Miscue analyses are performed in a similar fashion.

Figure 3.13 This chart shows how to use running records and miscue analysis to form and work with small groups.

Purpose	Instructional Setting	Kind of Text	How Often	Considerations
Determining a benchmark reading level	Testing kids one-on-one	Unfamiliar text/"cold read"	Two to three times a year, including the beginning and end of the year	No teaching is done; just use the "script" for administration
Observing which reading strategies kids are using or confusing, based on what you've already taught	Small-group instruction as part of "warm-up" or familiar reading	Slightly familiar text	May do with one child each time you meet with a small group	Use a teaching point, helping a student see what he or she is doing well or needs to try

I also use running records during small-group instruction. These are done frequently with individuals as part of the warm-up before kids read a new book. Here, a child reads a *familiar* text, usually the one read the last time I met with this group. It should not be overly familiar, or it will skew the information you get. I listen in and often use a teaching point to help reinforce a reading strategy a child is using or to emphasize something new I want that child to try as he or she reads that day in small group. This use of running records tells me how kids are handling the strategies I've been modeling and helps me determine how kids are doing on their own. This information helps me decide whether the student should be moved to another group or to a harder or easier level of text.

Planning to Meet with Groups

Listed below are some commonly asked questions and answers about grouping.

How Do I Form Groups at the Start of the Year?

Look at all your data. Setting up a flexible reading groups folder, as described in this chapter and shown in Figures 3.5, 3.6, and 3.7, can really help. It will allow you to look at each child as well as the whole class.

Place each child where you think he or she will fit best for now, and then be prepared to be flexible. You can move students from group to group using sticky notes as you're making these initial decisions. You can even place a student in more than one group, depending on the child's needs. For example, an emergent reader may meet in one group for letter identification work and in another group for phonemic awareness. A student reading on a second-grade reading level may meet in one group that is focusing on phonics at that level and in another group for fluency if the student needs both. Be flexible in placing students in groups.

You can always try a student in a group and then rearrange the groups based on your observations. Follow the lead of the child. Look for student success. It will guide you in the right direction. Know that there is more than one way to group students. Form your groups and then try them out. You'll be able to tell whether students are correctly matched to the texts and skills they need. Use both your formal assessment data and your observations to inform your grouping decisions.

How Many Groups Should I Meet with in a Day?

I think it's smart to begin with just one group a day once you begin small-group instruction. In first grade and up, this is usually after four to six weeks of school (when children have been trained to work independently at literacy work stations). In kindergarten it usually takes longer. After you are meeting with one group a day successfully, work with two small groups a day. Occasionally, you might work with three groups in a day, but this is probably not the norm. You need time for whole group *and* small groups. If you do too many small groups, you'll run out of time for some whole-group reading instruction, too.

Trying to see every group every day will not yield quality teaching. Remember, *quality, not quantity*. It's not about how many groups you can "fit into" a day. Rather, it's about meeting the needs of students in small groups. You'll want to plan your lessons daily for the next day's groups to keep with students' cutting edge of development and optimize learning. No classroom teacher should be expected to plan three or four small-group lessons for reading in a day *plus* whole-group reading instruction *plus* writing and math and science and social studies!

Note: *If* you are fortunate enough to have another teacher in the classroom to work with small groups alongside you (Title I, special education, etc.), it may be possible to work with every group daily between the two of you.

How Long Should I Meet with Each Group?

I have found that about twenty minutes per small group works well in first grade and up. In kindergarten I often work with students for about fifteen minutes. I prefer short lessons to long ones because I think students take more away from them. When lessons are short and focused, student engagement remains high and kids pay better attention. This also allows you to see more than one group if time is limited.

How Often Should I Meet with Each Group?

Generally, most teachers meet with their lowest readers more often. Most schools ask teachers to work with their struggling readers every day. Teachers are very caring people and want to treat all children fairly. But remember that fair is not always equal (a quote from my friend Judy Wallis). If you try to meet with every group every day, you'll burn out quickly. And often you'll find yourself just pulling a group and reading a book with kids, rather than being thoughtful about planning a lesson and teaching in that small group.

Figure 3.14 is a chart that shows how one teacher managed meeting with her small groups over a two-week period. She plotted this out on sticky notes, so she could move the groups around flexibly until she found a plan that worked. You'll notice that she is often meeting with students on consecutive days so that she can connect instruction for them. Her yellow group has her highest students. She meets with them only once a week since they are reading well above grade level. Her lowest group is the red group, and she meets with them four times a week. Her blue group needs more support than her green group, so she meets with them a bit more often.

How Can I Meet with My Lowest Groups Every Day?

The reality in most classrooms is that it is very difficult to meet with your lowest students *every* day in small group because you'll run out of time very quickly. One possibility is to meet with those children four days a week and, on the fifth day, meet with them individually for a few minutes during independent reading to have a brief conference with them.

Another idea is to find hidden pockets during the day during which you might meet with this group. For example, you might be able to meet with them for fifteen minutes as kids are entering your room in the morning. If they know you'll be there to work with them, they may make the effort to get right to class. The rest of the class can do morning jobs and get ready for the day while you meet with this group for some extra attention.

In some classrooms there are several low groups, or the majority of kids are reading below

Figure 3.14 Sample small-group schedule.

Day of Week	Monday	Tuesday	Wednesday	Thursday	Friday
Week 1	RED YELLOW	RED BLUE	RED BLUE	BLUE GREEN	RED GREEN
Week 2	RED YELLOW	RED BLUE	GREEN BLUE	RED BLUE	RED GREEN
Note: Please do not copy this schedule as is. This is just one sample.					

grade level. This, again, is reality for some teachers. If you're one of them, you may have to meet with three groups a day on many days, finding and using the pockets of time mentioned above. This works best in a self-contained classroom.

You may also have to assign students to particular literacy work stations as interventions, planning very carefully which students go to which work stations for practice. For example, if you have a low group that needs fluency practice, you might plan for them to go to the buddy reading station (to practice orally reading easy text with a partner) or to the recording studio (to tape-record themselves reading orally, then listen to and self-evaluate it) or to the computer station (to work on a fluency program). See the section "Links to Literacy Work Stations Practice" in Chapters 4 through 8 to help with this planning.

How Do I Keep My Groups Straight— Who Read What, Lesson Plans, and So On?

Use a small-group lesson-planning notebook as described in this chapter and in Chapter 2. Keep written lesson plans and jot down which books were read in each group. Some teachers also keep a sticky note in this plan book where they jot down the date and title read by this group.

Don't worry if you occasionally have a child in a group tell you he or she has already read a book. Odds are the child will improve during this reading of the text! I always refer to familiar books as "old favorites." Tell the student he or she will be an expert on this book after reading it again. Just ask the child to please not give away what happens in the book so that everyone can enjoy it fully.

Regrouping Flexibly

Another question I'm asked daily is, "When do I move kids in or out of groups?" Again, I use a combination of both formal and informal assessments.

As you meet with children in small group, you will get to know them much better than if you worked with them only in whole group. You will know who is improving in fluency or phonics skill. You will see who still needs help with deeper comprehension or vocabulary development. Use this knowledge combined with your formal data. For example, if you're using DIBELS, you will be asked to monitor your struggling students' progress every few weeks. Use this data in combination with what you're noticing them doing as readers and writers.

Pay attention to what students are doing as readers with regard to phonemic awareness, phonics, comprehension, vocabulary, and fluency, as well as what they do as writers. Use the Reading Levels and What to Focus on in Lessons chart found in Appendix B to help you make decisions about reading levels. I always think, "Is the child able to do this on his or her own, or must I give support?" When a child consistently demonstrates use of the skills and strategy at a level with increasing independence, I try the student at a higher level. My goal is for kids to be doing *more* of the work than I do in the small-group lesson. I'm providing minimal support, so the student will develop independence over time.

Once students are working solidly on grade level, instead of trying to move kids to higher and higher reading levels, I prefer to go deeper and expand their reading of a variety of genres at that level. Also, I work with them on writing at that level. Students who are great writers are usually great readers. Paying attention to what writers do helps students better comprehend and read more fluently and with more accurate decoding. Looking at how words are spelled helps kids with decoding or phonics. Examining text structures and word choice used by writers helps readers with comprehension and vocabulary. Noticing how writers use punctuation to communicate a message improves reading fluency.

See the chart When Do I Move a Student into a Different Small Group? in Appendix A for additional help.

Grouping Emergent Readers

Grouping emergent readers looks somewhat different than grouping students who are reading. Here are some things to think about when working with children just learning to look at and work with print. Remember, these students are *not* nonreaders; they are *emergent* readers. No matter their grade level, they are just learning to work with print.

- You might place emergent readers in a group to work on the following:
    - phonemic awareness (see Chapter 6)
    - oral language development
    - letter learning
    - rhyming and other aspects of phonological awareness
    - concepts about print
- Emergent readers may be in a variety of groups, meeting some days to work on phonemic awareness and other days on concepts about print, or a combination of the two.
- Emergent readers need to be "reading" text, even if it is shared reading of Big Books or buddy reading little books used previously in shared reading. They need to feel like readers. Even students with as few as about ten letters and sounds can begin to learn to read. Their reading of little books will look different from that of students who are already beginning to read on their own. You will need to give more support to them as emergent readers.
- Keep watching their reading and writing progress at literacy work stations and during independent writing time. They often show you what they understand about print as you watch them "read" Big Books and poems with a partner at work stations. Likewise, look at their writing; when they begin to use letters to represent sounds this will show you what they're starting to understand about phonics.
- You might use the strips from the Reading Levels and What to Focus on in Lessons chart included in Appendix B on your flexible groups folder.

Simply cut them out and put Velcro on the back. They can be used to help you remember which students need to focus on what in small groups.

Reflection Questions for Professional Conversations

1. How have you formed small reading groups in the past? What worked well? What would you like to change? What are one or two new things you might try?
2. Discuss your use of both formal and informal assessments for forming small groups. Which are you most comfortable with? Why? How might you improve your use of both methods?
3. Talk with a colleague about using anecdotal notes to help with grouping. Collect some notes and share them with each other. Think about how these can help you form groups, plan lessons, and conduct parent conferences. Share ways that you're finding are helping you keep these notes useful and organized.
4. Share ideas with your grade-level team about formal testing. Note: Don't hold a gripe session! Think about what you can do to make testing easier and more valuable. How can you use the data gathered to inform your instruction? Meet with an administrator or literacy coach for help, if needed.
5. Make a flexible reading groups folder. Try it for a while and share what's worked with another teacher.
6. Work with a colleague to form your flexible groups (or to regroup them). Use the data you've collected. Ask each other questions and help each other make decisions about where to place children. Then be flexible and adjust as needed.

For Further Information on Grouping

Consult the resources that accompany any formal testing you are doing. Most of these have suggestions for grouping.

Comprehension

Mr. Lausch has formed a small group of five students in his second-grade classroom. He tells me that these students have some basic comprehension, but they don't think deeply. They often just decode and don't seem to be thinking about what they're reading. This group needs lots of support to help them think through inferences in the text, so he has asked me, his literacy coach, to show him what this kind of teaching looks like.

This group is just starting the book *Four on the Shore*, by James Marshall. It is easy enough for them to decode and will require deeper thinking, since this author's books are filled with wit and subtle humor. To help them focus their thinking, I begin by reviewing what they'll be thinking about as they read fiction—characters; setting; problem; solution; beginning, middle, and end; and author's purpose. I have these posted on a retelling glove; this visual really gets their attention. (See Figure 4.1.) The children are familiar with all these elements but have not applied them to their reading. I tell them that reading is *thinking* and that I'll help them with their thinking as they read today.

Figure 4.1 Retelling glove for fiction provides a scaffold to guide kids' thinking while reading stories.

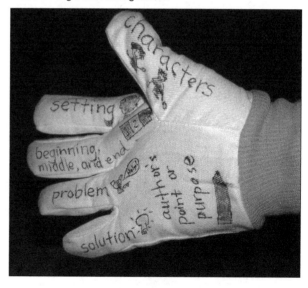

We use the cover to infer that there are four characters having a campout at a lake. Then I have them turn to page 3, look at the picture, and *think* before reading. I ask them to find out the names of the four characters and figure out which is which, using the picture again to help them infer. As they read quietly, I listen in to individuals. They decode accurately and with some fluency.

After they read, the group names Spider, Sam, and Lolly as three of the characters. They use the pictures and explain how they know who each one is. They infer *why* Spider got his name. (His hair looks like spider legs in the picture.) However, they have trouble figuring out who the fourth character is, since he hasn't been named in the text. They can only see his legs dangling from a tree in the picture. The text says, "'Spider,' said Lolly. 'Your little brother is getting on my nerves.'" They have trouble figuring out who's talking, so I ask a few questions to scaffold their thinking:

"If it says, 'said Lolly,' who's talking?"
"Who's Lolly talking to?"
"So, whose little brother is it?"

These questions support their inferences, and they figure it out. The children in this group need lots of support to help them think, but they *can* do it. I set the bar high, and they know I expect they *will* comprehend. I don't take, "I don't know" as an answer. I just ask another, more supportive, question to help them figure it out.

They tell me that this book is kind of hard and they must think. They're starting to get it. I ask, "What did we use to help us figure it out?" They respond with, "We used the names, the words, the pictures of the characters, and our brains. We were thinking."

Delighted that they are trying to comprehend, I ask them to read the next four pages. Before they read, they tell me they will *think*. I give each of them a sticky note and have them place it at the bottom of page 7, where they will stop today. Next, I tell them to read and find out the name of the little brother and where they're going. I ask them to write their predictions of what might happen next in the book on their sticky note when they finish. While they read independently, I listen in to indi-

viduals and have brief conversations with each about what they've found out so far. I'm amazed at how much better they're doing.

After they all finish, we have a small-group discussion. They are so excited, because they've understood what they've read. Their predictions are accurate. They're making personal connections; they've figured out what will probably happen next . . . and it makes sense. I close the lesson by asking, "What was different today?" Their responses include, "We were thinking and tried to help ourselves. Writing down helped me think. So did the cover. We used our brains." I remind them that every time they read, they must do the same thing. Then they'll understand it just like they did today. They look forward to reading the next chapter.

Mr. Lausch and I debrief after the lesson. He's very impressed with the level of thinking his kids did. "Teaching comprehension sure is a lot of work," he notes. "You really expected my kids to do it, and they did. I can see that I gave them too many of the answers in the past." He decides to model with the retelling glove in whole-group instruction and then move it to small group for reinforcement.

What Is Comprehension?

Comprehension is understanding. It involves thinking and can be likened to a conversation between the reader and the text. It can be basic, as in understanding a general message, or deep, as in inferring and generalizing ideas. Comprehension first develops as listening comprehension in infants and toddlers as they listen to the world around them and begin to respond.

In the classroom, I start by teaching comprehension in whole group. I model comprehension strategies—such as making connections, questioning, visualizing, inferring, determining importance, making generalizations, and summarizing—while I read aloud engaging, high-quality literature to students. Once students demonstrate listening comprehension, they can learn (with support and guidance) to transfer those same skills to the act of reading comprehension.

At first, they will need to read text that is easy enough for them to decode so they can use more of their mental energy to understand, or comprehend, what they read. In small group, I make sure students are reading at their instructional reading level, or text that is no harder than one they can read with 90 to 94 percent accuracy, some fluency, and some basic comprehension. If the text is too hard for them to decode, they'll have to use too much thinking power for phonics. And they'll have no brainpower left for comprehension. Think about the students in Mr. Lausch's group. Their brains weren't used to thinking about comprehension, but they could be trained to do so when the decoding wasn't too difficult.

Comprehension is important because it is the goal of reading. If we do not understand what we read, then why would we want to read? In kindergarten I was taught Spanish in an "enrichment" class. In high school, I also studied Spanish. Today, I can *decode* Spanish, but I don't *comprehend* what I've "read." Therefore, I don't say I can *read* Spanish; instead, I say I can *decode* this language. I have no comprehension of what I've read, because I don't have the vocabulary and the oral language to support my decoding.

This is one of the greatest dangers in our reading instruction . . . that we think we're teaching *reading* when in actuality we've essentially taught *decoding*. Teaching comprehension is critical to ensure that students understand what they've read. I'm not just talking basic recall here, but am referring to a deeper understanding of why the characters acted like they did in a fiction book or how students might use the facts gleaned from reading an informational text.

Some educators think it's a good idea to teach kids to decode first and then teach them to comprehend. My recommendation is that we should teach comprehension from the start. We should be modeling how to comprehend in our daily read-

aloud and shared reading sessions with students. All text we ask students to read should make sense so they get used to thinking about everything and anything they read.

Along with comprehension, we must also consider vocabulary. As students move into higher levels of reading, they often lose meaning because they skim over new vocabulary. See Chapter 8 on vocabulary teaching for more ideas and then integrate them into your comprehension lessons as needed.

Comprehension Research at a Glance

Before the 1980s, many teachers, including myself, were very good at *testing*, not *teaching*, comprehension. More recent research has shown us what to do to teach students how to comprehend. Here is a summary of some general comprehension studies you might find helpful when planning comprehension instruction:

■ Comprehension strategies can be taught effectively through think-alouds (Bereiter and Bird 1985).

■ Rosenblatt's (1978) theory of transactional analysis says that the reading of any work of literature is an individual and unique occurrence involving the mind and emotions of a particular reader.

■ Good comprehenders use a range of comprehension strategies to deepen and enrich their understanding of what they are reading (Pressley, El-Dinary, and Brown 1992).

■ Those who comprehend well are aware of their own thinking processes and make conscious decisions to use different comprehension strategies as they read, especially when they detect problems in understanding what they are reading (Baker and Brown 1984).

■ Good readers attribute successful comprehension to effort more than to ability. They believe they can understand if they apply the right comprehension strategies (Brown 2002).

- Stronger comprehenders use their background knowledge to identify or make connections among ideas in what they are reading (van den Broek and Kremer 2000).

- Weak comprehenders may not recognize inconsistencies between what they read and their background knowledge. Instead, they may ignore or modify information in the text so they can hold on to their current understanding, even if it is incorrect (Beck and McKeown 2001). ·

- Readers who ask themselves questions during or after reading are able to identify comprehension problems sooner and more accurately (Davey and McBride 1986).

- Having students generate their own questions, combined with detailed, explicit instruction and sufficient opportunity to practice the strategy, increased their comprehension and the ability to recall what they'd read (Pressley and Woloshyn 1995).

- Explaining what they've read to each other in their own words increases students' comprehension (Klingner, Vaughn, and Schumm 1998).

- Teaching readers to draw visual displays to organize the ideas found in what they are reading helps them remember what they read and can produce stronger comprehension in subjects such as social studies and science (Armbruster, Anderson, and Meyer 1991).

- Allington's (1983) study found that most of the time students should be reading texts they can decode with a very high level of accuracy to improve comprehension.

- In addition, the National Reading Panel Report (NICHD 2000) recommends the following to help students comprehend:
  - Monitoring comprehension
  - Using cooperative learning
  - Using graphic and semantic organizers
  - Answering questions

- Generating questions
- Understanding story structure
- Summarizing
- Making use of prior knowledge
- Using mental imagery

Who Needs to Meet in Small Groups for Comprehension?

Every student can benefit from comprehension instruction. Essentially, every time I meet with a small group to read a text, comprehension is the ultimate goal. To scaffold them and help them be successful, I choose text where students have some basic comprehension.

Students who are good decoders but can't tell you what they've read need extra small-group instruction on how to comprehend. If you're using an assessment such as DRA or an informal reading inventory (IRI) and find the students decode on grade level but can't retell what they've read, those students need small-group work with comprehension, too. Likewise, if you're using an assessment like DIBELS that does a quick measure of comprehension, use that data to form groups with students low in retelling for extra work on comprehension.

Often overlooked are kids who have some basic comprehension but don't go any deeper with their thinking. These students will greatly benefit from small-group instruction with a focus on deeper comprehension, such as inferring.

Above-level readers can also learn to go deeper in their thinking in guided small-group lessons with a focus on comprehension. Work with them on determining importance in nonfiction, understanding humor and deeper plots in fiction, and building background knowledge when they read texts for which they have little schema. I prefer to help kids think more deeply, rather than to keep pushing them through higher and higher reading levels once they are reading on grade level.

I also use writing to help kids comprehend better. Once they can write fluently enough that it

Figure 4.2 Kindergarten children write responses to a book read the day before in small group.

doesn't interfere with their reading, I often have them use sticky notes or graphic organizers to record what they're thinking to help them retain those ideas. Sometimes we write a response together after reading. I find that this helps them interact with the text—like having a conversation with the book as they read it.

Possible Focus for Lessons

There are many possibilities from which you might choose a focus during a small-group lesson for comprehension. The National Reading Panel (NICHD 2000) researchers recommend the following kinds of comprehension strategy instruction to help readers become purposeful and active. Good readers use these steps, in combination, to make sense of text:

- *Understanding text structure.* This is often overlooked in nonfiction but overused as an isolated review, or a check, *after* reading in fiction. I like to teach students how to think about characters, setting, problem, solution, and beginning/middle/end of a story *before*

and *during* their reading, as well as *after*. Likewise, teaching them how to identify nonfiction text structures, such as cause and effect, description, question and answer, and time order and sequence, can improve their comprehension of nonfiction.

- *Asking questions.* This comprehension strategy helps students learn to generate and ask inferential questions to propel their reading forward.
- *Answering questions.* It's important to teach kids to answer questions about the details and inferences of the text. I am careful to focus more on *thick* questions that require deeper thinking and have potentially layered responses rather than *thin* questions that require only one-word answers.
- *Summarizing.* This is tough, since it requires kids to first have basic comprehension and also determine which ideas are most important. Here, we focus on helping readers learn to identify and remember the main things from the text read.

While reading, students who use these steps improve their comprehension as they interact with the text:

- *Using schema/making use of prior knowledge.* This is often a good place to begin with comprehension instruction. Students make use of their personal experience and schema (background knowledge) to help them understand what they are reading. They often do this *before* reading as they preview the text as well as *during* their reading.
- *Visualizing/using mental imagery.* As they read, kids who best understand form vivid mental pictures. They often see, hear, taste, smell, and feel what's going on in the book. "I feel like I'm in the book with the characters" is how one third grader described this to me. Visualizing improves understanding and helps children remember what they read.

In addition, students can be taught the following to increase comprehension:

- *Monitoring.* It's important to learn to stop and reread when your mind wanders or meaning breaks down. Successful readers think about their thinking and are aware when it's not working so well.
- *Inference.* Many teachers throw up their hands in frustration on this one. Students can be taught to think through modeling and expecting that they can and will infer. I've found it helpful to build on their knowledge when teaching inference. When you can help kids connect what they know to what the text says, they can begin to infer.
- *Graphic organizers.* I like to use these as tools for thinking. When students have trouble comprehending, I often show them how to use graphic organizers as reminders and recording devices for what they're thinking. Graphic organizers can help to "hold" their thoughts while they're reading.
- *Deeper meaning.* This includes higher-level thinking, including generalizing, determining importance, synthesizing, and analyzing what was read. Use of quality questioning will help push kids' thinking deeper.

Figure 4.3 Third graders record their thinking on graphic organizers as they read to help them comprehend more deeply.

Figure 4.4 Sample graphic organizer.

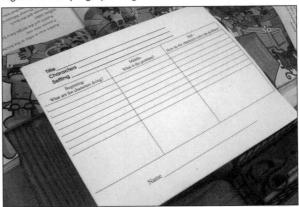

Choosing Materials

I think it's important to include a variety of text, including fiction *and* nonfiction, for comprehension instruction in small group. This is a great place to expand students' reading interests. If you have students who always choose a certain type of book, you might stretch their horizons by guiding their reading of a different kind of book. For example, if they usually read books about animals, guide them into mysteries for a new experience. Children who comprehend over a wide variety of text are more proficient than readers of just one type of book.

I've found that choosing books based on students' interest and background knowledge improves their comprehension greatly. It's very difficult to comprehend something you're not interested in or know nothing about. Many of the struggling readers I've worked with have preferred nonfiction to fiction. So in small group, I often offer nonfiction—based on topics kids love, like animals or cars or volcanoes—to children who normally avoid reading like the plague.

If I mistakenly choose a text that is too hard, I tell the group that I didn't do a good job with book choice (trust me, they've done the same) and choose a slightly easier book so they'll experience success. If you know your students well—their reading levels, their interests, their stamina—this information will carry you far in choosing the best books to use with them in small group. Remember to think about what they already know and build upon that to help them better comprehend.

⠿ The Lessons ⠿

Text Structure Lesson

Things to Think About

■ The type of lesson described below can help students learn how to comprehend *nonfiction*. I like to first teach about various structures of nonfiction, such as question and answer, time order, description, cause and effect, and problem and solution during whole-group instruction. Then it is easier for students to apply that learning in small-group lessons like the one that follows.

■ After reading books with these nonfiction text structures, you might teach students to write using the same structures.

■ You might also teach lessons related to *story* structure with fiction books, focusing on characters; setting; beginning, middle, and end; or problem and solution, like the opening lesson in this chapter.

Before the Lesson

Miss Rodriguez teaches kindergarten. Today she will meet with a group of four children who are reading on level and progressing well. Instead of trying to push them through higher reading levels, she chooses to go deeper and help them with comprehension by teaching about text structure. The book she selects is *Who's Hiding?* by Rozanne Lanczak Williams. It has a question-and-answer format, which is an easy text structure for emergent readers to understand. Every other page has a question, followed by an answer on the following page. Miss Rodriguez knows the children will enjoy reading this nonfiction text, since they are interested in animals and the world around them. She takes a few minutes

to read through the book and jots down a simple lesson plan. (See Figure 4.6.) Having a plan will help her stick with her comprehension focus during the lesson. (A template for planning for comprehension in small group can be found in Appendix C.)

She plans to take notes on Ella and Piper as they read today, as well as anyone else should the need arise. So she takes an index card with each child's name on it and distributes these around the table to mark where each child will sit. She'll have the cards at her fingertips if she wants to write down anything particular she noticed the students doing as readers today. (See Chapter 2 for more ideas on organizing for note taking.)

During the Lesson

Miss Rodriguez calls Caden, Ella, Piper, and Max to a small round table while the rest of the children go to their literacy work stations. The four eagerly sit down at their appointed places, ready to read. Miss Rodriguez gives each of them a book bag filled with several familiar books, and they all choose a book and begin to read independently. This is part of their routine, and they know just what to do. She listens in to Ella read her book and takes a few notes about her reading on her card. Then she asks Ella to tell her a little about the book. Miss Rodriguez expects comprehension of her beginning readers.

Next, she tells the children they will be reading a new book today. She hands each a copy of *Who's Hiding?* She reads the title to them and leads a brief discussion about the cover. They talk about who's hiding (a fish) and who's after it (a shark). This leads to thinking about *why* the fish is hiding. The kids agree that it doesn't want to be eaten, and that the shark is much bigger than the little fish. Caden says it's like the book *Swimmy*, which Miss Rodriguez has read aloud to the class recently. The teacher smiles at his connection and says that Swimmy was helping the other fish hide, just like on this cover picture. Max, who loves animals and often watches nature shows, adds, "The shark is a predator. It wants to eat the little fish." Miss Rodriguez uses

Max's word and says, "You will be reading about several predators in this book. On each page an animal is hiding from another one. What other animals might hide from a predator like the little fish?" The children volunteer ideas—bugs hiding from snakes and birds, fish hiding from eagles, deer running away from cheetahs. They are very interested in this nonfiction topic and are ready to read.

Miss Rodriguez points to the word *Who's* on the cover and has the children run their fingers under it while reading it with her. She tells them it's going to be on many of the pages and means *who is*. She also tells them there will be a pattern in the book. One page will ask who's hiding from an animal, and the next page will tell the answer. It's a question-and-answer pattern and will help them read and understand the book. They look at the first two pages together, and she points out the punctuation and how it differs. Finally, Miss Rodriguez tells them to read and find out who's hiding from whom and think about why. She reminds them to make the pictures and the words match and make sense as they read.

Each child reads the little book aloud at his or her own pace. They don't read together in unison or take turns. Miss Rodriguez wants each of them to read it on their own. Because of her rich but brief book introduction, the children are confident and try to read the book as independently as possible. She moves around the table and listens in to individuals, prompting as needed. Piper reads, "Who's hiding from the bird?" Miss Rodriguez notices that Piper glances at the picture and then at the word for confirmation and praises this checking. "You looked at the picture and the word to make it match. Good checking." Piper beams and keeps going. "A c-a-t, cat. Cat? That's not a cat. It's a bug." Miss Rodriguez helps Piper look at this long word, *caterpillar*, and back at the picture. "Oh, it's a caterpillar," says Piper. "That makes sense." Her teacher listens to her reread this page and then moves to the next child. She jots down a note about Piper's reading on an index card. (See Figure 4.5 for her notes.)

Figure 4.5 Mrs. Rodriguez's anecdotal notes on Piper.

Piper

11/30 - paying more attention to print

12/2 - really enjoying reading new books

12/7 - SC on caterpillar - said "cat," but checked picture & read through word - wow!

Miss Rodriguez continues to listen in to individuals, prompting and supporting each for just a minute or so. When some of the children finish early, she reminds them to read it again and read it so it sounds really interesting. She tells them to make it sound like a question when they read each question page.

They end the lesson with a brief but lively discussion about the animals and who was hiding from whom. They figure out that the hiding animals were usually smaller than the predators and that the animals lived in different environments, like the ocean and the woods. Miss Rodriguez praises them for checking the pictures and the words and making it make sense. They reread the book together one time, and Miss Rodriguez helps them raise their voices at the end of each question. They like this pattern and decide they'd like to write a question-and-answer book next time they meet.

After the Lesson

Miss Rodriguez collects the note cards and returns them to her small-group lesson-plan notebook while the four students she just met with move to their work stations. She also jots down a quick reflection about today's reading. Her children can read the management board for literacy work stations independently and know just where to go. It's on a nearby pocket chart. They find their names and read the icons telling them which station to

Figure 4.6 Lesson Plan for Text Structure

⁑ Lesson Plan for Text Structure ⁑

Group: Ella, Piper, Max, Caden

Focus: COMPREHENSION

☐ monitoring ☐ schema ☐ asking ?s ☐ visualizing ☐ inference

☐ summarizing ☑ text structure ☐ graphic organizers ☐ deeper meaning

Warm-Up: Familiar Rereading   **Listen to:** Ella   **Title:** *What's the Weather Like Today?*

Today's Book: *Who's Hiding?* by Rozanne Lanczak Williams   **Level:** end of kindergarten/C

BEFORE READING

Genre: nonfiction

Book Intro:

- Read title to them. *On each page, an animal is hiding from another one. Look at the cover. Who's hiding? Why? What other animals might hide from each other for protection?*
- Point out *Who's* on the cover and discuss that it stands for *who is*. *Who's will be in the book a lot and will ask a question.*
- Tell that the book has a question-and-answer pattern. Show the punctuation.

Set Purpose for Reading:

Read to find out: *which animal is hiding from which. Why?*

DURING READING

Prompts:

- *What makes sense there? Check it.*
- *Use the picture. Does that match the word you read?*
- *You read a question. What will probably come next? (an answer)*

Notes: Piper

AFTER READING

Discuss:

- *Name an animal from the book that was hiding. Who did it hide from? Why?*
- Discuss the pattern the writer used. *How could we use this pattern to write? What could we write about next time using questions and answers?*

REFLECTION

Kids liked the Q/A format of this book. Write with this pattern next time. Use other animal names. Find other books with *who* in them (for large and small group). Make question words chart with class. Use in science, too.

move to next. Another group of children arrives at her small-group table, and she directs them to get out their books for familiar rereading.

At the bottom of her lesson plan (see Figure 4.6), Miss Rodriguez notes that they will write a question-and-answer book next time they meet.

She will also look for other books with *who* in them for both shared reading during whole-group time and small-group reading. Question words are tricky, but she knows her kindergartners are ready to start recognizing and using these in science as well as language arts. She'll make a list of question words with her class to use as an anchor chart during whole-group instruction. Then she'll move it to the writing station. Some of her students will probably begin to write question-and-answer books after she works with this in small group.

Monitoring Lesson

Things to Think About

- Monitoring means checking. Emergent readers often stop while reading. When they do this, I like to label their behavior by saying, "You stopped. Good checking. How can you help yourself?" Your goal is for them to learn to reread and fix it up.

- Monitoring lessons are good to use with students who decode well but don't pay much attention to what they're reading. They must learn to stop and think about if they've understood what they've read so far.

- Monitoring is often used in combination with other reading strategies, such as schema, as you'll see in this lesson.

- Once children can write so that others can read and understand what they've written, you might have them use sticky notes to jot down brief notes about what they're reading. This often helps them slow down and pay attention.

Before the Lesson

Mrs. Washington, a first-grade teacher, will meet with Jamaal, Reid, Tarik, and Bryson today in small group. They can decode, but they often don't monitor, or think about, their understanding of what they've read. So she chooses a book for which they have lots of background knowledge—*Families*, by

Margie Burton et al. These students all have families and know lots about them, and this should help their comprehension. It's hard to understand something you don't know much about.

As she plans the lesson (see Figure 4.7), Mrs. Washington decides to have this group use sticky notes to jot down their thinking as they read. Recently, she attended a workshop where this technique was shared, and she's eager to try it. She will limit the number of sticky notes to three each so they don't get hung up with just playing with them. Mrs. Washington has just modeled how to use sticky notes in whole-group instruction while she was reading aloud a book, so her students have seen how to use them to write down their thinking. She hopes that writing down some of their thinking will help them stop and think about what they're reading, rather than just decode the words.

During the Lesson

Mrs. Washington introduces the new book, *Families*, by reading the title and looking at the cover with her small group. She asks them what they already know about families, and they share a bit about their own. They tell about black and white and Chinese and Mexican families.

Their teacher tells them that as they read today she wants them to think about how the families in the books are *like* theirs. She gives them each three sticky notes and tells them to write down what they are thinking as they read. She reminds them not to just read the words but also to *think*. When they get to the end of a page, they should think about how this family is like theirs. They should write down ideas of how they're alike.

As they read on their own, Mrs. Washington listens in to individuals. They are doing great with both decoding and fluency. Comprehension is definitely where she needs to focus. She listens in to Reid. He reads, "There are many kinds of families. Some are small. Some families are big." He gets ready to turn the page. Mrs. Washington stops and

Figure 4.7 Lesson Plan for Monitoring Comprehension

⠿ Lesson Plan for Monitoring Comprehension ⠿

Group: Jamaal, Reid, Tarik, Bryson

Focus: COMPREHENSION

- ☑ monitoring
- ☐ schema
- ☐ asking ?s
- ☐ visualizing
- ☐ inference
- ☐ summarizing
- ☐ text structure
- ☐ graphic organizers
- ☐ deeper meaning

Today's Book: *Families* by Margie Burton et al.   **Level:** mid–first grade/F

BEFORE READING

Genre: nonfiction

Book Intro:

- ■ Read title. *What do you know about families? What words might you find in this book?*
- ■ Give three sticky notes to each. *Write how your family is like those in the book as you read.*
- ■ *Think while you read. If you don't remember what you just read, stop and reread.*

Set Purpose for Reading:

Read to find out: *how your family is like the families in the book.*

DURING READING

Prompts:

- ■ *What does that make you think of?*
- ■ *What did you find out?*
- ■ *How is your family like that? Write it on a sticky note to help you remember.*
- ■ *What can you do to remember what you just read? Yes, read it again and think.*

Notes: Reid and Tarik

AFTER READING

Discuss:

- ■ *How is your family like one in the book? How is your family different?*
- ■ *Did you stop and reread today? Where? How did it help you?*

REFLECTIONS

Using sticky notes helped them stop and think. Some reread. Try this again. Let them know it's okay to reread.

asks him how this is like his family. He tells her and then writes on his sticky note, "My family is big but not fat." She prompts others to write what they are thinking. They write things like, "My family lives in an apartment" and "My dad don't live with me any more and I have a big family." "My family dos't live together." (See samples in Figure 4.8.) Mrs. Washington has to prod and remind them to jot down their connections. But they are successful and don't fuss about having to write. It seems as though these young readers realize this writing is helping them understand what they've read.

Figure 4.8 Kids' sticky note samples from *Families* lesson.

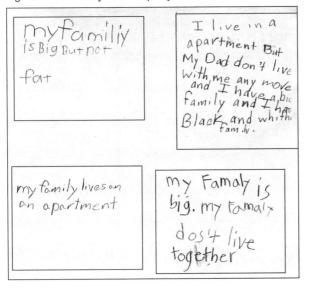

When their teacher ends the lesson by discussing how their families are like the families in the book, they have lots to share. Jotting down notes on the sticky notes helped them stop and monitor their thinking. Their comprehension improved greatly today. Mrs. Washington knows they will have to keep practicing this skill until it becomes automatic. Eventually, they won't need sticky notes to jot down their thinking.

After the Lesson

Mrs. Washington is pleased with how this lesson went. Her students needed quite a bit of prompting to stop and think, but they did so much better today and she is encouraged. Practice makes permanent. The children felt successful, which will help them to remember how thinking helped them understand. Writing on a sticky note engaged them, and Mrs. Washington will use this technique again next time. She'll also be sure to choose a book to which students can easily relate. This helped to improve comprehension as well.

Schema/Characters We Know Lesson

Things to Think About

■ Books in a series work well for this type of lesson. Kids get to know the characters in one book and can connect their knowledge to the next.

■ After you've guided the reading of one or two books in a series, many children will take off and read others on their own.

■ Some books have the characters listed in the front of the book with a little sketch and each one's name. This is a great comprehension support. The Woodland Mysteries series from the Wright Group is an example of this type of text for students reading at the second-grade level or above.

■ Reading books with fewer characters is easier than comprehending books with multiple characters.

■ Schema relates not just to known characters but to anything kids know that can help them better understand what they are reading. The following lesson is just one example of a schema lesson. Schema is also referred to as *background knowledge*.

Figure 4.9 Before reading, the teacher introduces the new book and builds schema/prior knowledge for comprehension.

■ Again, more than one reading strategy is employed. In the lesson that follows, children will use schema and a graphic organizer, as well as visualizing. However, the instructional focus will be on helping them use their schema.

Before the Lesson

Mrs. Davis teaches third grade. The group with which she'll be meeting includes students who enjoy chapter books but are reading slightly below grade level. She's decided to focus on helping them make connections, or use their schema, from text to text since they're starting to enjoy reading books in a series. If they can read this book with minimal support, she'll encourage them to read other books in the series during independent reading, which should improve their comprehension and reading stamina.

While listening to them read prior to today, Mrs. Davis has noted they are decoding well and starting to read with better fluency. They've been learning to read with different voices to match the characters in their books. The last book they read in small group was *Dinosaurs Before Dark* from the Magic Tree House series. So for today they will read another book in the series. As they read, Mrs. Davis will have them make a character map and think more deeply about what they know about the main characters who are in all these books, to better understand the story.

During the Lesson

When they come to the reading table, the children are excited to see that they'll be reading another Magic Tree House book. They enjoyed the last one they read in small group. They read the title, *Pirates Past Noon*, and tell what they already know and think will happen in this book. Mrs. Davis tells them they are using their *schema* to predict and infer. They have been learning how to do this in whole group, too, and they make the connection.

Then they work together to quickly fill out a character map about what they know about Jack

Figure 4.10 Teacher-made character map about Jack and Annie.

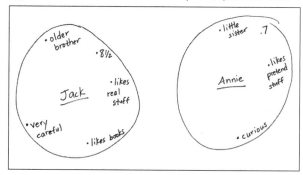

and Annie, the main characters in this series. (See Figure 4.10.) Mrs. Davis records their ideas and models how to make the map. Each child makes his or her own map to match. She draws a circle for each character and lists what they know about each inside the circle, showing their *schema* for the character. She tells them to use this as they read and check to see if the characters act the same way in this book. She also encourages them to jot down new information they get about each character as they read. They can write this on the outside of each circle to show that it is new information.

As they read the first two chapters silently, Mrs. Davis listens in to each read a bit aloud in a quiet voice. She listens for their fluency and decoding, and she prompts them as needed. She also asks them to tell if and how their schema for the characters matched what they already know. She has them jot down anything new they learn about either of the characters outside the circles on their maps.

They talk about the book when they are done reading. They discuss Jack and Annie and how they behaved. Ava says they acted just like she expected, and it really helped her understand. Andrew adds that he realized Jack likes to take notes and wrote that on his map. The rest of the kids agree and add it to theirs, too. Emily notes that this book was really easy for her to understand today, because she was thinking about what she already knew about the characters and could easily predict what would happen next.

Figure 4.11 Lesson Plan for Schema

:: Lesson Plan for Schema ::

Group: Emily, Ava, Joshua, Andrew, Ryan

Focus: COMPREHENSION

☐ monitoring   ☑ schema   ☐ asking ?s   ☐ visualizing   ☐ inference
☐ summarizing   ☐ text structure   ☐ graphic organizers   ☐ deeper meaning

Today's Book: *Pirates Past Noon* by Mary Pope Osborne   **Level:** end of second grade/M

BEFORE READING

Genre: fiction/fantasy

Book Intro:

■ Read title and look at covers. What do they already know? Tell them to use their schema to think about what might happen in the book.

■ As a small group, make a character map of what they already know about the main characters, Jack and Annie, before reading.

Set Purpose for Reading:

Read Chapters 1–2 to find out: *how Jack and Annie behave. Is it what you expected? How does it relate to the last book you read about them? Add to your character map.*

DURING READING

Prompts:

■ *What are you learning about _____?*

■ *Is this how you expected this character to act? Why or why not?*

■ *What else have you found out about this character?*

Notes: Joshua

AFTER READING

Discuss:

■ *How was this book like the other Magic Tree House book we read?*

■ *How was it different?*

■ *Share what you learned about Jack and Annie. Look at your character map. Did you learn anything else about them? What?*

■ *How did your schema about the characters help you understand what you read today?*

REFLECTION

They did well with understanding both the characters and the beginning chapters of this book. Guide the reading of Chapters 3 and 4. Check in with Ryan and Andrew to be sure their understanding is deep enough.

After the Lesson

Mrs. Davis is delighted with the kids' responses to these first chapters of their new book. She decides to read a few more chapters with them in small group and then let them finish it on their own and discuss it in a literature circle format. She will guide the reading of two more chapters and then plan to release control to them to finish it. They are moving toward independence, which is her goal for them as readers, writers, and thinkers. She'll continue to have them use their character maps, adding any new information they find. It should help to guide their thinking.

Using Graphic Organizers Lesson

Things to Think About

- In this lesson, students will use one kind of graphic organizer, an annotated list, to keep track of multiple characters. You'll want to expose students to a variety of graphic organizers and teach them *how* to choose one that will help them better comprehend. For example, they might use a Venn diagram to compare and contrast information. But they might use a web to chart facts or ideas that focus on a particular topic.

- As you model with a graphic organizer in whole-class reading (through read-aloud or shared reading), you might place several laminated copies of that same organizer in a file box on your small-group table. Then as kids need a graphic organizer to help them keep track of their thinking in small group, let *them* choose the one they think best fits the information. They can use these to record their thinking on them with dry erase pens. And when finished, the sheets can be erased and reused. (See Figure 4.12.)

- I use graphic organizers as scaffolds to help kids remember and better comprehend what they're reading. Eventually, many of these may become permanent thinking structures in

Figure 4.12 Graphic organizers stored in a file box can be easily accessed during small group. Students learn to choose which organizer will help them think more clearly about their reading.

students' brains. As a proficient reader, I occasionally still use a graphic organizer to help me understand, especially when there are multiple, complex characters in a story, as in this lesson.

Before the Lesson

Mrs. Wu is planning to meet with a group of third graders who are above-level readers. She has noticed that many of them are reading books with multiple characters during independent reading time, and they sometimes get the characters confused. So she has selected a fourth-grade-level book called *Ten Kids, No Pets* by Ann M. Martin. She was very careful when searching for an above-grade-level text, because many books touch upon themes that she feels are too mature for her third graders. It's a delicate balance to find something more challenging *and* appropriate for her students. This book looks like fun and it is about a topic of great interest to children their age—trying to persuade parents to get a pet.

Mrs. Wu fills out today's lesson plan (see Figure 4.14) and will begin by introducing the book and how to keep track of multiple characters. Most of the other students in her classroom don't need this strategy yet, so she'll introduce the graphic organizer only to this group for now. After she introduces the book and the strategy, she'll ask these five children to meet in a literature circle to discuss Chapter 1 after they read it independently today. To help guide their discussion, she types questions as listed on her plan, and will give each a copy to use to help them prepare for their literature circle or book club group.

During the Lesson

Mrs. Wu gathers Amelia, Jacqueline, Matt, Ryan, and Daniel around her small-group table and hands them the new book she's chosen for today. Often, she has the children choose from several books when meeting as a literature circle or book club. But today she has picked a particular book, since it has multiple characters and an interesting chapter structure (each chapter is the name of a character in the book).

The students quickly preview the text by reading the front and back covers, and begin to talk as a small group. "This looks like it will be good." "Ten kids. Wow! That would be cool to have a family like that." "I wonder if they'll get a pet. I bet they will." "This sounds kind of like a funny movie."

Mrs. Wu sits back and smiles as she listens to their talk. This group functions very independently, since its members all read above grade level and are used to having discussions about their reading. She directs their attention to the table of contents and talks with them about why it might be set up that way. The kids figure out that these are probably the ten kids and wonder about the eleventh name, since there are eleven chapters.

Then their teacher tells them that she's chosen this book because it has so many characters. She

asks them if they ever have trouble keeping up with all the characters in a book. Several share titles they've read and how they got confused with some of the characters. Mrs. Wu explains that this also happens to her as an adult reader, and she shows them how she sometimes keeps a character list to keep track of the people in a book. (See her list in Figure 4.13.) Recently, she read *Persian Pickle Club*, by Sandra Dallas, and used this strategy herself. The kids are somewhat amazed that even their teacher had to do this. It makes them more open to the idea, since most of them are used to reading with ease and don't normally have to respond to a reading challenge. They read a page together, and Mrs. Wu models how they might keep a character list for this book.

Then they return to their desks and read Chapter 1 independently. Mrs. Wu has given them each a list of discussion questions to guide their reading. They use it to prepare for the discussion. She has asked Amelia to lead the group talk today.

Figure 4.13 Teacher's character list from her personal reading.

Persian Pickle Club by Sandra Dallas	
• Rita -	married to Tom - city slicker
• Agnes T. Ritter -	single & miserable - Rita's sister-in-law
• Queenie Bean -	main character & narrator - childless - married to Grover
• Mrs. Ritter -	Rita's mother-in-law
• Opalina Dux -	odd
• Ada June Zinn -	married to Buck - good cook
• Septima Judd -	drives old Packard - married to Prosper
• Ceres Root -	
• Ella Crook -	best quilter, small, single, lives alone - kind of a widow
• Ben Crook -	left Ella in hard times - now found buried in field!
• Nettie Burgett -	married to Forest Ann's brother, Tyrone
• Forest Ann -	widow
• Rev. Olive -	annoying
• Velma Burgett -	Nettie's daughter - never attends - wild
• Lizzy Olive -	not a member - preacher's wife - gossips

Figure 4.14 Lesson Plan for Using Graphic Organizers

⠶ Lesson Plan for Using Graphic Organizers ⠶

Group: Amelia, Jacqueline, Matt, Ryan, Daniel

Focus: COMPREHENSION

☐ monitoring   ☐ schema   ☐ asking ?s   ☐ visualizing   ☐ inference

☐ summarizing   ☐ text structure   ☑ graphic organizers ☐ deeper meaning

Today's Book: *Ten Kids, No Pets* by Ann M. Martin   **Level:** fourth grade

BEFORE READING

Genre: humorous fiction

Book Intro:

■ Read title and look at covers. Make predictions.

■ Tell them this is a book with multiple characters. Ask them how they keep track of the characters when there are lots of them in a book. Show how to make a list of the main characters and jot down brief notes to keep them straight. *I often do this as a reader, but only when there are many characters and I get confused.*

■ Look at how the chapters are organized. Each is titled with the name of a character. *Authors sometimes title chapters with characters' names to help you learn more about that character and his or her perspective.*

Set Purpose for Reading:

Read Chapter 1 to find out: *information about each main character. If you start to get confused, you might keep a character list and a few notes about each. You can refer to it as you need to.* Read a bit with them and model how to do this. Give them discussion questions to think about as they read and to guide their conversation after they read.

DURING READING

Prompts:

None with this group. They will read on their own during small-group time and then meet as a literature circle. They'll use the questions below, typed, for them to guide their discussion.

Notes: Amelia will lead the group discussion today.

AFTER READING

This group will meet independently as a literature circle to discuss the questions below. I'll listen in to their discussion today.

Discuss:

■ *What did you learn about the characters?*

■ *Did you ever get confused about the characters? Where? How did you keep them straight?*

■ *Share your graphic organizer, if you made one, and tell how it helped you better understand what you read.*

■ *Which character was most interesting to you? Why?*

■ *Why do you think the author named the chapters after people? How might that help you better understand this book?*

REFLECTION

The character list worked well for most today. Check in with each of them this week during independent reading time and remind them to use this, as needed, to keep track of multiple characters in their books.

While they read, Mrs. Wu walks around the classroom, checking in on students at their literacy work stations. After a few minutes, she confers with individuals in her small group to see how their reading is going. Several are keeping a character list. But she notices that Ryan hasn't written anything down. When she asks him how his reading is going, he admits that he did okay at first, but then he started to get confused. He shows Mrs. Wu where he got mixed up. On page 13, there are suddenly neighbors coming to say good-bye. Mrs. Wu asks him what might help. He decides to go back and scan what he's read so far to make a character list. She stays with him for a moment for support, just in case he needs help. He does fine, so she moves on.

The students read for about fifteen minutes and then meet to discuss what they read today as a literature circle. They take their notes and their questions along back to the small-group table, sit in a circle, and discuss what they read. Often, literature circle groups meet on the floor without Mrs. Wu, but today she wants to observe and see how they're doing with keeping track of the characters.

Amelia begins to lead the discussion by asking, "What did you learn about the characters today?" Matt begins to share a bit about Abbie, also known as Abigail, like in the chapter title. Several kids share what they learned about this girl, the big sister. Daniel says that Abbie reminds him of his big sister, Renee. They talk about several of the other characters, too. Mrs. Wu intervenes after a while because she wonders whether they used a character list and whether it helped them keep track of the characters.

Ryan shares that at first he didn't think he needed a list, but then he got mixed up on page 13 and went back, scanned, and began a short list. He says it did help him. Others share their lists and they notice similarities and differences. Amelia asks if anyone had a favorite character, and they take turns sharing. Mrs. Wu thanks them for participating and sends them back to their desks after about fifteen minutes. It is time for the class to wrap up small-group and literacy work stations time.

After the Lesson

Mrs. Wu quickly jots down a note in the reflection space on her lesson plan. She is pleased with the way today's meeting went. Literature circles are working well with this group. Spending a few minutes with the group, in the *before*, *during*, and *after* reading segments today made sense. She'll have them continue reading a few more chapters and then check in with the group as they meet in a few days. She doesn't always meet with her literature circles; they often meet independently of her. But because she introduced a new strategy, she will check in with them next time, too.

Asking Questions Lesson

Things to Think About

- This type of lesson will help kids learn to stop and reflect on the questions that form in their minds as they read.
- I like to remind them that readers who ask questions keep their reading moving forward.
- I think it's important to focus on "real" questions that emerge during the reading, not just "test" questions that may appear on a standardized state assessment. Authentic questions help students see that they are responsible for their own comprehension. You'll want to ask students some "test-like" questions so they understand what these are asking on state assessments, but don't limit questioning to only this kind.

Before the Lesson

Mr. Miller plans to meet with five students who are reluctant readers in his urban second-grade class. They read slightly below grade level and often barely comprehend. He has been focusing on asking questions for several lessons with this group to help them better understand what they read. He has been modeling how to ask questions as a reader in whole-group instruction as well. The last time this group met, they began reading an informa-

Figure 4.15 Lesson Plan for Asking Questions

⠵ Lesson Plan for Asking Questions ⠵

Group: Michael, Hannah, Brianna, Joseph, Emma

Focus: COMPREHENSION

☐ monitoring   ☐ schema   ☑ asking ?s   ☐ visualizing   ☐ inference
☐ summarizing   ☐ text structure   ☐ graphic organizers ☐ deeper meaning

Warm-Up: Familiar Rereading   **Listen to:** Emma   **Title:** *How Did This City Grow?*, pp. 1–9

Today's Book: *How Did This City Grow?* pages 10–end   **Level:** early second grade/J

BEFORE READING

Genre: nonfiction/informational text

Book Intro:

- Read title on page 10. *This is the question the author will answer in this section. Use the words and the photos and the captions.*
- *Continue to jot down questions you have as a reader. They'll help you keep reading. Try to find the answers. If they're not there, you might read other books to find your answers.*
- If they finish early, they might write captions for a photo in this section on a piece of white six-line correction tape placed under the photo.

Set Purpose for Reading:

Read to find out: *the answer to the question in the title, How did this city grow?*

DURING READING

Prompts:

- *What questions are you thinking about as you read?*
- *Did the author answer your question? What did you learn?*
- *What questions do you still have?*

Notes: Brianna

AFTER READING

Discuss:

- *How did this city grow?*
- *What questions did you have? How were they answered?*
- *What do you still want to know?*
- *How did asking questions help you understand what you read?*

REFLECTION

Some of the kids had more questions than others. They can use more practice. Try a mystery next. This genre will naturally lead them to ask questions. Get books on the inventions, including cars.

tional text, *How Did This City Grow?* They live in a city, and they enjoyed the start of the book.

During the Lesson

Michael, Hannah, Brianna, Joseph, and Emma meet with Mr. Miller at a small table located where their teacher can easily peruse the room. They take a few minutes to reread the first half of the book, which they read yesterday. This will help their fluency and their comprehension. Before they begin to reread, Mr. Miller asks, "What question were we trying to answer yesterday as we read?" The students look at the contents page and tell him, "How did this city start?" It's the title of the first part. They all reread silently while Mr. Miller listens to Emma read a bit quietly to him. He asks her about what she read, and she tells him how this city was built in the middle of the state, is near lots of water for drinking and transportation, and had a railroad, which brought many people there. He asks her if she has any questions. She says, "I wonder how they got all the stuff to make the buildings. Who built them?"

Before the group reads the rest of the book, Mr. Miller reminds the students that yesterday they were focusing on questions readers ask as they read. He has Emma share some of hers. They talk a bit about possible answers to her questions. Then they read the title of the next part, "How Did This City Grow?" They briefly make predictions. Mr. Miller gives each of them several small sticky notes and tells them that as they read, they may have questions. These questions are good, because they help direct the reader forward. He encourages them to jot down questions on sticky notes as they read. He reminds them that their questions will help them to keep on reading. He also tells them to find out the answer to the question in the title.

As the children read, Mr. Miller listens in briefly to as many as possible for the next few minutes and looks over their questions jotted on their sticky notes. They are doing fairly well. They like the sticky notes, and he is pretty sure their questions are helping them think more about the text.

After reading, they share what they found out about how the city grew. They also share the questions they had while reading—*What kinds of jobs did they get? When were cars invented? Why were the roads not good?* They discuss some answers to their questions. Some of them decide to do further research to learn about when cars were invented.

After the Lesson

Mr. Miller reflects on how the kids handled the reading of this book. They had good comprehension, and jotting down their questions seemed to help them be more thoughtful. He's pleased that some of them wanted to read more to find out about the invention of cars. He plans to go to the library and find some books about early cars and a few about other inventions as well. Then he'll look for another book where questions will naturally propel these readers forward. Perhaps a mystery is a good choice, so he'll visit his school's leveled-book library after school.

Visualizing and Vocabulary Lesson

Things to Think About

- As students move to higher reading levels, they will need to visualize more. But don't wait until there are no pictures to teach them to visualize. A few pictures can still help them visualize, especially if the topic is somewhat unfamiliar.

- I've found it helpful to teach children to visualize in whole-group instruction before moving them into doing this more independently in small group. Having them do a quick sketch of what they picture can help them stay engaged with the task.

- You'll want to consider vocabulary when helping students visualize. I like to remind students that many times they'll have to reread and think about meanings of specific words to clarify their pictures.

Figure 4.16 Lesson Plan for Visualizing

✖ Lesson Plan for Visualizing ✖

Group: Kyla, Rachel, Jared, Isaiah, Jack, Gabriel

Focus: COMPREHENSION

☐ monitoring ☐ schema ☐ asking ?s ☑ visualizing ☐ inference
☐ summarizing ☐ text structure ☐ graphic organizers ☐ deeper meaning

Today's Book: *One Day in the Alpine Tundra* by Jean Craighead George   **Level:** end of third grade/P

BEFORE READING

Genre: fiction/nature writing/diary

Book Intro:

■ Read covers. Ask where the alpine tundra is and what lives there.

■ *This is written like a diary by a boy in the Wyoming mountains. What do you think it's like there?*

■ *Read Chapter 1 and visualize what it's like there. Pay attention to the details and you'll have a clearer, more detailed picture as you read. This will help you better comprehend. There will be lots of new words. Mark new words with highlighter tape and try to figure out what they mean. Use the pictures in the book and the words around them.*

■ Read the first paragraph together and model this.

Set Purpose for Reading:

Read to find out: *what it's like in the alpine tundra. Pay attention to new words.*

DURING READING

Prompts:

■ *What are you picturing?*

■ *Which words best helped you visualize?*

■ *What else do you see?*

■ *What do you think that word means? What can help you?*

Notes: Jared and Isaiah

AFTER READING

Discuss:

■ *What was it like in the alpine tundra?*

■ *What details did you picture?*

■ Discuss new words and what they mean.

REFLECTION

This text was challenging for some due to many new words and limited background knowledge. Look for a short video clip on the alpine tundra to show next time we meet.

Before the Lesson

Ms. House teaches third grade. She is working with a group of students who are reading solidly on grade level, and she wants to take their thinking deeper. So she has chosen a new book, *One Day in the Alpine Tundra*, by Jean Craighead George. They have been learning about habitats in science, and this will fit nicely. She isn't always able to make what they read in small groups match what they're studying in content areas, but occasionally, like today, it does, and she is pleased.

Ms. House reads the first few chapters and decides this will be a perfect book to help students use visualizing as a comprehension strategy. She notes there are many new words, so she'll be sure they pay attention to the vocabulary to help them visualize. (Note her lesson plan in Figure 4.16.)

During the Lesson

Following her plan, they read the book covers (front and back) and discuss what an alpine tundra is. They quickly make connections to what they're studying in science, using their schema. As students become more proficient, they learn to integrate comprehension strategies as they read. She briefly introduces the book, telling them it's a diary written by a boy in the Wyoming mountains, and tells them to practice visualizing and adding to their schema as they read. She reminds them to pay attention to the details and the new vocabulary to help them create a clear picture.

After modeling how to do this by reading the first paragraph together, she has the children read silently on their own. She listens to individuals read a bit and talks with each about his or her picture and its details. She prompts as needed, using some of the questions she's written on her plan.

Following their silent reading, they talk as a small group about what they pictured and understood. There are quite a few new words they came across, and they discuss what these meant and how this changed their mental picture. They are eager to read more about the alpine tundra.

Figure 4.17 A third-grade teacher listens in to individuals read a bit and checks their comprehension, too.

After the Lesson

Ms. House jots down a brief reflection about the lesson on her plan. The group did fairly well, but their schema for the alpine tundra is limited. She decides to look online for a video clip about this habitat. Her school subscribes to unitedstreaming.com, so she should be able to access a short clip about the alpine tundra that will really help her kids' comprehension. In addition, she'll find a few books from the school library that she'll show the group next time they meet. If they're interested, she'll add these to her classroom library for browsing during work stations time.

How Do I Assess/Check for Comprehension?

I have found that the best way to find out if students comprehend what they read is to talk with them. Having a conversation about what they read gives me valuable information about the depth of their understanding. I ask questions, as needed, to help them go deeper, but I try to avoid turning it into a question-and-answer session. That often makes kids rely on me to ask questions. The more they talk, the more I learn. From my work with many teachers and children, I've learned that struggling comprehenders often learn to sit back and let the teacher do all the talking. Often, in desperation, teachers simply tell students (rather than wait patiently for students to tell them) and thus, students learn that if they just sit there quietly their teachers will do the work for them.

Another way I check students' comprehension is to look at any notes they recorded while reading. If you had them jot down thoughts on sticky notes, you can look at these. Or if you had them use a graphic organizer, look at what they wrote there. Simply collect these at the end of small-group time and take a glance at them.

Some teachers feel comfortable only if they've used a formal, objective comprehension measure, such as a multiple-choice format, after students read. This is very time-consuming and isn't always available to accompany *everything* students read. You might use these periodically, but don't be fooled into thinking that you can teach a story from your core program all week, then give the kids a multiple-choice worksheet on it and totally assess their comprehension that way. By the time they do the worksheet, they've already "learned" the story and may test out higher in comprehension than they actually are. In this case, it would probably be better to give them a worksheet with an on-grade-level passage and comprehension questions that you haven't already "taught with." And see how they do independently. This will give you a better picture of their reading comprehension of on-grade-level text. What if they're reading below grade level? Then they shouldn't score very well, because they can't read on that level. The grade will reflect it.

Other teachers use a retelling rubric to assess comprehension. An excellent one is included with the DRA. Some school systems create their own comprehension rubrics. There are professional books available with rubrics, such as Linda Hoyt's

Revisit, Reflect, Retell: Strategies for Improving Reading Comprehension (1999) and *Make It Real: Strategies for Success with Informational Texts* (2002). Vicki Benson and Carrice Cummins' *The Power of Retelling: Developmental Steps for Building Comprehension* (2000) also includes retelling rubrics.

What to Look For and How to Take Notes on Comprehension

Along with measures such as the ones mentioned above, you might find it helpful to take anecdotal notes on comprehension. Some things you might look for are described in Figure 4.18.

Some Prompts for Comprehension

I've found that when a reader gets stuck, it's helpful to have some things to say to help prompt the child to take action (rather than my just giving him the word or the answer). See Figure 4.19 for some examples of what you might say to help a child think and do the comprehension work.

Links to Whole-Group Instruction

I have found that my small-group lessons move faster when I link what I do there to lessons previously taught in whole group. For example, if I want kids to write on sticky notes to record their thinking while reading, I model that strategy in whole group before ever expecting kids to apply it in small group.

If you want kids to make connections to what they're reading, show them how to do this in whole group. You can use a read-aloud book and pause briefly to show them places where you make connections to the text. Don't overdo it, though. When working with younger children, I sometimes put my hand on my head to show that this is what I'm thinking (and not what the book says).

Figure 4.18 Aspects of comprehension and what to look for when taking anecdotal notes.

Aspect of Comprehension	What to Record/Look for	Sample Notes You Might Take
■ monitoring	■ Note if the child is rereading or self-correcting (noted as SC) when meaning breaks down.	■ SC several times to make sense ■ *waffle /SC* *waddle*
■ using schema/making connections	■ Look for meaningful connections and jot down what the child said. ■ Or save his sticky notes.	■ *I know someone just like that character, so I know exactly how he felt.* ■ *That's where I live. I've seen that place.* ■ makes simple connections, but they don't help with understanding
■ asking questions	■ Notice if the child questions and if the questions propel the reader forward. Again, post the child's sticky notes onto your note card.	■ asks thoughtful questions ■ needs help with asking questions
■ visualizing	■ Have the child tell what he can see in his head, especially when there are limited or no pictures. ■ Store a child's sketch with your notes.	■ vivid pictures ■ needs help with visualizing ■ told me he had a movie in his mind and described what he saw today
■ inference	■ Note deeper meaning, rather than surface understanding.	■ still having trouble with this—isn't making connections ■ relies only on background knowledge, not the text ■ is inferring well
■ summarizing	■ Think about whether the child tells what the text was mostly about, rather than lots of little details.	■ too many details—parts, not the whole ■ summarizes using most important parts
■ using text structure	■ Look for whether the student understands and can explain how the text works.	■ identifies and recognizes text structures like descriptions in nonfiction (NF) ■ needs work on identifying and using text structure
■ using graphic organizers	■ Look at what the child records and see whether it is on target. Save a representative sample.	■ using graphic organizer for story helped comprehension ■ missing key information—keep trying
■ deeper meaning	■ Record comments and questions from kids that show evidence of deeper thinking.	■ starting to think more deeply ■ surface understanding

If you want kids to use sticky notes to record their connections, model this in whole group, too. Show them how you jot down a thought on your sticky note, and be explicit about how you place it in the book so it sticks out and you can find it easily after you're done reading. *Strategies*

Figure 4.19 Prompts to Help Students Self-Monitor Comprehension

What Child Is Having Trouble With	Possible Teacher Prompts
■ monitoring	■ *You stopped. Is it making sense?* ■ *What have you read about so far?* ■ *Rereading is smart. When you don't understand what you've read, go back and read it again.*
■ using schema/making connections	■ *What does that make you think about/remind you of? How does that help you understand what you're reading?* ■ *What do you already know about ___? How can that help you?*
■ asking questions	■ *What are you wondering about as you read?* ■ *What questions do you have?* ■ *Did the author answer any of your questions? Where?* ■ *What questions do you still have?*
■ visualizing	■ *What are you picturing? What do you see/hear/smell/feel as you read this?* ■ *Which part helped you see something more clearly?*
■ inference	■ *What might happen next? What else might you find out?* ■ *Why do you think . . . ?* ■ *Join together what you know with what the words say. What are you thinking now?* ■ *What does the author mean? How did you figure that out?*
■ summarizing	■ *If you wanted to tell a friend about what you just read, what would you say? Don't give away the whole thing. Just tell what it was mostly about.* ■ *What are the most important parts?*
■ using text structure	■ *What kind of structure did this author use? question/ answer . . . problem/solution . . . compare and contrast . . . time order* ■ *How can that help you understand what you're reading?*
■ using graphic organizers	■ *What kind of graphic organizer might help you better understand what you're reading? How could that help you?* ■ *Try a graphic organizer that might help you think about what you're reading and help to organize your thoughts.*
■ deeper meaning	■ *Why? What else are you thinking?* ■ *How could that have happened?* ■ *Tell me more.*

That Work (Harvey and Goudvis 2000) and *Reading with Meaning* (Miller 2002) both include practical ideas on teaching comprehension to primary students, especially in whole-group instruction.

Here are some ideas of how to model comprehension strategies in whole-group instruction. There are also sample lesson plans for whole-group comprehension instruction in Appendix C for your reference.

Monitoring

- As you read aloud, stop occasionally and have kids check for understanding by talking with a partner about what they understand so far.

- Model how to read a section, or a page, and stop and think about what you read using picture books, Big Books, poems stanza by stanza, chapter books, and textbooks.

- When you make an error and self-correct while reading aloud, point it out to kids and tell them you're monitoring or fixing it up to make it make sense.

Using Schema/Making Connections

- Share some of your connections as you read aloud, but don't stop on every page and overdo this one.

- You might jot some of your connections on sticky notes to model how to do this.

- Explain how your connections help you better understand what you've read (see sample whole-group lesson plan in Appendix C).

Asking Questions

- Model how you ask questions about what will happen next, who a character is, what a word meant, what just happened, etc., during read-aloud.

- Again, you might show how you jot down your questions on sticky notes to make you aware of your thinking.

- Write question marks on sticky notes and post them on the page where it made you ask a question as you work with a text in shared reading; then remove the question mark when the question is answered.

- Focus on *thick* questions, or ones with multi-layered response possibilities, rather than *thin* (one-word-answer) questions.

Visualizing

- You might do a quick sketch on the board to show what you're visualizing as you read a book aloud (or have kids do this and then share their sketches with each other).

- Or read aloud a page or two from a picture book, have kids close their eyes and think about the picture in their minds, and then show the pictures to see whether it's what the illustrator pictured.

- Use poetry to teach visualizing; it's short and often not illustrated. Highlight words that help paint a visual image while doing shared reading (see the sample whole-group lesson plan in Appendix C).

Inference

- I often make a chart showing that inference is a combination of background knowledge/ schema and what the words (or pictures if there are no words) say (see Figure 4.20).

- Ask kids to infer using pictures with no words; show them they used what they know plus the clues from the picture.

Figure 4.20 Anchor chart made with students helps them understand how to infer.

■ Even young kids can infer from oral examples related to things they know. (*Meg has a new puppy. She leaves the front door open. What do you think might happen?*)

■ Model how to infer and name it inferring when kids help you do so. (*Sam, you're inferring. It didn't say that in the book, but you figured it out using what you know plus the words.*)

Summarizing

■ Start with read-aloud books and write summaries together in shared writing to model this process (see the sample lesson plan in Appendix C).

■ Tell kids to practice telling what happened in the story by pretending they're talking to someone who hasn't read the book and doesn't want to know all the details because he wants to read it.

■ Sometimes we break down summarizing by telling a sentence about what the beginning was about, a sentence about what the middle was mostly about, and a sentence about the ending.

Using Text Structure

■ Show kids how both fiction *and* nonfiction work by charting with students what each may include (see Pam House's sample charts in Figure 4.21).

■ As you model how to read informational text in read-aloud and shared reading, add to a chart of nonfiction text features and text structures, as shown in Patty Terry's first-grade anchor chart (see Figure 4.22).

Using Graphic Organizers

■ Model how to fill out graphic organizers as you read aloud fiction and nonfiction.

■ Think aloud about why you use a particular graphic organizer. (*I'll use a web, since this piece has facts about a particular topic. I'll use a Venn diagram to chart what I'm learning, because this*

Figure 4.21 Charts made with students about how to read fiction and nonfiction during whole-group instruction.

Figure 4.22 A nonfiction-text-features chart, made over time with students during whole-group instruction, can be referred to during small group, too.

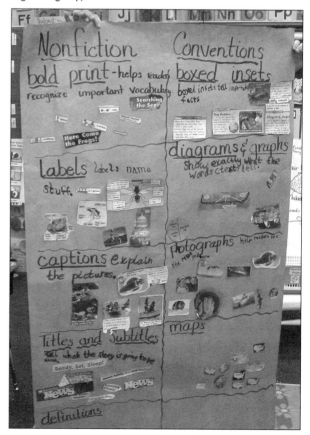

Figure 4.23 Deep Thinking Questions

- What did I learn from reading this that the book didn't even say?
- What's the most important thing I read? Why is that important?
- What was interesting? What was important?
- What might I try that I learned from reading this?
- What else did this book make me think about?
- Why did the author say that? Why did the author use those words?

article compares reptiles and amphibians. I'll use a character map to help me better understand how each main character acts in this story.)

Deeper Meaning

- Model how to think at a deeper level, including generalizing, determining importance, synthesizing, and analyzing what was read using quality literature with themes that provoke thinking.

- Use quality questioning to push kids' thinking deeper (you might post questions for kids to help them think more deeply—see Figure 4.23).

Links to Literacy Work Stations Practice

After modeling comprehension lessons in whole group and having students practice applying these in small groups, I've found success giving them additional practice with comprehension at literacy work stations. Figure 4.24 describes some stations for students to go to where they'll be practicing comprehension.

Links to Standardized and State Testing

Most state reading tests evaluate students' reading comprehension. Generally, these tests don't just focus on basic comprehension. They extend to deeper thinking, especially questions that involve inference.

I've found that learning the academic language used in tests can help some children comprehend better on those tests. For example, if a test question says, *What's the best summary of this piece?* and students don't know what *summary* means, they will not have a very good chance of answering correctly. For this reason, I often structure the questions I ask when discussing a story to sound like the way they might be asked on a test. This helps to familiarize students with the terminology they will encounter in tests.

If your state posts release tests or samples of questions, use these to help prepare your students for the kinds of thinking they'll need to do when they take these tests. Having taught in Texas for almost thirty years through the TABS, TEAMS, TAAS, *and* TAKS tests, I am very familiar with how the language and rigor of our test has changed over the past years. I make it my business to know what the most recent tests have included, since these are posted on our state department website, and I use the test "question stems" with kids at all grade levels, including kindergartners (as appropriate). I believe that even if you don't teach a grade that's "tested," you should be aware of and use that academic language with your students orally. There's much we can do as primary teachers to help support intermediate teachers who are responsible for giving these tests.

Comprehension Cautions

I'm careful not to focus *all* my attention on comprehension. It is certainly very important and rather tempting at times. In fact, it's the goal of reading. But if kids can't decode, their comprehension will suffer. Reading fluency must also be considered, since this has been shown to increase comprehension. And vocabulary has a huge influence on students' comprehension. As their reading levels

Figure 4.24 Literacy work stations that support comprehension.

Literacy Work Station	What Kids Do Here to Practice Comprehension	How This Station Supports Comprehension
Classroom Library	■ Choose just-right books for independent reading. ■ Talk about books read with others. ■ Recommend books to each other. ■ Use graphic organizers/questions for discussion.	■ Setting up a library with your kids can help them choose the right books. Talking about books and responding to them with others increases comprehension.
Listening Work Station	■ Listen to and comprehend a recorded story, informational piece, or poem. ■ Talk with others about what they heard. ■ Interact with what they heard by writing personal responses. ■ Use graphic organizers to help them understand.	■ Listening comprehension is an easier task than reading comprehension. Listening to a book frees up the brain to think about the text, rather than having to decode every bit. Adding responses to listening helps kids interact with what they've heard, which improves comprehension (especially if the teacher has taught students how to think about text).
Buddy Reading Work Station	■ Read a bit at a time together and talk about it. ■ Help each other as they read, especially to figure out the meaning if and when comprehension breaks down.	■ Buddy reading promotes working with a partner to figure out new words and comprehend. Reading a bit at a time and then talking about it helps readers monitor and fix up their comprehension.
Poetry Work Station	■ Illustrate a poem. ■ Read a poem and think about the picture in your mind.	■ Illustrating a poem helps students visualize, which is a helpful comprehension strategy. Poems are short and are often fun, which makes them more appealing to struggling readers to try to comprehend.
Drama Work Station	■ Retell a story or informational piece to demonstrate understanding. ■ Act out what was read to deepen understanding.	■ If you can dramatize what you've read, you're demonstrating understanding. It helps passive readers become more active.
Big Book Work Station	■ Dramatize the Big Book while reading.	■ See above.
Writing Work Station	■ Write a response to a piece read aloud in class. ■ Write book reviews or letters of recommendation to friends about what they've read.	■ Writing clarifies thinking, and comprehension is thinking. Reading what others have written about books they've read often prompts kids to read these books, too.
Computer Work Station	■ Answer questions about books they've read. ■ Use software programs like Kidspiration to demonstrate understanding through graphic organizers.	■ The computer often gives immediate feedback, which can give encouragement to students who are struggling with comprehension.

Figure 4.25 Graphic organizers are posted and used at a variety of literacy work stations to aid students with comprehension.

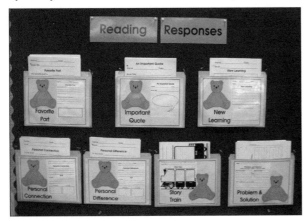

increase, vocabulary becomes more and more important to comprehension. In fact, I often focus on comprehension and vocabulary simultaneously.

I never settle for basic comprehension. I don't ask *thin* questions, ones with one-word answers. You can push your kids' thinking deeper by expecting them to come up with more. Ask good questions, *thick* ones with multilayered possibilities, especially questions that include the words *why*, *what made you think of that*, and *how do you know*. And help students pay attention to new vocabulary and what those words mean.

Reflection Questions for Professional Conversations

1. What have you learned about teaching comprehension that you'll try in the next few weeks?

2. Who comprehends well in your classroom? How can you help them think even more deeply?

3. Who is struggling with comprehension? What can you try that will support their taking more ownership for their understanding?

4. Which elements of teaching comprehension have you taught well? What could you focus on more?

5. How are you using writing to help students comprehend? What else might you try to link reading and writing and deepen comprehension?

6. How do you see vocabulary affecting your students' comprehension? Refer to Chapter 8, on vocabulary, for more ideas.

For Further Information on Teaching Comprehension

Benson, V., and C. Cummins. 2000. *The Power of Retelling: Developmental Steps for Building Comprehension.* Bothell, WA: Wright Group.

Harvey, S., and A. Goudvis. 2000. *Strategies That Work: Teaching Comprehension to Enhance Understanding.* Portland, ME: Stenhouse.

———. 2001. *Strategy Instruction in Action.* Video series. Portland, ME: Stenhouse.

Hoyt, L. 1999. *Revisit, Reflect, Retell: Strategies for Improving Reading Comprehension.* Portsmouth, NH: Heinemann.

———. 2002. *Make It Real: Strategies for Success with Informational Texts.* Portsmouth, NH: Heinemann.

Keene, E. 1997. *Mosaic of Thought: Teaching Comprehension in a Reader's Workshop.* Portsmouth, NH: Heinemann.

Miller, D. 2002. *Reading with Meaning: Teaching Comprehension in the Primary Grades.* Portland, ME: Stenhouse.

———. 2002. *Happy Reading! Creating a Predictable Structure for Joyful Teaching and Learning.* Video series. Portland, ME: Stenhouse.

5

Fluency

Five students are seated around a table with the teacher, ready to read the folktale *The Three Little Pigs*. It is an easy text and a familiar story, because they will be working on fluency today. Before they read, the children preview the cover and make predictions using the title, picture, and their background knowledge. As the teacher guides this conversation, she reminds them that today she wants them to practice reading fluently—reading with interesting voices. She asks them about the characters they expect to meet and how each voice might sound. Then the children begin to read, each at his or her own pace.

As the teacher listens in to individuals, she notices that Ruben is trying out a deep voice for the big bad wolf. She listens and then responds, "You sound just like the wolf. It sounds interesting. How does using the wolf's voice help you understand what you're reading?" Ruben tells her that he is thinking about what it would be like to be that wolf and he is picturing a mean, sneaky character. He continues to read a bit more and sounds even more convincing as the wolf.

The teacher moves on to Madison. She is trying out voices, too, but is confused about who is saying what. She doesn't quite understand where to use different voices. The teacher asks, "How can you tell when a new character is talking?" Madison replies, "I keep getting mixed up." So the teacher points out the quotation marks and reminds her of the lesson she'd taught during shared reading recently. The teacher says, "When we read the Big Book version of *Little Red Riding Hood*, remember how we used highlighter tape to mark the quotation marks so we could be sure to say those parts differently? Then we looked at the words after it to see who was talking." A glimmer in Madison's eyes shows she is making the connection. They look at a sentence together. "Oh," says Madison. "Here are those marks, and I see *said the pig* after them. That means the pig is talking." She continues to read a bit using the voice of one of the pigs. The teacher makes a note to revisit this at the end of the lesson. Then she moves on to see how the other students are doing with their fluency.

Figure 5.1 Teacher reviews how to read dialogue before kids read in this small-group lesson for fluency.

After the students have finished the book, the teacher leads a short discussion about what happened in the story and how the children understood the different characters by using different voices. Several children volunteer to read a favorite part, using the character voices. The teacher ends the lesson by praising the students for trying out different voices as they read today and reminds them to keep doing this the next time they read. She glances at her notes and this reminds her to ask Madison to tell the group how she knows which character is saying what. Then the teacher tells the students to practice reading this book again with their partner at the buddy reading station the next time they are there; she will add this book to the buddy reading materials.

After the group goes on to their work stations, the teacher makes a brief note on her lesson plan sheet: *Kids read with different voices; keep practicing; Madison—quotation marks and who's talking.* She plans to revisit fluency several more times with these students in small group, so they'll take on this strategy and use it even when she's not sitting with them.

What Is Fluency?

Fluency is not just speed. It's a combination of several factors—rate or speed, prosody or phrasing, expression, intonation, and pacing—along with comprehension. In the lesson above, the teacher focused on expression and intonation, but rate entered into it, too. Choppy reading is certainly not fluent. When teaching kids to read fluently, there are several aspects to consider, according to fluency researcher Tim Rasinski (2003).

Accuracy in Word Recognition (Decoding)

Kids must be able to decode accurately in order to gain fluency. You'll want them to be reading books at approximately 95 to 99 percent accuracy when helping them develop fluency. This means that if you listen to a student read aloud a text with one hundred words, the child should make errors on no more than five of those words (or fewer). You can easily check for accuracy in word recognition by doing an IRI (informal reading inventory) or a running record and computing the student's accuracy level using this formula: Number of words in the text divided by number of words read correctly equals accuracy percentage.

$$\frac{95 \text{ words read accurately}}{100 \text{ words possible}} = 95\% \text{ accuracy}$$

Automaticity in Word Recognition (Reading Rate)

A second fluency component is automaticity (or quickness) in word recognition. In addition to reading accurately, students should effortlessly recognize the words they see in print. Most states now require that you determine a student's reading rate on a grade-level passage in words correct per minute. You can glance at your watch (with a second hand) or use a timer. Beware, though, because a timer can make kids nervous. I'm often asked why we have to do this. We're simply checking to see if the reading is automatic. This is important because it frees up the brain for the important task of comprehending the text. If students use too much of their cognitive processing power trying to decode the words, there is little fuel left to think about what they've read. Assessing fluency in words per minute is a quick, easy measure. Here are the suggested rates of reading according to the TPRI (Texas Primary Reading Inventory):

- by the end of first grade—60 words per minute
- by the end of second grade—90 words per minute
- by the end of third grade—114 words per minute

Interpretive and Meaningful Reading (Expression, Intonation, Phrasing, Pacing, Pausing)

When students read, it should sound expressive and phrased, and include good pacing and pauses where appropriate. This is the third aspect of fluency. We hope that students are reading in an interpretive and meaningful way when they read silently. We can check for this kind of fluency by listening to them read orally. You will want to measure this aspect of reading with a rubric. (See Figure 5.2 and Appendix D for a sample.) The teacher (or the student himself) listens to the reader read grade-level material and scores the reading fluency according to descriptions provided in the rubric. This can be used both for teacher evaluation and student self-evaluation. When students can read with this kind of fluency, they usually show evidence of greater comprehension.

Fluency is a bridge between phonics and comprehension. When children can read with greater automaticity (fast, accurate decoding) and not spend so much brainpower trying to figure out how to read words, they are freed up to think more

Figure 5.2 Student's assessment of fluency—rubric filled in.

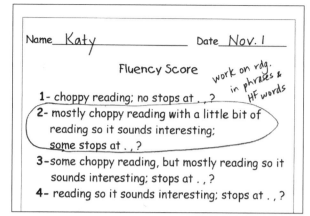

about what they've read, which leads to better comprehension. Thus, fluency instruction and practice can help students improve in comprehension over time. This chapter will examine ways to do this.

Fluency Research at a Glance

What does the research say about fluency and teaching for fluent reading? Here's a summary of some of the studies you might find helpful when planning instruction.

Importance of Fluency

- LaBerge and Samuels (1974) constructed a model of what it means to acquire this automaticity. They found that readers could devote only a limited amount of attention to any given task. The more attention readers gave to identifying words or decoding, the less attention they had left for comprehension.
- Johns and Berglund (2002), the National Reading Panel (NICHD 2000), and Pinnell et al. (1995) found that students who experience reading difficulties are most often not fluent.

How Fluency Develops

- Biemiller (1977–78) found that fluency develops gradually over time and through extensive reading practice.

- Nagy and Anderson (1984) and Richard Allington (1983) studied the reading behaviors of children outside the classroom and found that fluent readers simply read more text. A nonfluent reader may read only 100,000 to 400,000 words a year, but a fluent reader reads closer to 4,000,000 words a year.

- Allington (2005) found that students' fluency improved when they practiced on easy texts, books kids could read with 95 percent accuracy or above. To help students pay attention to phrasing, punctuation, and expression, he found that 99 percent accuracy was even better (so students aren't distracted by unknown words).

Fluency Teaching Approaches/Methods

- Two forms of reading practice where increasing fluency can be evidenced are repeated reading and guided oral repeated reading (NICHD 2000).

- Repeated oral reading with feedback is one of the best approaches available to increase fluency, but most of these studies have involved one-on-one work with a student and adult (Hasbrouck, Ihnot and Rogers 1999; Rasinski 1990; Smith and Elley 1997).

- Using repeated reading with a tape-recorded version produced significant gains in fluency (Blum et al. 1995).

- Rasinski's (1990) research found that having students read along orally as the teacher or another fluent adult reader reads the story is an effective type of fluency practice.

- Jay Samuels (2002) recommends that teachers pair students for oral reading to improve their fluency. First, each student reads a passage of text aloud to an adult. Then the student reads it again silently to himself. Next, he pairs with a partner, and they read the text to each other. Finally, each of them is paired with a new partner to read the passage again, but this final time, the partner provides feedback about how the reading sounds.

- Round-robin reading has not been proven successful in improving reading fluency according to Stallings' (1980) research. It does not give students a chance to improve their fluency through rereading. Fluency improves when students can apply the guidance their teacher has provided in rereading the same text.

- Telling students unfamiliar words as they come across them allows students to focus on constructing meaning and reading with fluency (Shany and Biemiller 1995).

- Taylor, Wade, and Yekovich (1985) found that helping students group words in a sentence into meaningful phrases improves fluency.

Who Needs This Kind of Small Group?

I have found that students who read in a laborious fashion are prime candidates for fluency work in small groups. Those who read word by word, kids who struggle over decoding long or new words, and those who read in a monotone voice all will benefit from small-group fluency work. Children who have a high score on fluency according to DIBELS or TPRI, two commonly used assessments, may look like they don't need fluency practice. But beware. Students who read super-fast but have no expression or phrasing and little to no comprehension need fluency help also. Students who skip punctuation can also benefit.

Possible Focus for Lessons

You will want to choose a focus for each fluency-oriented small-group lesson, but be sure to be flexible within your lessons and provide opportunities for comprehension and vocabulary development as well. Here are some possibilities to choose from:

- *Decoding words effortlessly and automatically.* Students who are able to easily decode words will be able to pay more attention to phrasing and expressive reading. Their brains will be freed up to think more about what they're reading, which will lead to greater comprehension. Focus on strategies that help students "chunk" words by reading parts of words, rather than decoding letter by letter. (Of course, if you're working with beginning readers, they may need to decode some CVC [consonant-vowel-consonant] words, like *cat*, sound by sound.) It's a good idea to record decoding errors using a running record or a miscue analysis, and look for patterns of words misread. See Chapter 7 for further ideas on teaching students to more easily decode.

■ *High-frequency-word work.* Practicing with sight words, or words that appear often in text, will often help students achieve greater fluency. Teaching with high-frequency words and expecting students to spell these words correctly in their writing (as well as read these easily and accurately) will improve some students' fluency as well. High-frequency words are very important, especially for beginning readers, because they give the child an anchor—a known—to hold on to when solving new words. Knowing some words automatically contributes greatly to reading more fluently.

■ *Reading the punctuation.* Some students zip and zoom through text without ever stopping at the punctuation. They are like poor drivers who coast through stop signs and run red lights. Skipping punctuation interferes with meaning. Help students see the purpose of punctuation. The author put it there intentionally to give meaning to the text.

■ *Reading in phrases.* This is sometimes called prosody. It adds rhythm and cadence to the reading. It makes reading sound interesting and, again, creates meaning. You'll want to look carefully at the kinds of text you choose if your students have difficulty reading in phrases. I've found it works well to begin by

choosing books that are written in phrases that stop at the end of the line to support students' reading across the line. Show them how to move their eyes more quickly across the line to the end of a phrase.

■ *Reading with intonation and expression.* Expressive reading is music to the ear and helps the mind visualize more effectively. Students who read word by word often have no pictures in their heads at all. Teach them to vary their voices by changing pitch, dialect, and even speed as they portray events and information. Students who read with intonation and expression usually comprehend much better than those who read in a flat, monotone voice.

■ *Reading dialogue.* This is often a fun way to teach kids to read with expression. Show them how to change their voices when different characters speak. By doing so, they have to think about each character and what he or she is really like. This dramatic reading improves comprehension.

■ *Regulating the speed of reading.* Teach students how to vary the rate at which they read. While reading, they should speed up their reading when the action is exciting and slow their reading down when they want to illustrate that something is suspenseful. Don't become overly concerned about their speed here, as long as they are reading expressively. Remember that the goal of fluency is to help children comprehend (not to read as fast as they can)!

Choosing Materials

There are several things to consider when choosing materials for teaching fluency in small-group instruction. The first factor is to choose books at students' easy reading level—at least 95 percent accuracy. These may seem easy, but the text should not be so difficult that the child struggles on too many words. Since fluency includes reading accurately, be sure the text doesn't present much work for decoding. This way the child can feel successful and experience what it feels and sounds like to be a fluent reader. Success breeds success!

If you're trying to help students read in phrases, use even easier text, such as familiar books or those they can read with 99 percent accuracy. I've also found it helpful to use books that are written in phrases that end at the end of a line. This provides special scaffolding or support to help a child know where to pause.

You might look for kid-friendly text layouts when working on fluency. Larger print looks easier to read and is less intimidating than smaller print. Less print on a page looks friendlier than lots of print on a page. Do everything you can to help children be successful when reading fluently.

Find texts on topics students can easily relate to. When they can instantly make a connection with a book, students will be more likely to read it with enthusiasm.

Look for familiar stories with repetitive phrases in the dialogue when teaching students how to read dialogue. Folktales and fairy tales are especially good for this. When the big bad wolf says, "Let me come in or I'll blow your house down!" over and over again in *The Three Little Pigs*, students are more inclined to read faster and with better expression.

As you choose books for fluency instruction, you'll want to gradually decrease the support and present text that's a bit more challenging. But remember, fluent reading comes from reading lots of easy text. So be sure to begin with text that is no harder than 95 percent accuracy, especially when you're working with fluency instruction, so the reader has fewer decoding challenges.

∷ The Lessons ∷

By now, you're probably thinking about how to put all this information together in small-group lessons

for fluency. The following section gives examples of how you might think about grouping students, choosing a focus and matching texts, as well as what you might try in a variety of lessons. A lesson-plan template for fluency is used in each one. A reproducible copy of this form can be found in Appendix D if you'd like to use it to write your own fluency-focused small-group lesson plans.

Join me as we take a field trip to visit several classrooms where the teachers in a variety of grade levels are making decisions about teaching for fluency in small groups. Think about how you might apply these ideas to the students you work with in your room. Each lesson centers around a fluency focus and gives ideas for things to think about when deciding on a particular focus, as well as what that teacher does before, during, and after the lesson. Each teacher's lesson plan is included for a handy reference.

High-Frequency-Word Lesson

Things to Think About

- This kind of lesson is usually most suitable for beginning readers. But it may be used with children who are having trouble taking on more difficult high-frequency words, such as *friend*, *said*, *people*, *because*, or *thought*.
- Choose books that have many high-frequency words children already know.
- Limit the number of new high-frequency words in the lesson to one or two, so the text remains relatively easy and can be read fluently. Be sure those high-frequency words are used often in the book to promote practice of those words and increase automaticity.
- Build on the students' known words by practicing them with a few new high-frequency words *before* reading the new text. You might play a high-frequency-word game like Concentration, Sight Word Bingo, or a simple flash card game.

Figure 5.3 Teacher models and students make and write high-frequency words to help them with fluency.

■ Or have students make the new high-frequency words (just one or two) with magnetic letters. Then have them mix up the letters and make it again. You might also have them write it fast on a dry erase board. Be sure they build words or write them from left to right. Encourage them to do these tasks fast to build automaticity. This warm-up should take only five minutes or less. When the children know how to play the game well, you might move it to a literacy work station for future independent practice for these students. Put the materials in a Ziploc bag with these students' names on it.

Before the Lesson

After school, Mrs. Oliver, a first-grade teacher, looks at her anecdotal notes taken during small-group instruction and independent reading conferences over the past two weeks, surveying them to see who might benefit from a temporary small group for fluency. She decides to include five students who are all reading on grade level but still read choppily. She chooses an easy text, *Five Senses*, by Robyn Opie, from the Sun Sprouts series, for their next book. The

class has been studying about this topic in science, so they have lots of background knowledge for this text. This book is a bit easier than the level most of them have been reading in, but Mrs. Oliver has noticed that their fluency isn't as strong as it needs to be. It's tempting to keep moving them into harder text, but she resists.

She chooses high-frequency words from this book that will be easy for the group (*my, can, see, if, things*), and two newer high-frequency words (*with, are*). Then she uses blank white index cards and a black marker to create a set of high-frequency-word cards to use in a warm-up game. She jots this idea on her lesson-plan template along with Danitra's name for warm-up reading. She needs a bit more information on this child's fluency. See her lesson plan in Figure 5.4. Note that she highlights high-frequency (HF) words as her fluency focus.

During the reading of today's book, she'll be sure to take a few notes on Roberto, too. He is a quiet child and it's hard to get good information on how he's doing as a reader. She will jot notes on a sticky note with his initials at the top and then transfer this to the anecdotal note section of her small-group notebook later on. She'll be sure to listen in to other children as well and prompt them for fluent reading, but Roberto is the one she will really be sure to take notes on. This will free her up so she can interact with as many children as possible in the small group.

During the Lesson

It's time for small groups, so Mrs. Oliver calls her new group together and tells them they will be meeting to work on their fluency, reading so it sounds more like talking. She listens to Danitra read *The Chick and the Duckling* from her reader, while the others read other familiar stories for a warm-up. Mrs. Oliver makes notes of words Danitra gets stuck on. (See Figure 5.5.) She'll place these in the anecdotal note section of her small-group reading notebook later. Some of the words might need to be added to the word wall.

Figure 5.4 Lesson Plan for High-Frequency Words

∷ Lesson Plan for High-Frequency Words ∷

Group: Danitra, Dominick, Roberto, Katy, Sam

Focus: FLUENCY

☐ fast decoding   ☑ HF words   ☐ punctuation   ☐ phrases
☐ intonation and expression ☐ dialogue   ☐ adjusting rate

Warm-Up: Familiar Rereading   **Listen to:** Danitra   **Title:** *The Chick and the Duckling*

Today's Book: *Five Senses* by Robyn Opie   **Level:** early first grade/E

BEFORE READING
Book Intro:

■ Play high-frequency-word flash card game (*if, with, are, my, things, can, see*)
■ *These words are in this book—read them fast!*
■ Read title. *What will this be about? A girl tells how she can use her senses. What are her five senses?*
■ *Read it fast, so it sounds like talking. Remember the words we used in our game today. They are in the book. Read them fast.*

DURING READING
Prompts:

■ *That's a word you know. It's a word-wall word. Read it again, fast!*
Notes: Roberto

AFTER READING
Discuss:

■ *What could the girl feel/see/hear/smell/taste?*
■ *What would happen if she couldn't use one of her senses? Choose one and tell what might happen.*
■ Talk about how kids sounded as they read. Review any sight words that presented difficulty, using the cards.

REFLECTION
HF-word flash card game went well. Play again. Include *with, out, of*. Reread book tomorrow. Find another book with these words in it.

Danitra's fluency is still a little choppy, so Mrs. Oliver reminds her to read faster the next time. She reads the last sentence to Danitra and has her read it again. "That sounds just like talking!" Mrs. Oliver tells Danitra. "Remember to try that while you're reading today."

The high-frequency-word flash card game goes well. The first child to read the word gets to hold on to it. They go through the cards twice in less than two minutes. Mrs. Oliver reminds them to read the book fast, so it sounds like talking. She lays the high-frequency-word cards

Figure 5.5 Teacher's sticky notes recording student's trouble-some words during fluency lesson.

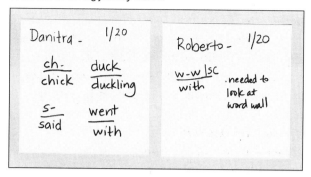

on the table so the children can refer to them if needed.

Following a brief book introduction using the notes on her lesson plan, Mrs. Oliver listens to the kids read individually while the others read on their own. This is the heart of her small-group lesson. She reminds them to read the book over again if they finish. She listens to Roberto first and jots down a few notes on his reading. (See Figure 5.5.) He is rather slow on the first page; he pauses at the word *with*, and Mrs. Oliver points toward the index cards used in the warm-up game. He says, "w . . . w . . . with." She tells him that it's a word-wall word and will be in this book often. "Say it fast next time you see it," she reminds him. Roberto chimes in, "with." He rereads the page, faster this time and then continues to the next pages. When he gets to page 5, he glances at *with* in the book and on the card and reads it. Then he rereads the page. Each time he reads it successfully, he is adding to his repertoire of high-frequency words and increasing his automaticity.

Mrs. Oliver listens in to several other students and notices their fluency is better than before. This easier book is working to build fluency. She interacts with each for a minute or so and helps them read it faster. With one, she reads the page and then has the child read it with her. Then he reads it on his own. With another, she says, "That's a word you know," when the child pauses on *are*. The child finds it on the previous page and reads it correctly.

The children discuss the book after reading, and their comprehension is very good. This is a concept they know a lot about and are very interested in. At the end of the lesson, Mrs. Oliver tells the children they are beginning to sound more fluent today, that they sounded more like they were talking. She shows the flash cards *with* and *are*, and has the children read the words fast. She reminds them that these words will be in lots of the books they read and they'll have to remember them quickly. Then she tells them to practice reading this book in their book bags during independent reading time. If they are at buddy reading during literacy work stations time, they can practice rereading it there, too.

After the Lesson

Before calling another group to her table, Mrs. Oliver jots down a brief reflection about today's lesson. See her reflection at the end of her lesson plan in Figure 5.4. She'll ask the group to reread this book tomorrow and perhaps begin a new book. She will need to visit the book room to choose several more texts with these high-frequency words in them. She is pleased with the success of this lesson. She was thoughtful in both her group choice and her book choice. These are elements that make small group work effectively.

Phrasing Lesson

Things to Think About

- Be sure to include comprehension as well as working on reading rate in this kind of a lesson.
- Don't use a stopwatch when teaching a small-group lesson on reading rate. It might make kids focus more on how many words they're reading than on comprehension. Reading rate is important, but just listen for it rather than time it when teaching.
- You might choose a book written in phrases to help children with phrased reading initially.
- Encourage students to read across the page with their eyes, rather than point to every

word with their finger. Finger pointing to every word often creates word-by-word readers. If kids get lost on the page, try a book with fewer words per page. Or have them slide their finger across the page. Tell children to use their finger if they get stuck on a word, but then move their finger out of the way so they can read faster. (Note: Emergent readers need to use their finger to point to each word to help them pay attention to print. After students have established one-to-one matching or tracking of words, they should be encouraged to read with their eyes to promote greater fluency.)

Before the Lesson

The group in the following lesson was selected because the teacher, Mr. Jones, noticed that each of them need help with phrasing. If his whole second-grade class had been having trouble with reading in phrases, he would have done more modeling in whole group. However, based on his anecdotal notes and recent fluency assessments, he knows that eight of his twenty-three students need practice with phrasing. Some are reading in monotone voices, others are reading word by word. He has decided to divide them into two groups for phrasing practice to give them more individualized attention. One group is reading on lower levels than the other. The lesson plan that follows is for these children. His second group working on phrasing will be engaged in a similar lesson with a text that is slightly more difficult, since they have less trouble decoding.

Mr. Jones will stick with this focus for several lessons, because he knows that reading in phrases takes a lot of practice. He begins by choosing a book that is very easy (99 percent accuracy) and is written in phrases to give extra support for phrased, fluent reading. It is *Morris the Moose*, an I Can Read book by Bernard Wiseman. There aren't too many lines of text per page, which should help rid the children of finger pointing. And it's a funny story

that the children will delight in. If they enjoy this book, he'll point them to other books in the I Can Read series. In fact, he'll make a basket for the classroom library with this label on it and encourage kids in this group to browse these during their time at the classroom library as well as during independent reading. See his lesson plan in Figure 5.6.

During the Lesson

While the rest of the group reads familiar books from a basket of books they've read recently, Mr. Jones listens to Brianna read one. He does a running record, noting her miscues and self-corrections so he can reflect on it later. He notices that she wants to use her finger to point to every word, just as he suspected, and jots this down. He tells her to try reading with her eyes instead of her finger and see if she can read faster. It works, and they're both delighted! When she gets stuck on a word, her finger goes back on the page, and he tells her that's okay since she's using it to help her look closely at the word. She self-corrects and continues to read, taking her finger away. He reminds her to make her eyes move quickly across the page and her fluency begins to improve. After she's finished, he has her do a short retelling of the few pages she's read to check her comprehension.

Then the group looks at today's book together. *Morris the Moose* is a new book, but it's a very easy one and is written in phrases. The children read the title and make predictions. Students pay close attention to the teacher's demonstration of moving his eyes quickly across the page and reading in phrases. They laugh when he reads word by word and points with his eyes. And they realize that many of them have been doing this when they read. They are ready to attempt to read in phrases on this book. The text layout is so supportive that the teacher knows they'll succeed. He tells them to read to the bottom of page 17 and write a prediction of what might happen next on a sticky note.

As he moves from child to child, listening in to each one read a bit, Mr. Jones is pleased to see how

Figure 5.6 Lesson Plan for Phrasing: Day One

⠶ Lesson Plan for Phrasing: Day One ⠶

Group: Brianna, Ted, Jack, Lauren, Devon

Focus: FLUENCY

☐ fast decoding ☐ HF words ☐ punctuation ☑ phrases
☐ intonation and expression ☐ dialogue ☐ adjusting rate

Warm-Up: Familiar Rereading   **Listen to:** Brianna   **Title:** *The Apple Tree*

Today's Book: *Morris the Moose* by Bernard Wiseman   **Level:** early second grade/J

BEFORE READING

Book Intro:

■ Read title and make predictions using the cover.

■ *Morris is a moose and has some problems. Read to find out what Morris' problem is. Read to the sticky note at the bottom of page 17.* (Put one in each book to remind kids to stop and think here.) *Read to page 17 and write your prediction of what you think will happen next.*

■ Show kids how the text is written in phrases. Ask them to watch my eyes as I read the first sentence. (Read it word by word and then again in a phrased way.) *What did my eyes do? How did it sound?*

■ Tell them that this is reading fluently, and that it will help their reading sound better and help them understand more as they read.

■ *Remember to read to the end of page 17 and write your prediction. Read it fluently.*

DURING READING

Prompts:

■ *Move your eyes across the page fast. Read it in phrases. Make it sound like talking.*

Notes: Devon

AFTER READING

Discuss:

■ *What was the character, Morris, like? What was his problem?*

■ *What was your prediction at the bottom of page 17? Why did you think that?*

■ Discuss their phrased reading and how they did. Get kids to share what helped them.

■ Have each choose a favorite part and read it fluently to the rest of the group. Others give them feedback.

REFLECTION

Their fluency improved, but they weren't very solid on good predictions. Do more teaching about predictions in whole group and be sure to call on these kids. Have them reread this part and think more about the characters.

much more fluently they are reading. Their eyes are, in fact, moving more quickly across the page and they don't sound so robotic. He jots down on a sticky note that this book is perfect for Devon and is supporting his reading in a phrased, fluent way. Most finish reading much more quickly than normal and have time to jot down their predictions.

After they've read, they discuss it. They have a basic understanding of Morris, the main character, but their predictions are weak. Mr. Jones talks with them about how they sounded today, and they all think they've done much better. When he asks them what helped them, they say, "I moved my eyes across the page to the end of the line." "I didn't use my finger unless I got stuck on a word." "I read in phrases!" They are on their way to improved fluency.

After the Lesson

Mr. Jones realizes that this was the first time they really worked on reading in phrases, so they may have been focusing more on their phrasing than on their comprehension. He decides to have the students reread this book the following day and think more about comprehension. They will still focus on reading in phrases, but they will revisit predictions, too. He makes a quick note on the Reflection section of his lesson plan and decides to meet with this group again tomorrow to continue reading and rereading *Morris the Moose*.

See the plans Mr. Jones wrote for day two on his Lesson Plan for Phrasing in Figure 5.7. Notice that students will reread the text from day one in a slightly different way, with emphasis on making it sound interesting and thinking about the characters. This should aid comprehension as well as strengthen fluency.

Intonation and Expression Lesson Plan

Things to Think About

- Text that evokes strong emotions is easier to read with intonation or expression. You might

use a funny or a sad book, especially if it relates to something the children have experienced.

- A book with a few questions or exclamations can help students read with greater expression if you point these out and show them how to read these punctuation marks.
- If you're teaching kids to read in phrases, linking to reading them like the characters might say them often helps children to read so it sounds like the character would talk.
- I've found that using a bit of echo reading can directly model for children what they should sound like. I'm sure to do it just for a bit, though, so they can try this out on their own, too.

The Lesson

Yesterday, Mr. Jones worked with this group on reading in phrases. He still wants to continue having the students practice this, but he also wants them to think about what they're reading to be sure their comprehension is strong. So today, he will meet with them again, still focusing on phrasing. He will suggest that they think about the character, Morris, whom they understood well yesterday, and try to read it like Morris might say it. He'll point out the exclamation points and words written in capital letters to help children read it with better intonation, expression, and phrasing. See the lesson plan in Figure 5.7.

Reading Dialogue Lesson

Things to Think About

- Reader's theater scripts and plays are great for practicing how to read dialogue. See suggested resources of these kinds of materials in Appendix D.
- You might want to take the role of a theater "director" in these kinds of lessons, guiding the "actors" to read their parts more dramatically and with greater fluency.

Figure 5.7 Lesson Plan for Phrasing: Day Two

:: Lesson Plan for Phrasing: Day Two ::

Group: Brianna, Ted, Jack, Lauren, Devon

Focus: FLUENCY

- ☐ fast decoding
- ☑ intonation and expression
- ☐ HF words
- ☐ dialogue
- ☐ punctuation
- ☐ adjusting rate
- ☑ phrases

Warm-Up: Familiar Rereading   **Listen to:** Ted   **Title:** *The Apple Tree*

Today's Book: *Morris the Moose* by Bernard Wiseman   **Level:** early second grade/J

BEFORE READING

Book Intro:

- Quickly review what they learned about Morris yesterday as they read. Ask them what they learned about reading fluently, too.
- Divide the group in two. Have half of them be Morris and half be the cow. Model how to read across the page in phrases and with intonation and expression to make it sound like talking. Tell them that thinking about making the character talk will help them read in phrases and understand better. Read page 5 aloud and have the "Morris" kids echo read it. Then read the "cow" part on page 6 and have those kids echo read that. Repeat with several more pages until kids have the gist of this. Point out how to read the exclamation point.
- Tell them to reread the first 17 pages today, thinking about what Morris and the cow might say and do. Remind them to read quickly across the page in phrases and sound like the characters are talking. Ask them to think about what might happen next (after page 17).

DURING READING

Prompts:

- *Move your eyes across the page fast. Read it in phrases. Make it sound like talking.*
- *Read it with excitement when you see an exclamation point.*
- *Your reading helps me know how that character feels.*

Notes: Jack

AFTER READING

Discuss:

- *Did Morris sound different than the last time you read this? How?*
- *What was your prediction at the bottom of page 17 today? Why did you think that?*
- Discuss their phrased reading and how they sounded. Get kids to share what helped them.
- Have each choose a favorite part and read it fluently to the rest of the group. Others give them feedback.

REFLECTION

Their fluency improved and so did their predictions. Continue to call on these kids in whole group for predictions in read-aloud. Finish reading the book tomorrow. Continue with phrased reading using books written in phrases. *Henry and Mudge* might be good.

Figure 5.8 Lesson Plan for Reading Dialogue

⠶ Lesson Plan for Reading Dialogue ⠶

Group: Tommy, Aaron, Miguel, Sharee, Lucy, Mike

Focus: FLUENCY

☐ fast decoding   ☐ HF words   ☐ punctuation   ☐ phrases

☐ intonation and expression   ☑ dialogue   ☐ adjusting rate

Today's Book: *Pignocchio* by Donna Alexander   **Level:** mid–second grade/L

BEFORE READING

Book Intro:

■ Read title together, showing how to break names into chunks.

■ Kids make predictions. Tell what they know about Pinocchio.

■ Look at pages 2–3. Discuss how to read a play. Read names together.

■ Have kids read scene 1 silently to page 8.

- -

■ Kids choose part to read aloud. Use first five parts. Have two of them read Narrator 1 together.

DURING READING

Prompts:

■ *Who's talking here? Read it like the character would say it.*

Notes: Mike

- -

■ Direct their oral reading, giving support and feedback to make it sound like the character.

AFTER READING

Discuss:

■ Discuss pages 2–7. Describe each character and how he or she feels. *How would that make them sound as they spoke in this play?*

- -

■ Share how the dialogue sounded. Kids give feedback to each other.

REFLECTION

Reading a play went well. Continue tomorrow. Still need to show them how to transfer this to independent reading.

■ You might mix students with differing reading levels in a group for reading dialogue if you can find materials with parts written at different levels. Be sure each student has a part that is easy enough for him or her to read fluently.

The Lesson

Six students are seated at the table with their third-grade teacher, Ms. Belinski. She has just formed this group to help children work on reading dialogue more fluently. These children read at a variety of reading levels, but they all can use help with reading character parts more fluently. The teacher has chosen four students who were working in a recent group on decoding long vowels and other tricky vowel patterns. They have been making progress but could use fluency practice. Ms. Belinski has also noticed two other students needing help with reading dialogue as she's listened in to them during independent reading conferences. Figure 5.8 shows her lesson plan for their first meeting together.

Note that she has students read scene 1 silently first, then orally, to build fluency. There are two before, during, and after reading segments in this lesson. Each is divided by a dotted line to help you follow the sequence. The teacher introduces scene 1, and students read it silently while she listens in during their reading. After they read scene 1, they discuss the characters. Then they choose parts to read aloud, the teacher directs their oral reading, and they end the lesson by giving each other feedback about their reading.

Adjusting Rate Lesson Plan

Things to Think About

- You might look for text that has parts that naturally speed up or slow down, according to the action in the book. Suspenseful stories lend themselves well to this kind of reading practice. So do speeches.

- You might use poetry for this kind of lesson, particularly poems that evoke strong emotions or describe exciting events such as sports or weather.

- Use this kind of lesson once students can read in phrases and are using some intonation and expression. Build upon what they already know how to do, and take fluent reading to a dramatic level.

- After children have learned to read in this way, they might practice and then perform dramatic readings for an audience, such as the rest of the class, parents, the principal, or another classroom.

The Lesson

In this third-grade classroom, there are three students who read several grades above level. The teacher often feels like it's hard to provide time and opportunity to stretch these students in their reading, so she's chosen them for this fluency group. She wants to teach them how to read more dramatically, so they can grow as readers and perhaps show other students how to do this, too. They've been studying about Martin Luther King, Jr., since it's his birthday. She locates the text of his *I Have a Dream* speech and an audio recording online. She chooses a section of the speech and prints a copy for each student, and cues up the audio recording to that segment.

When she meets with the group, she gathers the children around a computer and gives each a copy of Dr. King's speech so they can follow along as they listen to it. Before they listen and follow along, the teacher cues them in to what she wants them to pay attention to as they listen and then, later, read. She tells them to listen to how Dr. King slows down his voice to emphasize certain parts and how he accelerates his voice as he shows excitement and hope. Her lesson plan is in Figure 5.9.

The following day, the teacher uses Dr. King's speech again. This time the students listen and follow along, reading orally with Dr. King. Then they read it on their own, each reading it aloud in a quiet voice so they can hear how they sound. The teacher listens in to individuals and prompts for and coaches each on varying the reading rate. After the reading, she asks them if they noticed anything new in the speech today. Then they take turns reading a section of their choice orally while the other students give feedback. They have enjoyed reading this speech and would like to read more. They decide to meet in a literature discussion group and read another of Dr. King's speech

Figure 5.9 Lesson Plan for Adjusting Reading Rate: Day One

⠶ Lesson Plan for Adjusting Reading Rate: Day One ⠶

Group: LaShawn, Tonya, Mariel

Focus: FLUENCY

☐ fast decoding   ☐ HF words   ☐ punctuation   ☐ phrases

☐ intonation and expression   ☐ dialogue   ☑ adjusting rate

Today's Book: *I Have a Dream* speech by Martin Luther King, Jr.   **Level:** fifth grade

BEFORE READING

Book Intro:

- Look for Martin Luther King, Jr.'s, *I Have a Dream* speech online, and cue up final part of speech. Look at photos of MLK, Jr., and discuss what kids already know about him and this speech.
- Hand out speech to kids and have them follow along and listen for how Dr. King slows down his voice and speeds it up to make his point. They might take notes on their copies of the speech to show this.
- Listen together and talk about what we notice about how he adjusts his rate.
- Have students read the speech silently and independently.

DURING READING

Prompts:

- *Speed up the parts that show his hope and excitement.*
- *Use pauses to build anticipation and show his concern.*

Notes: LaShawn

AFTER READING

Discuss:

- Discuss how it felt to read this speech after hearing Dr. King read it.
- Ask what they found themselves doing as readers. Discuss how they changed their reading rate, where, and why.

REFLECTION

Students really enjoyed this lesson and paid close attention to reading rate. Tonya is very interested in civil rights and loved the speech. She'd like to read more. Maybe give this to her for independent reading and use at the computer station.

excerpts that the teacher will find for them on the Internet. They would like to perform this speech for the rest of the class, so they plan to meet during literacy work stations time at the drama station to practice and prepare.

How Do I Assess or Check for Fluency?

In each of these small-group lessons, fluency assessment plays a crucial part. It helps the teacher know where to move next with each student—in forming groups, in choosing a lesson focus, and in choosing texts for students to practice reading in small groups.

To assess a student's fluency, you'll want to listen to the child read a short bit of text aloud one-on-one. In these lessons, this was accomplished by the familiar rereading section at the start and/or during the reading of that day's text in small group. I think it's important to take notes about a child's fluency, so I can remember exactly what the child did or didn't do as a fluent reader. I'm often asked what I write in those notes, so I've included some tips in the next section, "What to Look For and How to Take Notes on Fluency." I always have the child retell what was read or answer questions about the selection to check for comprehension, too, after I listen for fluency.

As stated earlier, some assessments, such as the DIBELS and the TPRI, require that you use a stopwatch to time how fast students read. When listening to students read aloud to check for fluency in a lesson, it is not necessary to always use a stopwatch. Remember that reading rate is part of fluency. DIBELS and TPRI use a stopwatch to give you a quick assessment of fluency, and since rate is the easiest thing to observe, it is the main measure you will get in using these assessments. You may choose to do more informal assessments of fluency by simply listening to students read aloud to you periodically and making notes such as those in this next section. You can also use the fluency score rubric in Appendix D.

What to Look For and How to Take Notes on Fluency

Along with objective measures like the ones mentioned above, subjective measures can be very useful. You'll find it helpful to take notes on fluency. Figure 5.10 describes some things you might look for.

Some Prompts for Fluency

When listening to a student read, your prompts or what you say to the child can provide the right amount of scaffolding to help him or her read more fluently. I've found it helpful to remember that my job in the small group is to help the child solve his or her own problems and come out of the experience reading more fluently. My prompting can make all the difference for the child. As the teacher, I am there to lend support, but not to do the work for the student! Prompting is the power of small-group instruction. Figure 5.11 describes some things you might say to the child, depending on what you notice the child is having some difficulty with.

Links to Whole-Group Instruction

If you want to help students improve in their oral reading fluency, there are many things you can model in whole-group instruction. Remember that you'll need to model these kinds of lessons several times in order to help students learn *how* to use these reading strategies. Using explicit language as listed in the previous section and as noted on the prompting sheets in Appendix D can help students transfer the strategy both in small-group instruction and, eventually, during their independent reading. Listed below are some ideas for how to teach for fluency in whole group.

Building Accurate Decoding

- Do Making Words lessons (see Patricia Cunningham's book listed at the end of this chapter).
- Do shared reading of Big Books with some nonsense words or onomatopoeia (see sample lesson plan in Appendix D).

Creating Automaticity

- Do shared reading of Big Books and poems and show kids how to move their eyes quickly across the page to the end of the line or phrase.

Figure 5.10 Aspects of fluency and what to look for when taking anecdotal notes.

Aspect of Fluency	What to Record/Look for	Sample Notes You Might Take
■ Decoding words effortlessly and automatically	■ Notice the amount of effort needed in decoding.	■ *no trouble with decoding*
■ High-frequency words	■ Record miscues like those to the right. ■ Find out words known so you can build on them in future lessons.	■ *of we* *if when* ■ *knows and, to, with, by, my* ■ *new: here, are*
■ Accurate decoding	■ Record miscues like those to the right. ■ Look for patterns in decoding errors.	■ *bush sig eat* *tree sign eight* ■ *errors make sense, but don't look right* ■ *uses beginning and ending sounds, but ignores middle* ■ *confuses long-vowel patterns (ea eigh)*
■ Reading the punctuation	■ Notice if the child pauses/stops at punctuation or just keeps reading. ■ Note if this seems to affect comprehension.	■ *Skipped over periods several times, especially in the middle of sentences* ■ *Is affecting comprehension*
■ Reading in phrases	■ Note if the child reads smoothly in phrases or choppily.	■ *Word-by-word reading* ■ *Not smooth*
■ Reading with intonation and expression	■ Think about how the child's expression sounds.	■ *Makes the reading sound interesting* ■ *Reads with enthusiasm and great interest*
■ Reading dialogue	■ Listen to how the child changes his or her voice when reading different character parts.	■ *Reads in a monotone voice*
■ Regulating the speed of reading	■ Does the reading rate slow down to build suspense or speed up to show excitement?	■ *Reads too fast*

■ Do some echo reading or choral reading of poems and short pieces of text, pointing out to the class how to read quickly and smoothly (see sample lesson plan in Appendix D).

Developing Interpretive and Meaningful Reading

■ Do reader's theater or read plays with the whole class, modeling how to read with interesting voices that match the characters (see sample lesson plan and resources for plays/reader's theater in Appendix D).

■ Read aloud and have kids tune in to *how* you sound—your pacing, phrasing, the way you change your voice when you read with different characters' voices.

Links to Literacy Work Stations Practice

After modeling fluency lessons in whole group and having students practice applying these in small groups, you'll want kids to have additional practice

Figure 5.11 Prompts for Fluency

What Child Is Having Trouble With	Possible Teacher Prompts
Decoding words effortlessly and automatically	■ *Read through the word quickly and think about what makes sense.* ■ *Use the parts you know and read it fast.*
Doing high-frequency-word work	■ *That's a word you know.* ■ *It's a word-wall word.* ■ *It's a spelling word.*
Reading the punctuation	■ *Stop at the periods.* ■ *Make your voice go up at the end of a question.* ■ *Read it with excitement.* ■ *Someone's talking. Sound like that character.*
Reading in phrases	■ *Think about where you'd pause if you were talking.* ■ *Read to the punctuation and stop.* ■ *Read it in phrases.*
Reading dialogue	■ *Who's talking here?* ■ *Read it like the character would say it.*
Reading with intonation and expression	■ *Make it sound interesting.* ■ *Make your voice go up at the end when there's a question mark.* ■ *Read it with excitement when you see an exclamation point.* ■ *Your reading helps me know how that character feels.*
Regulating the speed of reading	■ *Speed up the exciting parts.* ■ *Use pauses to build anticipation.*

Figure 5.12 Modeling how to read quickly across the page with a pointer in shared reading of a Big Book teaches students to read in phrases.

with fluency at literacy work stations. Here are some stations for students to go to with direct links to fluency:

Links to Standardized and State Testing

Students who can read fluently can read faster (with greater automaticity) and with better expression. They are thus able to have more brainpower free to think about comprehension. Most standardized and state reading tests focus on comprehension, not fluency. But some reading tests are timed. Fluency will make a huge difference in a timed test. Children will be able to read more text in a shorter amount of time and will not tire so easily when taking a reading test.

Figure 5.13 Work station that supports accurate decoding.

Literacy Work Station	What Kids Do Here to Practice Fluency Strategies	How This Station Supports Fluency
Word Study Work Station	■ Use hands-on materials to blend sounds to make words, using phonics patterns being studied (letter tiles, magnetic letters, letter cubes, etc.) ■ Do word sorts that match phonics patterns being studied	Decoding words automatically helps students with their reading fluency. They can read faster when they don't have to stop and sound each word out, letter by letter. Be sure to have kids practice with phonics patterns you've been studying in whole-group and small-group instruction.

Figure 5.14 Work stations that develop automaticity in word recognition (reading rate).

Literacy Work Station	What Kids Do Here to Practice Fluency Strategies	How This Station Supports Fluency
Word Study Work Station	■ Play games with high-frequency words that encourage automatic recognition, such as Concentration, Memory, or Hangman.	Working with high-frequency words can help students read more automatically as they quickly recognize more words embedded in text.
Buddy Reading Work Station	■ Read familiar or easy text with the support of a more fluent buddy to increase reading rate.	Oral reading practice, combined with instruction on how to read fluently, can improve reading fluency.
Big Book Work Station	■ Read familiar or easy text with the support of a more fluent buddy to increase reading rate.	Oral reading practice, combined with instruction on how to read fluently, can improve reading fluency.
Listening Work Station	■ Listen to an audio book read at a fluent reading rate to provide a good model of reading rate. ■ Follow or read along in the audio book as it is read aloud fluently.	Listening to a fluent reader on a recording provides a model for students who are learning to read more fluently. Oral reading of favorite parts gives students opportunities to practice reading fluently to an audience.
Recording Studio Work Station	■ Record one's reading. ■ Listen to one's reading and do a self-evaluation for reading rate, using a reading fluency rubric. (See Appendix D.)	Listening to one's oral reading and evaluating it can make students more aware of their reading fluency. Combined with fluency instruction, this can improve reading fluency.

Fluency Cautions

Fluency is an important part of reading, but be careful not to teach for fluency at the expense of comprehension. As I work in classrooms across the country, I sometimes see teachers working with kids to read faster, thinking this will automatically produce gains in comprehension; however, it's important to put as much effort into teaching comprehension as into teaching for fluency.

Remember, when teaching for fluency, rate is just one factor. Be sure to also look at students'

Figure 5.15 Students at the buddy reading work station enjoy reading for fluency.

Figure 5.16 Third grader uses a listening device to help her "hear" her fluency at this station.

Figure 5.17 Work stations that help students practice interpretive and meaningful reading.

Literacy Work Station	What Kids Do Here to Practice Fluency Strategies	How This Station Supports Fluency
Buddy Reading Work Station	■ Read together familiar or easy text expressively. ■ Listen to a partner read expressively and give each other feedback on fluency. ■ Use a reading fluency rubric.	Repeated reading builds oral reading fluency. Using a reading fluency rubric can increase students' awareness of their fluency and help them know what to focus on improving in their practice.
Big Book Work Station	■ Read familiar or easy text with the support of a more fluent buddy to improve expressiveness. ■ Use highlighter tape to mark the punctuation and then read and stop at the punctuation.	Repeated reading builds oral reading fluency. Support of a more fluent reader can provide feedback and a good model for fluent reading. Paying attention to punctuation while reading can improve expressive reading and comprehension.
Listening Work Station	■ Listen to a recording (fiction, nonfiction, or poetry) read at a fluent reading rate to provide a good model of expressive reading. ■ Follow along using the text as it is read aloud fluently.	Hearing a text read aloud first as a model, followed by repeated readings, can improve oral reading fluency.
Reader's Theater or Drama Work Station	■ Choose parts and read a reader's theater script with expression. ■ Retell or reread a familiar book with expression.	As students use expression, their phrasing and intonation generally improve.
Poetry Work Station	■ Read poems in phrases expressively. ■ Work on rhyme and rhythm.	See above.

Figure 5.18 Reading reader's theater scripts and using a flannel-board builds both fluency and comprehension.

Figure 5.19 Students record their reading of a familiar book, then play it back and listen for their fluency.

expressiveness while reading. And again, always take time to talk with them about what they read, so you have not ignored comprehension. Don't give students the false impression that reading fast is reading fluently. They will do what you model. Show or tell them what is important. Fluency includes decoding accurately, reading rate, expression, intonation, phrasing, pacing, *and* pausing.

Reflection Questions for Professional Conversations

1. What do you notice about your students' reading fluency? Is this something most of your students need help with, or do just several kids need fluency practice?

2. How are you currently assessing fluency, and how often? How is this information helping you? Which ideas from this chapter can you use to accelerate your students' reading fluency?

3. How are you currently teaching fluency in whole group? What aspects of fluency have you been focusing on? What else might you try?

4. How are you currently teaching fluency in small group? What aspects of fluency have you been focusing on? With whom? What else might you try?

5. What can you take from whole-group fluency instruction and apply to practice with support in a small group? Who needs this small-group instruction?

6. Tape-record yourself working with a small group for fluency. Listen to the students. Listen to your prompts. What's going well? What do you want to change? Why? You might use the prompts shown in Figure 5.11 for help.

For Further Information on Fluency Instruction

Try some of the following for more information on teaching for fluency:

Brand, M., and G. Brand. 2006. *Practical Fluency: Classroom Perspectives, Grades K–6*. Portland, ME: Stenhouse.

Cunningham, P. 1994. *Making Words*. Carthage, IL: Good Apple.

Opitz, M., and T. Rasinski. 1998. *Good-bye, Round Robin: 25 Effective Oral Reading Strategies*. Portsmouth, NH: Heinemann.

Rasinski, T. 2003. *The Fluent Reader*. New York: Scholastic.

Phonemic Awareness

Mrs. Bird is sitting around a table with four of her kindergartners. They are engaged in a phonemic awareness lesson—playing with sounds and a few letters. She begins with sounds only, no print attached. She sings a little song the children know to the tune of "Row, Row, Row Your Boat." They happily join in: "Say, say, say the sound. Say the sound of *m* . . ." Then she sings the following words and asks them if they start with *m* or not. If they do, the children give a thumbs-up; if not they give a thumbs-down. She uses the words *mom, man, cat, me*. And they end with "Say the sound of *m*." They repeat the song with the sounds of *r* and *t*. To keep things lively, Mrs. Bird begins a new game. These children know several letters, so she tells them they will use what they're learning about letters and sounds to play Toss the Cube. She has a large plastic cube with letters on it that they are learning. Frederick rolls it and an *m* comes up. Mrs. Bird tells him to trace the letter and say the sound (not the letter name, since her objective is to work with sounds). He says, "\m\." Then she asks him to say a word that starts with \m\. She gives him several

examples—*Mike, my, me.* Frederick says, "milk." Each child takes a turn quickly tracing the *m* on the cube, saying "\m\" and a word that begins with that sound. Then it's Alicia's turn to pick a new letter. She rolls the cube and gets *s*. She says "\s\, sun" and is followed by the other children tracing the *s* and saying the sound, followed by other words that begin with this sound—*Sammy, sit, seven.* They go around the circle several times with this one, since kids love this sound . . . *silly, six, said, sick, summer, spring.*

Mrs. Bird praises the children for their sound knowledge. She tells them that boys and girls who know sounds can use these to learn to read. Then she pulls out a favorite Big Book, *The Itsy Bitsy Spider.* The children ask if they can help read it. She gives them their own pointers, and they help her point to the words while they read/sing it together. On the cover, Alison says, "I see *s*." As they read the title, Mrs. Bird stretches out the \s\ sounds and points to them to show the children how speech sounds map onto letters and can be used to help us read. They read the Big Book together and after-

Figure 6.1 Lesson Plan for Mrs. Bird's Phonemic Awareness

⠞ Mrs. Bird's Phonemic Awareness Lesson Plan ⠞

Group: Frederick, Alicia, Elayna, Julio

Focus: PHONEMIC AWARENESS

☑ sound matching—Activity 1   ☑ initial sound isolation—Activity 2 and 3

☐ final sound isolation   ☐ medial sound isolation

☐ sound blending   ☐ sound segmenting   ☐ sound addition, deletion, or substitution

---

Activity 1:

Sing song to tune of "Row, Row, Row Your Boat." Use sounds of *m, r, t*. Kids put thumbs up if word starts with that sound; thumbs down if not. Kids sing along.

Say, say, say the sound.	*mom, man, cat, me*
Say the sound of (*mmmmm*)	*run, boy, red, rag*
(*mom, man, cat, me*)	*tie, tug, toy, bag*
Say the sound of (*mmmmm*).	

Activity 2:

Play Toss the Cube. Kids toss letter cube (with letters *m, r, t, s, p, f* on it).

Kids take turns saying words that start with that sound.

Use mirror, if needed, for kids to look at their mouths to make that sound.

Then ask, "What's the sound that starts these words?" and say several words with that sound.

Activity 3:

Read together *The Itsy Bitsy Spider* Big Book. After reading, find words that say *sssss* and *mmmm*. Ask where they hear that sound . . . at the beginning, middle, or end of the word.

Prompts:

■ *Do you hear the sound of _____?*

■ *Where do you hear it? At the beginning, the middle, or the end?*

■ *Look at my mouth. Make your mouth look like this when you say _____.*

Notes:

REFLECTION

Kids did really well. It was easier for them to hear sounds at the beginning of words than at the end. They're ready to start isolating sounds at the end of words, too.

---

ward, Mrs. Bird asks them to look for \s\ and \m\ in the book. She uses the sounds rather than the letter names. She wants children to attach *sounds* to the letters, so they can start to understand the alphabetic principle—that speech sounds can be represented by letters.

What Is Phonemic Awareness?

Due to the developmental, foundational nature of both phonological and phonemic awareness in helping children learn to read, many of the lessons in this chapter focus on children in kindergarten and first grade. We'll take an in-depth look at some of the groups in Mrs. Bird's kindergarten classroom, whom we met in the opening lesson of this chapter, to see how she plans and teaches for hearing and manipulating the sounds of our language. We'll also meet Ms. Wu, a first-grade teacher; and Mr. Diaz, who teaches second-grade English language learners, and see how they work with phonemic awareness in small groups.

Phonological awareness and *phonemic awareness* are related terms that are often used interchangeably by teachers. However, they do not mean exactly the same thing. *Phonological awareness* is an umbrella term that refers to an understanding of spoken words, and includes an awareness of words, syllables, rhymes, and individual sounds. Figure 6.2 shows a phonological awareness continuum. Rhyme awareness is a part of phonological aware-

ness and is a stepping-stone for children on the way to developing phonemic awareness. When students have learned to rhyme, it is a signal that they're ready to manipulate smaller units of speech, down to *phonemes*—the smallest units of speech a word can be divided into.

It's important for young children to learn to rhyme because it helps them understand that words are made of parts that can sound the same. A child who can rhyme can hear the sounds in words *and* tell where they occur. Later, this will help them read and write words more readily. They will understand that *day* is like *play* at the end of the word, both in sound and letter patterns. Understanding rhyming words can also affect comprehension, so young learners must be able to differentiate between the meanings as well as the sounds of rhyming words.

There are several stages in learning to rhyme. You might want to keep track of students' rhyming development to help you plan instruction, like Mrs. Bird does. See Appendix E for a blackline version of Figures 6.6 and 6.7. You'll notice that Mrs. Bird has students at various stages of rhyming. Most of her students can hear and produce some rhyme, so she

Figure 6.2 Phonological Awareness Continuum

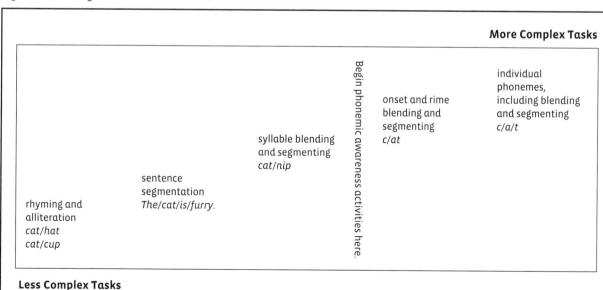

Figure 6.3 Kindergartners learn to sort these rhyming pictures in small group. Then they practice the same activity at the pocket chart work station.

can be written, which helps them develop concepts about print such as, print carries a message.

Recently, a kindergarten teacher asked me why it's important for her students to learn to blend and segment syllables. I explained that when children can hear these bigger sound chunks, it becomes easier for them to be able to map letters onto sounds and to understand that words are made of parts. A first or second grader who is trying to write a long word needs to know that *happy* has two parts. First, he must segment and write *hap*, and then he must hear and write *py*. Working with onset and rime also helps kids learn to segment smaller chunks. *Onset* is the consonant sound (or sounds) that comes before the *rime*, which includes the vowel and the letters to the right of it in a one-syllable word. For example, in *horse*, the onset is \h\ and the rime is \orse\. In *brain*, the onset is \br\ and the rime is \ain\.

Building on the foundation of all these phonological skills, students will start to develop *phonemic awareness*—the ability to play with those *smallest* speech sounds in language, phonemes. (For example, *cat* has three phonemes—\c\a\t\ and *show* has two phonemes—\sh\ow.\) In the opening lesson,

does whole-group rhyming activities where kids have opportunities to produce rhyme. In small group, she meets with Juan, Adrienne, Selina, Omar, Philip, and Amber to work on hearing rhymes. She is also helping them start to produce some rhymes.

As her children learn to rhyme, Mrs. Bird teaches them to listen to words that sound the same at the beginning—words like *Miss* and *Muffet*. Playing with alliteration also tunes children in to the sounds our language makes. In whole-group instruction, she reads aloud books, poems, and nursery rhymes that play with beginning sounds.

Another phonological task Mrs. Bird is teaching her kindergartners is to hear individual words in sentences by having them say a sentence and hold up one finger for each word. This makes them aware that our language is made up of words. She also shows them the space between each word, just like it is in print. She shows them how these words

Figure 6.4 This kindergarten teacher praises her students for hearing sounds in words as they work together on phonemic awareness in small group.

Mrs. Bird was helping her small group develop phonemic awareness.

As mentioned earlier, phonemic awareness is not the only component of early literacy instruction. Young children also need to learn about the following:

- phonological awareness, including listening, words and sentences, awareness of syllables, and playing with onset and rime
- concepts about print (print carries a message; print goes from left to right and top to bottom; there are spaces between words; words are different from letters; we read from the front to the back of a book; etc.)
- letter names, shapes, sounds, and formation

Providing children with rich language experiences that encourage active exploration and manipulation of sounds can develop phonemic awareness. This kind of instruction should celebrate oral language and tap into the magic and wonder of words.

Phonemic awareness activities may include

- sound matching
- sound isolation (initial, then final, then medial sounds)
- sound blending
- sound segmenting
- sound addition, deletion, or substitution

Activities that engage children and help them play with words may include

- reading and reciting nursery rhymes
- singing songs that play with sounds
- engaging in games that play with words
- sharing riddles and rhymes that focus on songs
- phoneme manipulation games

All phonemic awareness activities should begin with oral language. Children hear the words or see

Figure 6.5 In small group some kindergarten children play with language using nursery rhymes. Later, they work with nursery rhymes and manipulative pieces as they practice what they learned in small group at literacy stations.

pictures of objects. These activities should be playful, not done as drills. Phonemic awareness should begin with *sounds* in spoken words with no letters present. Over time, print can be added to phonemic awareness activities. As students learn to identify some letters, *these* letters can be used to show how the alphabet represents speech sounds. This gives children opportunities to understand and apply the *alphabetic principle*—understanding that the sounds within spoken words are represented in writing by letters, and that those letters represent the sounds rather consistently.

You do not need to teach phonemic awareness first and then teach letters separately. These can be successfully blended together to help children understand that words are made up of sounds that are represented by letters. Children can begin learning about letter-sound relationships and reading and writing some words while learning that spoken words consist of several sounds.

Figure 6.6 Mrs. Bird's rhyming groups folder.

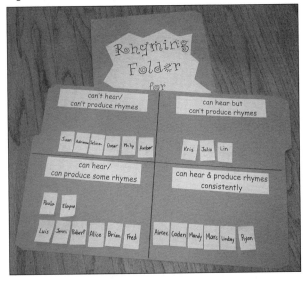

Figure 6.7 Mrs. Bird's Rhyming Stages Chart

Mrs. Bird's Rhyming Stages Chart	
can't hear/can't produce rhymes	can hear/can't produce rhymes
can hear/can produce some rhymes	can hear/can produce rhymes

Figure 6.8 Mrs. Bird's phonological awareness groups folder.

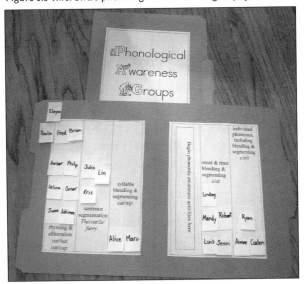

Phonemic Awareness Research at a Glance

Much research is available on the importance of phonemic awareness:

- Phonemic awareness is the most potent predictor of success in learning to read (Stanovich 1986, 1994).
- Lack of phonemic awareness is the most powerful determinant of the likelihood of failure to learn to read (Adams 1990). If kids cannot hear and manipulate the sounds of spoken words, they have trouble learning how to map those sounds to letters and letter patterns.
- Phonemic awareness is central in learning to read and spell (Ehri 1984).
- Phonemic awareness is a prerequisite to learning phonics (Liberman and Shankweiler 1979). If kids have phonemic awareness, they will learn to connect the speech sounds to letters more easily.
- Children who are taught to separate words into sounds and blend sounds into words are better at reading words (Torgesen, Morgan, and Davis 1992).
- First graders in whole-language classrooms who were taught to separate words into sounds read real words, nonsense words, and passages aloud better than those who were not taught to separate words into sounds (Uhry and Shepherd 1993).
- Phonemic awareness is both a prerequisite for and a consequence of learning to read (Yopp 1992).

Similarly, studies show the most effective ways to teach phonemic awareness:

- About twenty minutes a day, three to four times a week, will result in dramatic improvement for kids who need further development in phonemic awareness (National Reading Panel 2000).

- There are studies that support the use of phonemic awareness as a speech-related practice in the absence of print (Bentin and Leshem 1993; Hurford et al. 1994).
- Connecting phonemic awareness instruction to reading and writing increases its impact on reading achievement (Cunningham 1990).
- Learning to separate and blend sounds is not particularly effective without some letter-sound knowledge (Ball and Blachman 1988b; Lundberg, Frost, and Petersen 1988).
- Having children write words by listening for individual phonemes and identifying the letters that represent these sounds helps to teach segmenting and improves children's ability to recognize unfamiliar words (Ehri and Wilce 1987).

Here are some specific findings about teaching phonemic awareness from the National Reading Panel report (National Institute of Child Health and Human Development 2000):

- Beyond preschool, phonemic awareness instruction is most effective when printed letters are added to the speech sounds over time (and as children can identify those letters).
- Begin with easier levels of phonemic awareness such as identifying the initial sounds in spoken words. Progress to segmenting, blending, and deleting phonemes.
- Focus on one or two phonemic awareness skills at a time. More than this is less effective.
- Working with small groups of three to four children to teach phonemic awareness may be more effective than one-on-one tutorials.
- Studies that produced the strongest results engaged students with phonemic awareness activities between a total of five to eighteen hours.
- Emphasis should be placed on segmenting words into phonemes. Blending is important, too, but segmenting is most important.

- Use manipulatives to help students develop phonemic awareness. Have students move letters while pronouncing phonemes to produce maximum transfer to reading and spelling.
- Focus attention on how the mouth changes when pronouncing different phonemes to increase phonemic awareness.

Related to phonemic awareness, research by Marilyn Adams (1990) suggests the following considerations when teaching the alphabet:

- Teach upper- and lowercase letters separately.
- Begin with uppercase letters in preschool.
- Teach kids to form letters correctly to help them develop letter recognition.
- Use letter/keyword/picture displays to introduce letter-sound connections.

Students must learn the alphabetic principle—that letters are worth learning and stand for sounds that occur in spoken words.

Who Needs This Kind of Small Group?

Most young children enjoy playing with language if the teacher models this and shows how much fun it can be. Much of your phonological and phonemic awareness teaching will take place in whole group, and many students will develop phonemic awareness from this large-group teaching as well as from the language interactions they're having with adults at home. However, some children will probably have difficulty hearing and playing with the sounds of language. These are the students with whom you will want to work in small-group lessons for phonological or phonemic awareness.

You may also notice that students in your classroom are at different stages of phonological and phonemic awareness. You'll want to group kids with similar needs together for small-group instruction. You may want to make grouping folders for rhyming and phonological awareness, as pictured in Figures 6.6 and 6.8, to help you. You might use the blacklines in Appendix E to make these.

Possible Focuses for Lessons

Since phonemic awareness hinges on students' development of basic phonological awareness such as rhyming and syllable segmenting, I've included in this chapter several possibilities for phonological and phonemic lesson focuses, as well as sample lessons for both. The lessons are intended for small-group instruction, so students have increased opportunities for hands-on engagement. The more they participate in the lessons, the more they will develop phonological and phonemic awareness.

Possible Phonological Focuses

- *Rhyming.* Because this is a prerequisite skill for many other kinds of phonological awareness, you may want to start here. Remember that there are several stages in rhyming. Most four-year-olds will learn to rhyme as they play with language through nursery rhymes, poems, songs, and rhyming books. Others will need extra practice in small group.
- *Alliteration.* Here you'll be helping children listen for words that start with the same letter. Use books, nursery rhymes, and songs to do this.
- *Sentence segmenting.* At this point, students start to understand that sentences are made up of smaller units called words. You might have students hold up a finger for each word in a sentence as you're thinking of a message to write together.
- *Syllable blending and segmenting.* I like to begin with children's names. I have them clap the parts of their names, like *Thom-as*, starting with first names and then using last names. I also may ask them to clap the parts of a book title or an author's name before I read aloud.

Or I choose an interesting word from a book and clap it with them to see how many parts it has. To blend syllables, I like to call children by their names, such as *Bri-an-na* and have children say, "Brianna" while that child stands up or children point to her picture on a chart.

Possible Phonemic Focuses

When we focus on phonemes, we're targeting the *smallest* units of speech in a word. Some possible lessons include the following:

- *Onset-rime segmenting and blending.* These activities can be done in a playful way, too. You'll want to help students isolate the first part of a word from the rest of it. For example, play a game naming parts of your body. Point to your *leg* and say \l\eg\. Repeat with other one-syllable body parts, such as *nose, cheek, lips, mouth, neck, nail, toe, shin, calf, thigh, wrist, waist.*
- *Sound matching.* This is an easier phonemic awareness task. Here kids match sounds that sound the same. They might tell which word doesn't belong, based on the beginning sounds. Or they may generate words that start with that sound. Kids don't need to know alphabet letters to be successful here. They are focusing on the sounds. However, if they know some letters, you might add the letter to help them make the connection between the sound and the letter that represents it.
- *Counting phonemes in a word.* Use objects or pictures. Or just say a word aloud. Have children hold up a finger for each sound as they say the word slowly.
- *Blending phonemes to make a word.* Give children individual speech sounds, and they try to guess the word. For example, "I'm thinking of a word. I'll say it slowly and you guess it . . . \m\ou\se\." The kids say, "Mouse."

- *Isolating the beginning phoneme in a word.* This will help children move into the more difficult task of segmenting phonemes. Here, they'll isolate just the first sound. To do this, kids may repeat the first sound several times, such as in *c-c-c-car.*

- *Isolating the final phoneme in a word.* This is similar to the preceding task, except now the emphasis is on the last sound in a word. You might help students do "echo talk," having them repeat the last sound in a word. For example, "My name is *Deb-b-b-b-b.*"

- *Isolating the medial phoneme in a word.* This is the hardest of all for most kids to do, since it involves listening to the sound in the middle. Use words with only three phonemes here, such as *light, bag, hat, meal, soup, net, hug, feel,* and *name.* Have them tell the sound they hear in the middle of the word. Focus on the sound, not the letter.

- *Segmenting phonemes in a word.* Again we are playing with the sounds of words, this time using a more difficult phonemic awareness task. But if kids have been successful at the preceding tasks, this activity will be much easier. It does take a lot of practice for some children. Here they must take a word and break it into parts. It's easiest to begin with two-phoneme words, like *bee* and *two.* Use picture cards and objects to play with this task. Then move to three-phoneme words, and then to four. You might ask kids to add body motions to help; for instance, have them touch their head while saying the first sound, their shoulders during the medial sound, and their waist as they say the final sound.

- *Substituting one phoneme for another.* This is fun to do with songs or with kids' names. Take a familiar song, like "Mary Had a Little Lamb," and sing it with a new sound at the start of each word, such as *w.* You'd sing, *Wary wad a wittle wamb, wittle wamb, wittle wamb. Wary had a wittle wamb. Wits weece was white was* *whoa.* (This will work only if the kids really know the original version.) You might also play a game where you take the first sound and change it to another. Again, use something familiar like the parts of their body. Have them point to their leg as you say, "Leg. \L\e\g\. Let's put \m\ where the \l\ is and we'll have . . ." They reply, "Meg." "What would *nose* be? Point to your nose. *Nose.* \N\ose\. Let's put \m\ where the \n\ is and we'll have . . . (*mose*)."

To help students segue from phonemic awareness to phonics, try the following:

- *Deleting phonemes from words.* This is much easier to do once you've attached some print to the sounds. For example, if you tell kids to say *plop* without the *l,* that's much easier to do if you can see the print. This is not the goal of phonemic awareness. Most of the research points to phonemic segmentation, not phoneme deletion, as being key to children learning to read.

Choosing Materials

You won't need many materials for teaching phonemic awareness, since many of the activities are devoid of print. But you might want to use some manipulatives to help children play with language, such as the following:

- colored blocks
- teddy bear counters
- plastic chips
- Elkonin boxes (a box stands for each speech sound)
- small objects for sorting and naming
- pictures of familiar objects for sorting and naming
- handheld mirrors (for children to look at their mouths while articulating sounds)

- chart showing how your mouth looks when you say a sound

At the early stages of phonological awareness, when you're working with rhyming and alliteration, you'll want to use books and songs that include rhyme and word play. Don't move on to the phonemic awareness lessons until children understand how to rhyme, segment sentences into words, and clap their names by syllables, and are beginning to be able to separate onsets from rimes. Add letters once children are able to divide words into individual speech sounds and they can identify some letters. Using letters they know attached to phonemes they hear can help children understand how these letters can be used to represent speech sounds in reading and writing. As you add print, you might want to consider also using these materials:

- magnetic letters
- letter tiles
- dry erase boards and markers

:: The Lessons ::

Now that you understand the relationship between *phonological* and *phonemic awareness*, we'll take a look at some lessons you might use to teach children in a small group who need help learning these skills. We'll begin with some less-complex *phonological* tasks, such as rhyming, and then move into *phonemic awareness* lessons. The *phonemic awareness* lessons have an asterisk (*) by them to help you differentiate them from phonological lessons.

Rhyming

Things to Think About

- Do these lessons only with children who need extra help with rhyming. Use the rhyming stages folder to help you determine who needs what. Work with your students where they

are. If kids can already rhyme, you don't need to do this in small group.
- For children who are having difficulty learning to rhyme, you might use familiar books from read-aloud that include rhyming words so students have a base on which to build, as demonstrated in this lesson.
- It's okay if children make up nonsense words that rhyme. You may have to provide a beginning sound to help them produce a rhyme.

Before the Lesson

Mrs. Bird, the kindergarten teacher we met in the opening of this chapter, has several children who either can't hear or can't produce rhymes (see her rhyming folder in Figure 6.6), despite all the whole-group lessons she has taught focusing on rhyming. I ask her to show me the materials she's been using to teach rhyming. She has lots of stuff—rhyming picture cards, rhyming games, little books with a rhyming word on each page—but none of these materials seem to have helped this small group of children learn to rhyme.

Mrs. Bird also shows me a set of nursery rhyme Big Books that have one line of print per page and large colorful pictures. She says she's read them frequently with her class, and the children love them.

Figure 6.9 Materials used to teach rhyming.

Most of her students are English language learners, and she's been focusing on developing oral language with them. Most of her children can identify the rhyming words in these books, so we decide to try them with her small group. I'm thinking that the missing link may be finding something familiar for these children to help them use what their teacher has been trying to teach them about rhyming.

I offer to teach the lesson, and Mrs. Bird says she'd welcome the opportunity to observe her children and learn from my modeling. This will give her a chance to see what they may be able to do with a bit of scaffolding from a different teacher, since she has been stumped about what else to try with them. She will take notes, and we'll debrief after this short, focused lesson.

During the Lesson

I begin by showing the children several of the nursery rhyme Big Books. I tell them that we will read one of these together today and that they get to pick. Their faces light up, probably because they know these books. They are going to be successful— I can tell from the start. I ask them to choose a Big Book and name the title. They select *Jack and Jill*. First we read the title and look at the cover, talking about the pictures and what will happen in this book. They say, "Jack falls down. He gets hurt." We begin to read together, enjoying the pictures and the language—"Jack and Jill went up a hill." While I read, I point to the pictures of Jack and Jill and the hill. This helps to build vocabulary and add meaning to the rhyme. Then I say, "Do you hear any rhyming words? Rhyming words sound the same at the end." I reread the page, emphasizing the words *Jill* and *hill*. One of the children smiles and says, "Jill, hill." Her teacher beams from the sidelines.

I reinforce the rhyming by saying, "Yes, those words rhyme. *Jill* and *hill* rhyme. They sound the same at the end. *Jill, hill.* Say them with me." All the kids repeat the rhyming words with me several times. I reiterate that they rhyme because they

sound the same at the end. All of a sudden, one of the children says, "*Jill, hill, bill.*" I respond enthusiastically that all those words rhyme and sound the same at the end. I repeat the words again and invite them to say these rhyming words in a playful singsong way. Another child chimes in, "*hill, will.*" They're starting to catch on.

We move on to the next page and read, "To fetch a pail of water." Again I point to the pictures showing them the pail filled with water. They look at the picture, and some of them say, "Pail of water," playing with the sounds of the words rhythmically as I have modeled.

On the next page, we read, "Jack fell down and broke his crown," and I ask if they hear any rhyming words. We reread it again, and I emphasize *down* and *crown*. I point to Jack falling *down* and to his head, explaining that they call his head a *crown* in this rhyme. I say, "*Down* . . ." and point to Jack's head, and they say, "*Head.*" I repeat, "*Down, head,*" and ask if they rhyme and sound the same at the end. Several of them shake their heads. We quickly read the page again. Again, I say, "Which words rhyme? *Down* . . ." Someone says, "crown." We repeat the rhyming words again, *down, crown*. I ask them if they can think of any other words that rhyme with *down* and *crown*. I repeat the words several times, as they join in with me. I supply \t\ to help them get started, and one says, "town." Then I give \g\ and some say, "gown." They are all smiles.

I decide to quit while I'm ahead. They've enjoyed playing with language in this Big Book, and I don't want to overstay my welcome. This entire lesson has lasted less than ten minutes. I could do another phonological task with them, but I choose instead to send two of them to the Big Book station where they can reread this book or several others. They may or may not play with rhyme. The other four can go to an extra listening station. Their teacher has a rhyming story on tape that they can listen to and join in with. It's short and will last about five minutes. This allows me to spend a few minutes walking around the room and observing

Figure 6.10 Lesson Plan for Rhyming

:: Lesson Plan for Rhyming ::

Group: Philip, Juan, Adrienne, Selina, Omar, Amber

Focus: PHONOLOGICAL AWARENESS

☑ rhyming   ☐ alliteration   ☐ sentence segmenting
☐ syllable blending and segmenting   ☐ onset and rime blending and segmenting

Activity 1:

Read together nursery rhyme Big Books. Let kids choose from *Jack and Jill, Little Miss Muffet,* and *Humpty Dumpty.*

- I read and have them fill in the rhyming word. Help them tell which words rhyme.
- If they can hear rhyme, help them produce more rhyming words.

Activity 2:

Send this group to work stations. Send Philip and Juan to Big Book to read these nursery rhymes once. Others go to listening station and hear rhyming story and help supply rhyming words orally.

- I walk around the room seeing how kids are doing at their literacy stations.

Prompts:

- *What rhymes with _____?*
- *It sounds the same at the end.*
- *_____, _____. Hear how they're the same at the end.*
- *(Jill), (b)_____. (Give first sound to scaffold rhyming.)*

Notes:

REFLECTION

They started to hear and identify some rhymes today, probably because the text was familiar. Several times, Philip, Juan, Selina, and Omar added a new rhyming word. Keep working on this. Use more of these nursery rhyme Big Books.

---

what the rest of the class is doing at their literacy work stations.

After the Lesson

I notice that children are working well at their stations. Mrs. Bird has done an excellent job of teaching routines in her classroom. This frees her up to work consistently with children in small group. The two children I sent to Big Books are reading and enjoying *Jack and Jill*. I hear them say some of the same things I said in my lesson—*Can you hear the rhyming words? Jill, hill.* They don't go much further

with the rhyming, but they now have an anchor they can hold on to when Mrs. Bird does rhyming lessons with them.

The children at the listening station are trying to finish the rhyme at the end of the sentence on the tape. They are enjoying the story and are making attempts at rhyming. The tape supplies the correct rhyming word, which gives the kids immediate feedback.

Mrs. Bird and I take a few minutes to debrief. She is delighted with how her kids did with rhyming today. When I ask her what she thinks made a difference, she says, "It's the familiar book. Most of the time I was trying to play rhyming games with them. There was nothing familiar there. They loved reading the Big Book with you."

Together we plan the next day's lesson for this group. She decides to do a similar rhyming lesson tomorrow. They'll reread *Jack and Jill* and add *Little Miss Muffet* or *Humpty Dumpty*. She liked the idea of a shorter lesson and then sending kids to a rhyming-related work station for a few minutes for additional practice. She says she'd never tried that before and really liked the way it worked. It will also give her a chance to see what the rest of the class is doing.

Sentence Segmenting

Things to Think About

- Keep these lessons brief. Use them to develop oral language as well as to help children think about sentences being made up of words. Try to get kids to use longer, more complex sentences as you go through the lesson.
- Use pictures with familiar objects and events. Or use familiar picture books so students can easily create sentences about them.

The Lesson

Mrs. Bird has children at many different levels of phonological awareness. There are four children who can benefit from some extra work with sentence segmenting. This will later help them as readers and writers, especially when they're learning to put spaces between words. They have to be able to *hear* word boundaries in order to mark them with spaces in their writing.

Today's small-group lesson is done through the ear. Mrs. Bird neither writes down their sentences nor shows them spaces. She just helps them *hear* words in sentences. This phonological awareness activity doesn't involve phonemes, the smallest speech units. It focuses on bigger chunks—words.

Mrs. Bird has chosen one of her class' favorite books, Paul Galdone's version of *The Three Little Pigs*. She tells her small group that today they're going to play a fun game called Push My Sentence. They will look at the cover of *The Three Little Pigs* and make up sentences about what they see in the picture. Mrs. Bird models this first. She says, "Let's read this book." She has five plastic teddy bear counters in front of her on the table, and each is a different color. She repeats her sentence, "Let's read this book" and pushes one bear forward each time she says a word. She leaves a space between each bear, too. After doing this, she gives each child a set of bear counters and invites them to say the sentence with her and push a bear forward each time they say a new word.

They take turns making up sentences about the cover illustration and pushing the bears forward to represent the words in each sentence. Mrs. Bird reinforces their actions by saying, "Every time you say a word, push a bear. These bears are like the words in your sentence." Karla says, "I see three pigs" and pushes forward four bears, one at a time. The other children repeat her sentence and follow Karla's lead. Although Mrs. Bird is focusing on sentence segmenting, she also uses this opportunity to develop language, so she adds, "Tell me more about the little pigs. Say a sentence telling what one of the pigs is holding."

Figure 6.11 Children segment sentences using teddy bear counters (a math manipulative). They push a counter for every word as they say a sentence. These can also be used to push sounds heard in individual words.

Figure 6.12 Lesson Plan for Mrs. Bird's Sentence Segmenting

⠿ Lesson Plan for Mrs. Bird's Sentence Segmenting ⠿

Group: Karla, Drake, Cecily, Daniela

Focus: PHONOLOGICAL AWARENESS

☐ rhyming   ☐ alliteration   ☑ sentence segmenting
☐ syllable blending and segmenting   ☐ onset and rime blending and segmenting

Activity 1:

Play Push My Sentence.

- Give each child various colored teddy bear counters.
- Show picture that has familiar objects/events in it. Use a few pages from a favorite book (*The Three Little Pigs*).
- Have kids take turns saying sentences about the picture.
- Have them push a colored bear forward each time they say a new word.

Activity 2:

Say or sing a nursery rhyme together.

- Use nursery rhyme charts, so kids can look at the pictures and see that spoken language can be written down.
- Tell them we'll clap each time we hear a new word. Have them clap on each word as we say the rhyme together.
- Use "Jack and Jill" and "Baa, Baa Black Sheep." (These have more one-syllable words to start.)

NOTE: Save for next time. Ran out of time today!

Prompts:

- *Listen for each word in the sentence.*
- *Clap on each word.*
- *_____ is just one word, not two.*
- *Push a counter each time you hear a word.*

Notes:

REFLECTION

Students did better today. Some still confuse two-syllable words, thinking each syllable is a new word.

Daniela says, "Flowers." Mrs. Bird patiently reminds her to use a sentence and helps her get started. "Use a sentence, Daniela. One little pig . . ." She asks the child to repeat her sentence starter and Daniela says, "One little pig is holding yellow flowers." They all say it together once to hold the pattern. Mrs. Bird quickly hands each child a few extra bears, and they all try to push their teddy bear counters while saying the sentence. Mrs. Bird notices some confusion on the word *little*. Some children think it is two words, so Mrs. Bird tells them that *little* is one word. They wouldn't say *lit* and then *lllll*. She says, "little" and pushes just one counter. They try again and do better.

They look at a few pages in the book and have fun making up sentences and pushing the counters. Mrs. Bird had planned another activity for today, but the children were so engaged with Push My Sentence that she decides to save the other game for the next time they meet.

Initial and Final Sound Isolation*

Things to Think About

- Start with sounds only. Focus on *where* the sound is heard. Then connect the print.

- Connect only *known* letters to the sounds. Don't overwhelm the students.

- Start with two-phoneme words, so children can be successful. Then build to three- and four-phoneme words over time.

- Do similar work with *medial* sounds after kids can hear initial and then final sounds. Medial sounds are harder for most young children to hear. Use three-phoneme words when having kids isolate medial sounds. If you have kids add print, use only consonant-vowel-consonant pattern words, like *big* and *top*.

Before the Lesson

Now we'll visit Ms. Wu's first grade. It is early in the year, and she is teaching whole-group phonemic awareness lessons. She has noticed that during these lessons, many students are successful, but a handful of kids can use additional help in isolating the individual sounds of words. So today she will work with four children on initial and final sound isolation. She knows that this will provide a strong foundation for the phonics work she will be doing with them this year. Until they hear the sounds, the letters will have little meaning.

These children know some letters from kindergarten, and they can rhyme, segment sentences and syllables, and even segment onset and rime. Ms. Wu knows that if they can learn to isolate sounds in words, they will have more success as readers and spellers this year. So her focus in this lesson is to help them hear sounds *and* identify where that sound is in a word. She chooses the sound of *t* to begin, since they all know this letter well. It is also in one of the kids' names in this group—Tyrone.

Ms. Wu writes her lesson plan, as shown in Figure 6.13. She gathers together her materials, including a two-by-three-inch card for each student with a *t* written in the middle. She also has sound box cards, made from three-by-nine-inch cardstock divided into three equal-size boxes with thick black lines. This lesson is simple and quick to prepare. Ms. Wu uses ideas from her teacher's edition, a testing intervention guide, and several articles she's saved and read from *The Reading Teacher*, the International Reading Association journal.

During the Lesson

Tyrone, Connie, Lamar, and Sammi join Ms. Wu at her small-group table. They love coming to group, because it is a time of day they all feel successful. Even though their friends are all at literacy work stations, they don't mind. Ms. Wu has established good routines, and they know they will also go to work stations after they work together in small group.

Ms. Wu has all her teaching materials at her fingertips to guarantee a fast-paced, smooth lesson. She tells her group that today they will play a sound game. They've played a similar game in large group before, and they're excited to begin. Ms. Wu gives each child a *t* card and asks them to name the sound, \t\. Tyrone says, "That's *t*, like in my name." Ms. Wu smiles and replies, "Yes, *Tyrone* says \t\ at the beginning of the word. \T\ is the first sound. Today I will tell you some words. You'll think if it has \t\ at the beginning of the word, like \t\ in *Tyrone*. If you hear \t\ at the start of the word, hold up your *t* card. If the word doesn't start with \t\, put the card behind your back. Ready?" You'll notice that Ms. Wu took every opportunity to use the sound of *t* to give children explicit instructions of what they'll be doing today.

Then she says, "tub." She repeats it, so they can really zoom into the sounds. They all smile and

Figure 6.13 Lesson Plan for Ms. Wu's Initial and Final Sound Isolation

⠶ Lesson Plan for Ms. Wu's Initial and Final Sound Isolation ⠶

Group: Tyrone, Connie, Lamar, Sammi

Focus: PHONEMIC AWARENESS

☐ sound matching   ☑ initial sound isolation   ☑ final sound isolation
☐ medial sound isolation   ☐ sound blending   ☐ sound segmenting
☐ sound addition, deletion, or substitution

Activity 1:
Give each child a letter card with *t* on it. Tell them to listen for the sound of *t* in each word. Sometimes \t\ will be the first sound. Sometimes it won't. If they hear \t\, they should hold up the *t* card. If the word doesn't start like \t\, they should put it behind their backs. Give them time to hear each word. Repeat it several times, if needed (*tub, tail, box, man, ten, top, tag, tug, can*).

Activity 2:
Repeat above. Tell them sometimes \t\ is the last sound in a word. They'll hear it at the end. Have them hold up the *t* if they hear its sound at the end of the word. Hide it behind their back if the word doesn't say \t\ at the end (*bat, bin, seat, leg, it, hat, it, ten, not, what, get*).

Activity 3:
Give each child a sound box card. It has three boxes on it. Tell them sometimes they'll hear \t\ at the beginning of the word. If they do, push the *t* card into the first box (show them). Sometimes they'll hear \t\ at the end of the word. Then push the *t* into the last box to show where they hear the \t\ sound (*tub, to, bat, hot, fit, ten, what, get, tooth*).

REFLECTION
This was tricky, but the sound boxes helped. Keep doing variations on this using known letters. Use one letter at a time for now.

hold up their *t* cards. She has them say *tub* with her and reiterates that *tub* has \t\ as the first sound. They repeat this game with the other words on her plan, which is on the table in front of her for reference. Ms. Wu has made the game easy and fun, and they are successful.

Next, she tells them the game will be changing a bit. Now they'll have to listen for \t\ at the end of the word. This is a little trickier. She gives them an example, *Connie*—another child's name in this group. She asks them if they hear \t\ at the end of

Connie. They shake their heads. "How about in *Matt*?" This child is also in their class, but not in this group. They show their *t* cards. They get the gist of this game quickly. Ms. Wu asks them what they want to do if the word does *not* end in the \t\ sound. They decide to turn it over, so the blank side shows. They play this game, and it is harder. But they start to catch on after a few words.

Satisfied that they are starting to hear a familiar sound both at the beginning and end of a word, Ms. Wu plays the last game with them. She tells the

Figure 6.14 Students listen to a word with *t* in it. They listen for the *t* sound and push the *t* card to show where this sound is heard in the word.

group that this time they will use their sound card and think about *where* the sound is in a word. If they hear \t\ at the beginning of the word, as the first sound, they'll put the *t* card in the first space of their individual sound card. If they hear \t\ as the final sound in the word, the last sound, they'll put the *t* card in the last space. They are ready to begin. Ms. Wu reminds them to listen carefully. She calls the words from her plan, one at a time, repeating each word several times and inviting the kids to join in saying each word with her. Then the children decide where the *t* card goes. They periodically look at each other's sound cards to see if they were right, and most of the time they are.

To end the lesson, Ms. Wu praises them for hearing the sounds and thinking about where these are in words. She tells them that when they can hear sounds, it will make both their reading and writing easier. She reminds them that when they write today, they can think about the sounds in each word they write and put the letter *where* they hear it in the word.

After the Lesson
Ms. Wu signals the rest of the class that it is time to change to their next work station by ringing a small bell. This is their sign to tidy up for the next group to come there. She has the children in her group help to put away the materials they used by returning their *t* cards to a labeled tackle box for the letter cards. They stack the sound cards and put them on the shelf behind Ms. Wu's table where she keeps other cards like these. Then they go to their work stations. They can easily read the management board posted on a door in their classroom. Ms. Wu takes less than a minute to jot down how the lesson went on the Reflection space of her plan. She'll sit down for a few minutes after school to plan what this group will do tomorrow when she meets with them. She puts her lesson plan back in the notebook where she keeps these on her table and pulls out her plan for the next group she will meet with.

Blending and Segmenting Phonemes*

Things to Think About

- Begin with blending two-phoneme words. When children can easily accomplish this, then have them blend three-phoneme words and eventually four-sound words.

- Blending is easier than segmenting for most children, so begin with this task. Once kids can successfully blend, move on to segmenting sounds in words.

- Add print to these lessons as you see it helps kids understand how sounds and letters work together. Remember that the emphasis on these lessons is the *sounds* and putting the *sounds* together or taking them apart. When introducing print in this kind of lesson, always use *known* letters, so students will be more successful.

- For children who still don't know all their letters, you can also teach lessons on letter identification in small group. But teach these new-letter lessons separately from your phonemic lessons.

The Lesson

We return to Ms. Wu's first-grade class. She has two groups that need help with phonemic awareness. This is her second group. (See her lesson plan in Figure 6.15.) Two of these students go to speech class, but Ms. Wu knows it is her responsibility to also teach them in small group. She doesn't just rely on the special teacher to meet the needs of these kids.

This group needs practice with blending and segmenting phonemes. Ms. Wu has administered the DIBELS, as directed by her school district. These children score low on PSF (phonemic segmentation fluency), so she is continuing to work with them on sound blending and segmenting. She knows that her persistence will pay off. They have been showing some progress, but still need more practice. Ms. Wu begins with a quick game of Name Blending. The children love hearing their names said sound by sound by their teacher, and then pointing to that child as they blend the sounds and say the child's name together. It is a fast, fun warm-up.

Ms. Wu tells them that today they will play Sound Blend Bingo. They are familiar with this game, since they've played it before. Ms. Wu takes the game from a shelf right behind her table, and the kids distribute the cards and the Bingo markers. Ms. Wu takes a picture card and names the object on it, sound by sound. It is a *sun*. She says, "\s\u\n\. Blend the sounds and say my word." The kids in her group all say, "sun" in unison. Those who have a picture of a sun mark their Bingo cards. Ms. Wu shows them the picture to check, and they continue playing in this way until a child calls out, "Bingo."

Before they can clear off their cards, Ms. Wu tells them not to start over. Now they'll play Reverse Bingo. She'll show them a picture she's already used. They'll name the picture (e.g., *sun*), name the picture slowly, sound by sound (\s\u\n\), and then remove the marker if they have the picture on their boards. She's mixed up these cards, so that ideally someone else will win

this time. The children have fun saying each word slowly, segmenting the phonemes, and removing markers from their boards. As predicted, another child wins this time.

As they clean up, Ms. Wu tells the group that they did a great job of blending and segmenting words today. She reminds them that this will help them with their reading and writing. When they have writer's workshop later in the day, she wants them to think of their words, say them slowly, and write the letters they know that make those sounds. She has chosen not to include print in today's lesson, but she is confident that they will start to make this transfer in their writing soon. She'll pay close attention to them today during writing time and remind them to say the words slowly. They're doing better at this each day.

Substituting One Phoneme for Another*

Things to Think About

- Phoneme manipulation helps kids really understand where sounds are in a word. Remember to have children play with phoneme substitution for sounds at different places in a word. Again, once they can do this with initial sounds, have them practice it with final sounds and then with medial sounds as well.

- Adding the print to these activities can make them easier for young children.

- This lesson may look like word families, but it's not. The emphasis here is on the *sounds* of the words, not the letters. It should focus on playing with the *sounds* to change the word into new words. Don't work with rhyming here either. That's not the purpose of the lesson. You want kids to leave with the understanding that they can make new words just by changing the sounds and where the sounds are located in a word. The print just helps them see *where* that sound is.

Figure 6.15 Lesson Plan for Ms. Wu's Sound Blending and Segmenting

⠶ Lesson Plan for Ms. Wu's Sound Blending and Segmenting ⠶

Group: Lana, Aimee, Tyler, Shaneka

Focus: PHONEMIC AWARENESS

☐ sound matching—Activity 1 ☐ initial sound isolation—Activity 2 and 3
☐ final sound isolation ☐ medial sound isolation
☑ sound blending ☑ sound segmenting ☐ sound addition, deletion, or substitution

Activity 1:

Play a quick game of Name Blending.

■ Say a child's name in the group slowly, phoneme by phoneme, and have kids name and point to that child. (\L\a\n\a\—Lana . . .)

■ Have kids' names on cards, too, and have them touch this child's name and tell the sound it begins and ends with. Then have them name those letters, too. (They touch Lana's name, point to *l*, say *lll*, and name the letter *l*. Then they repeat with the last letter.)

Activity 2:

Play Sound Blend Bingo.

■ Give each kid a Bingo card with pictures on it (two- to four-phoneme words pictured).

■ Choose a picture card and name it, phoneme by phoneme, without showing it to kids (like \m\a\n\).

■ They blend sounds to say the word and mark the picture on their Bingo boards if they have it (*man* and mark picture of a man).

■ Show the picture so they can check.

■ Play until someone gets Bingo. Don't clear the cards, though!

Activity 3:

Play Reverse Bingo.

■ Kids keep markers on their Bingo boards.

■ Teacher chooses a picture used in Activity 2 and holds it up (picture of a *cat*; teacher says the word *cat*).

■ Kids segment it, phoneme by phoneme (\c\a\t\). Then they remove the picture from the board. First one to clear the board wins.

Prompts:

■ *Put the sounds together. Blend them to say the word.*

■ *Say the sounds fast. Say the word.*

■ *Say the word slowly. Say it sound by sound.*

Notes:

REFLECTION

Kids loved these games. They did really well today. I think it helped using things that are familiar, like their names and the pictures. Good scaffolds for now.

Figure 6.16 Lesson Plan for Mr. Diaz's Sound Substitution

⁑ Lesson Plan for Mr. Diaz's Sound Substitution ⁑

Group: Ana, Marta, Monique, Frederick

Focus: PHONEMIC AWARENESS

☐ sound matching   ☐ initial sound isolation   ☐ final sound isolation
☐ medial sound isolation   ☐ sound blending   ☐ sound segmenting
☑ sound addition, deletion, or substitution

Activity 1:
Tell kids they'll be playing with sounds today.
- Give each child known letters (magnetic or letter tiles) *b, f, h, r, s, p.* Tell them they know these letters and each makes a special sound (*b, p, t,* and *d* are often confused).
- Then give each child a paper with Elkonin boxes stamped or drawn on it.
- Say *at.* Have them segment it \a\t\. Then help them write the letters *a* and *t* in the last two boxes to spell *at.* Have them point to each letter and say its sound.
- Then say *bat.* Ask them the first sound they hear in *bat.* Help them find the letter that says \b\. Have them push that letter in the first space. Then ask them to say each sound while touching it and blend the sounds to read the word, *bat.*
- Say *bat.* Tell them to take away the *b. Now what do you have?* (*at*)
- Add \p\ *to at. Now what word do we have?* (*pat*). They push the *p* in the first space.
- Repeat with *fat, rat, sat, hat.*

Activity 2:
If successful, try with substituting final sounds.

Activity 3:
Move to four sounds if they're successful with three.

Prompts:
- *Add _____ to _____. What's the new word?*
- *Take away _____. What word do you hear now?*

Notes:

REFLECTION
This is hard. Adding the print (known letters are key) helps a lot! Remember to focus on *sounds*, not the letter names.

The Lesson

For this lesson, we'll look at a group of second graders. They are in Mr. Diaz's class. He has many English language learners this year and has noticed that the children in this group (many of them from other countries) are confusing letters and sounds in their writing. They also are guessing at sounds in the middle of words, so he's decided to work with them phonemically rather than in phonics today. He wants to be sure they can *hear* the sounds, especially those that may not be in their native language, and learn to apply letters that match *in order*.

He uses Elkonin boxes and letter tiles. This group knows their letters and sounds, but it is the placement of those letters Mr. Diaz will focus on in today's lesson. He emphasizes the *sounds* in each word they will build, and the order in which they'll use these sounds. This is not a word-family activity. Instead, he wants children to play with the sounds and how they can manipulate them to make new words. See his lesson plan in Figure 6.16.

How Do I Assess/Check for Phonemic Awareness?

To form groups like the ones you met in the lessons above, the teachers used both informal and formal measures of phonemic awareness. These teachers were aware of how their students did when working with them in both whole and small group. You also will be able to tell when children begin to improve on phonemic awareness tasks as you work with them from day to day in a small-group setting. You might use the folders described earlier in this chapter and pictured in Figures 6.6 and 6.8 to keep track of how your students are progressing in their phonological awareness.

The Yopp-Singer, the Rosner, and the Roswell-Chall are all quick screening tests that take about five minutes to administer. Another assessment is the phonemic segmentation fluency (PSF) portion of the DIBELS. PALS (Phonological Awareness and Literacy Screening) and PAPI (Phonemic Awareness and Phonics Inventory) are two other formal phonemic awareness tests. Many states are mandating phonemic awareness assessments such as these in primary grades. Use what your school or district has asked you to administer, and also pay attention to your observations of students' phonemic development as you work with them in whole- or small-group settings.

What to Look For and How to Take Notes on Phonological (and Phonemic) Awareness

As you work with your students in small groups, you may want to take notes on how their phonological and phonemic awareness is progressing. Figure 6.17 will give you some ideas of what those notes might look like. Some teachers keep their notes in a special notebook after recording them on initialed sticky notes during their small-group lessons. Phonemic awareness is signaled with an asterisk.

Some Prompts for Phonological (and Phonemic) Awareness

Knowing what to say to help a struggling student solve a problem can help that child become more successful. The key is to use explicit language so the child knows what you want him or her to do and why that's important. Phonological and phonemic awareness tasks require very specific language because they are teaching as well as playing with the sounds of our language. Figure 6.18 describes some things you might say to help your students zoom in on what you want them to hear. Remember to always focus on the *sound* the letter makes, not the letter name, in phonemic awareness. This prompting sheet in Appendix E may be photocopied and stored in your planning notebook.

Links to Whole-Group Instruction

Many of your phonological and phonemic awareness activities will take place in whole group. (Sample whole-group lesson plans are included in Appendix E.) For most children, this will be sufficient modeling for them to learn about the sounds of language. Your goal in these lessons is to engage kids and help them play with words, so they learn

Figure 6.17 Aspects of phonological awareness and what to look for when taking anecdotal notes.

Aspect of Phonological Awareness	What to Record/Look For	Sample Notes You Might Take
■ rhyming	■ if child can hear and/or produce some or many rhymes	■ *can hear/can produce some rhymes* ■ *not identifying rhyming words in books* ■ *Jill/hill/bill—added to rhyming words in the book today!*
■ alliteration	■ if child can hear/identify words that begin the same in books and poems	■ *loved* Playful Purple Penguins ■ *is confusing rhyming words with words that start the same*
■ sentence segmenting	■ if child can determine word boundaries by clapping on each word or pushing a block for each word said	■ *pushes a block for each syllable, not each word—gets tricked by two-syllable words* ■ *can segment sentences orally*
■ syllable blending and segmenting	■ if child can clap syllables or blend syllables together to say words	■ *doesn't hear syllables—hears words* ■ *can blend two-syllable words, but has trouble with three-syllable words*
■ onset-rime segmenting and blending*	■ if child can separate the onset from the rime in a word or blend the parts together to say a word (no reading involved)	■ *is starting to blend onset-rime* ■ *segmenting onset-rime is difficult (run was \r\n\)*
■ counting phonemes in a word*	■ if the child can count the number of small sounds in a word	■ *can count phonemes in words with three sounds; more than that and she gets confused*
■ phoneme isolation (initial, final, medial)*	■ if the child can hear *where* the sound is in a word (beginning, end, or middle)	■ *still needs help with medial phoneme isolation* ■ *does great with initial phoneme isolation*
■ blending phonemes*	■ if the child can blend sounds to say a word	■ *said* sit *for \s\i\p* ■ *can blend three- or four-phoneme words well*
■ segmenting phonemes*	■ if the child can break the word apart into its smallest speech sounds, in order	■ *can blend, but segmenting is hard* ■ *said \m\t\ for mat*
■ adding, deleting, or substituting phonemes*	■ if the child can play around with speech sounds, adding and deleting them as directed (print helps with this task)	■ *does this when we add print, but has trouble doing this all orally*

that sounds can be manipulated in fun and interesting ways. Be sure to use lots of nursery rhymes, songs, games, riddles, and word play books as you explore phonemic awareness with your young learners. Here are a few suggestions to get you started:

Figure 6.18 Prompts for Phonological Awareness

What Child Is Having Trouble With	Possible Teacher Prompts
Rhyming	■ *What rhymes with _____?* ■ *It sounds the same at the end.* ■ *_____, _____. Hear how they're the same at the end.* ■ *(Jill), (\b\) _____. (Give first sound to scaffold rhyming.)*
Alliteration	■ *_____, _____ sound the same at the beginning.* ■ *What else starts like _____ _____?*
Sentence segmenting	■ *Listen for each word in the sentence.* ■ *Push the block for each word you hear.* ■ *Clap each word with me.* ■ *_____ is just one word, not two.*
Syllable blending and segmenting	■ *Put the parts together. Say the word.* ■ *Break the word into parts. Clap it with me.*
Onset-rime blending and segmenting	■ *Put the sounds together. Say the word fast.* ■ *Say the parts. I'll start and you finish. (cat . . . \c\ . . .)*
Counting phonemes in a word*	■ *Push a counter each time you hear a sound.*
Phoneme isolation (initial, final, medial)*	■ *Listen for _____. Where do you hear _____, at the beginning, the middle, or the end of the word?* ■ *Look at my mouth. Make your mouth look like this when you say _____.*
Blending phonemes*	■ *Put the sounds together. Blend them to say the word.* ■ *Say the sounds fast. Say the word.* ■ *Say the word slowly. Say it sound by sound.*
Segmenting phonemes*	■ *Say the word slowly.* ■ *Say it sound by sound.*
Adding, deleting, or substituting phonemes*	■ *Add _____ to _____. What's the new word?* ■ *Take away _____. What word do you hear now?*

Phonological Awareness (Working with Rhyming and Alliteration)

■ Read aloud books and nursery rhymes and have kids listen for words that rhyme (or have alliteration).

■ Have kids use a signal to show that words rhyme (or demonstrate alliteration).

■ Sing songs that rhyme and have kids jump each time they hear a rhyming word.

Phonological Awareness (Sentence and Syllable Blending and Segmenting)

■ Give short directions and have kids clap each word as they repeat the directions with you.

■ When modeling writing in front of children, create a sentence together, then clap each word in the sentence and count each word before writing the sentence on chart paper.

- When calling kids to the table (or carpet), call their names syllable by syllable and have them blend the parts together to say the whole names (see the syllable blending and segmenting lesson plan in Appendix E).

Phonemic Awareness (Phoneme Isolation)

- Use games as provided in your teacher's edition if you are using a core program.
- Use commercial games with pictures, such as Match and Clip from Lakeshore (see Figure 6.19).
- Consult idea books, such as those listed at the end of this chapter, for games related to phoneme isolation (see also the sample lesson plan for medial sound isolation in Appendix E).

Phonemic Awareness (Phoneme Blending and Segmenting)

- Use the overhead to show kids how to segment phonemes; use a transparency with sound boxes on it and show how to push a counter into each box to represent a speech

Figure 6.19 Match and Clip, a game from Lakeshore, is used to teach sounds. The teacher works with the sound (phonemic awareness) first and then adds the letter as children learn the alphabetic principle. Later, they will use these materials independently at the ABC work station.

Figure 6.20 Students segment words and push a teddy bear counter for each sound as they say each word (from the picture) slowly.

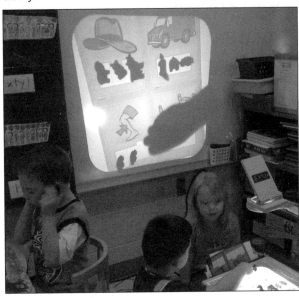

sound; use pictures instead of words (to keep the emphasis on sounds). (See Figure 6.20 and the sample lesson for phoneme segmentation in Appendix E.)

Links to Literacy Work Stations Practice

Much of the work you do with phonological and phonemic awareness will need to be done in whole- and small-group settings, due to the oral and aural nature of the activities. However, after you've worked with students in whole and small groups, there are a few things kids can practice on their own at literacy work stations (see Figure 6.21). Just know that many of these are quick activities, and children may need some other alternatives at these stations in addition.

Links to Standardized and State Testing

Children with strong phonological and phonemic awareness become successful early readers. Those

Figure 6.21 Work stations that support phonological (including *phonemic) awareness.

Literacy Work Station	What Kids Do Here to Practice Phonological and Phonemic Awareness	How This Station Supports Phonological and Phonemic Awareness
Listening Work Station	■ Listen to rhyming stories (or stories with alliteration) on tape. Those that stop and have kids supply the rhyming word (and then give the word) provide immediate feedback and are especially useful. You may want to make some of these. ■ Use a Listening Lotto game. Commercial games are available. ■ Make a tape with words that start with the same sound and are easy to draw (*sun, snake, star, spoon*). Kids listen and draw a picture of what they hear. Then they read the pictures, emphasizing the first sound of each word.*	This builds students' listening and speaking vocabulary as they hear stories read aloud on tape. It also gives them opportunities to play with rhyming and alliterative words. At the listening station, children can also listen for sounds made by objects when they play Listening Lotto.
Language Master Work Station	■ If you have a language master (machine), you can have kids work with rhymes, syllables, or phonemes.* You make the cards by reading and recording into the language master.	Some schools have old language masters lingering on shelves. Pull out this machine if you can find one and use it to record sounds for kids to blend and words to segment. It's the next best thing to having you in the station with them.
Names Work Station	■ Look at a student's photo, say the name, and clap the syllables. Then sort the photos by the number of syllables in the name. ■ Do the above with number of sounds in the name (phonemes).* ■ Sort by same beginning or ending sound.*	Using the most familiar words of all to the children, their names, they'll be able to play with these words, saying and sorting them in a variety of ways—by number of syllables or phonemes, or by same beginning or ending sounds. Print may or may not be included, depending on the skill level of your students.
Overhead Work Station	■ Use picture cards and sound boxes with counters to say words slowly and push the counters into the boxes to represent each sound.* ■ Match rhyming pictures or pictures that start or end with the same sound.*	This is an easy way to monitor how kids are doing with segmenting sounds or rhyming. You can easily look at what they're doing on the overhead to see if they're applying what you've taught in whole and group lessons.
Big Book Work Station	■ Use nursery rhyme Big Books. Kids read them and then say rhyming words. If possible, they can highlight the words, too.	This gives children a chance to revisit the Big Books you've used in whole or small group. You'll want children to practice exactly like they did when they were with you.
Pocket Chart Work Station	■ Use pocket chart with pictorial nursery rhymes like "One, Two Buckle My Shoe." See Figure 6.22.	Using pictorial nursery rhymes lets kids work with these without the print. This will help children focus on the sounds and rhythm of language. They should name the words that rhyme, much as you did with them in group.
Classroom Library	■ Use familiar books to say a sentence about a picture. Clap each word in the sentence. ■ Have a basket of rhyming books for them to "read." Make class books, too. ■ Do the same for alliteration.	Students can practice sentence segmenting, rhyming, and alliteration here.
ABC Work Station	■ Play sound-matching games, like Bingo or Concentration with pictures.*	If you've played this with students in whole or small group, they can practice isolating sounds in these games.

Figure 6.22 A student practices saying a rhyme and then finds the rhyming pictures using magnetic pieces at this work station.

students who find reading interesting and rewarding will usually continue to grow and become independent readers. Generally, children who are good readers do well on standardized and state tests for reading. Many states now institute phonological tasks as part of their evaluation of early readers' progress as well.

Helping children develop phonemic awareness, especially of *where* sounds are in words, can provide a foundation for later phonics learning and improved spelling. Understanding how words work makes both reading and writing easier and more fluent. And this can lead to greater comprehension—the ultimate goal of reading. Phonemic awareness training will have long-term benefits for your young readers and your readers with learning disabilities.

Phonemic Awareness Cautions

It's wise to look at phonemic awareness as *one* important part of the success formula for developing good readers. It is not a magic bullet that will guarantee instant success for all children. Remember that young readers need to also develop a strong oral language base, including learning rich words and using more complex sentences. The goal of phonological and phonemic awareness is to *play* with the *sounds* of language. Don't be tempted to turn these lessons into phonics teaching. *Phonemic* means smallest *speech* sounds. Have fun with these games and activities. Keep them playful, short, and sweet.

Be aware of the various stages of phonological awareness. Don't lump them all into one big category. You might want to keep a folder like the ones shown in the opening of this chapter to help you keep track of what your kids need in small-group instruction. You don't need to do all these lessons with every group.

Use these phonemic awareness activities as a tool to construct a foundation. Think of phonemes as the building blocks of language. Develop your students' sound base, one block at a time—from words, to syllables, to onset and rime, to individual phonemes. Help them understand *where* each speech sound is located in a word. Think of phonological and phonemic awareness as creating a sound map that kids can follow and use to plot out the letters, chunks, and syllables of words that make up our language.

Reflection Questions for Professional Conversations

1. What do you better understand about both phonological and phonemic awareness after reading this chapter? How would you explain its importance to a parent? To a colleague? Discuss with your grade-level team.

2. How are you currently assessing your children's phonological and phonemic awareness? How do you keep track of who needs what kind of small-group instruction in these areas? What new ideas might you try from this chapter? Share your ideas with a colleague.

3. What have you been teaching in whole group for phonological or phonemic awareness that might need to be taken to a small group for some children? Which children? Do they need to practice what you've been doing in whole group, or is there a prerequisite task you need to focus on with them in small group first? What task would that be?

4. What is the purpose of adding letters to phonemic awareness activities? Do you have any children who are ready for this? Which students? Which letters? How might you go about doing this? Discuss this with another teacher at your grade level.

For Further Information on Phonemic Awareness Instruction

Adams, M. J., I. Lundberg, B. R. Foorman, and T. Beeler. 1998. *Phonemic Awareness in Young Children: A Classroom Curriculum.* Baltimore, MD: Brookes.

Beck, I. 2006. *Making Sense of Phonics.* New York: Guilford.

Blevins, W. 1999. *Phonemic Awareness Activities for Early Reading Success.* New York: Scholastic.

Opitz, M. 2000. *Rhymes and Reasons: Literature and Language Play for Phonological Awareness.* Portsmouth, NH: Heinemann.

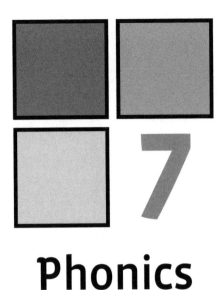

7

Phonics

Mrs. Georgas has gathered four of her second graders together for a lesson focused on helping them apply what they are learning about phonics. She has noticed that these children sometimes have difficulty figuring out words with two or three syllables. Although she has systematically been teaching phonics in whole-group lessons, this small group of children is still struggling at times with decoding longer words. She notices this when she listens to them read independently, and there is evidence in their writing, too, as they often switch letters around and leave off parts of longer words. This group has strategies for decoding shorter words, but long words seem to throw them.

Mrs. Georgas takes a few minutes at the start of her small-group lesson to review some of the phonics patterns and principles they've been studying in whole group. Recently, they have been learning about open and closed syllables, since many of the books they're now reading have multisyllabic words. She does a quick review of short and long vowel sounds by having the children read together a vowel chart with pictures and words on it. Then

they discuss what to do if they get stuck on a long word. They talk about searching through the word and reading it by syllables. Mrs. Georgas does a short review of open and closed syllables. Then she models by writing *permit* on her dry erase board. She asks a child to circle the first chunk or syllable he can find. He circles *per* and says \pur\. She points out that it's a closed syllable. Then she asks him to find the next part, and he circles *mit* and says, "It's a closed syllable and has a short vowel." Quickly, he blends the parts together to say *permit*. Mrs. Georgas tells them that's what they'll be practicing today as they read—looking fast through the word at each part, syllable by syllable.

She writes *cabinet* on the board, and another student quickly circles and reads *cab*, *in*, and *et* and then blends the parts together. This child notes that all the parts had closed syllables and short vowels. Others want a turn, so Mrs. Georgas gives them each a quick turn at *bravery*, *famished*, and *victory*. These are not words from today's book, but they are similar to the patterns students will need to decode in this nonfiction book. She has chosen not to give students all the hard words in the book, because she wants them to try to independently problem-solve new words so she can see how they do. If they need assistance, she'll be right there to prompt them and help them figure out the words.

Satisfied with the phonics review, Mrs. Georgas hands a copy of the new book, *Abraham Lincoln*, to each student in the group. They talk just a bit about what they already know about this kind of book (a biography) and about Lincoln and get ready to read the first chapter, "Childhood." The teacher points to the word *childhood* on the title page and tells the group that today if they get stuck on a longer word like this, they can use their finger to look just at the first syllable and read it, \child\ (just like when they circled the first part of *permit* on the dry erase board). They should use their finger to actually cover up the rest of the word, so they can see just *child*. After they read that part, they should cover it up and read the rest of the word, *hood* (like when they circled the second part of *permit* on the dry erase board). Finally, they should look at the whole word, using their finger as needed to read it. This should all be done very quickly! One child notes that *child* was a closed syllable and asks if it shouldn't be pronounced with a short *i* sound. The teacher

Figure 7.1 This teacher reviews how to decode words using open and closed syllables by modeling with a few words on a dry erase board before students read their new book in small group.

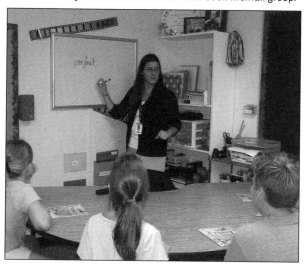

asks him if *chilledhood* would sound right, and he realizes that this isn't a real word. Mrs. Georgas tells them to always be sure that the word sounds right and makes sense—that sometimes all the rules don't work. Then she tells them to read the first chapter and find out facts about Abraham Lincoln's childhood. She reminds them to use their finger as needed to look at and read through the syllables of long words if they get stuck. They should think about the long and short vowel sounds but *always* make sure the word sounds right and makes sense.

Then she listens in to individuals as the rest of them read silently. She pays close attention to their decoding of longer words and notes that several of them use their finger to help them look through the words. When they have finished reading, they talk about what they read and share examples of how they figured out longer words today. They show her how they used their finger to move across a word and look at its parts. She reminds them to try this if they get stuck when reading independently.

What Is Phonics?

In the opening lesson, Mrs. Georgas focused on one element of phonics instruction—decoding longer words—with her second graders. Phonics is a method of teaching reading that emphasizes letter-sound relationships. It involves the associations between sounds and how they are represented by print. The goal of phonics is to teach students the most commonly used sound-spelling relationships so that they can decode all kinds of words. When children are using phonics, they can use what they understand about letters and their sounds to read and write words (not just do worksheets). They are applying the *alphabetic principle*—understanding that the sounds within spoken words are represented in writing by letters, and that those letters represent the sounds rather consistently.

There is a difference between *phonics* and *phonemic awareness*. Phonemic awareness is a prerequisite to phonics instruction. As we have noted,

Figure 7.2 Lesson Plan for Decoding Long Words

⠶ Lesson Plan for Decoding Long Words ⠶

Group: Scott, Dylan, Dustin, Arianna

Focus: PHONICS

☐ initial letters   ☐ final letters   ☐ short vowels   ☐ blending and CVC

☐ long vowels   ☐ vowel + *r*   ☐ funky chunks   ☑ long words

Warm-Up:

- Read vowel chart together to review long and short vowel sounds.
- Write word on dry erase board and have kids circle syllables, one at a time—*permit, cabinet, bravery, famished, victory.*
- Review open and closed syllables.

Today's Book/Writing: *Abraham Lincoln* by Lola M. Schaefer   **Level:** mid–second grade/L

BEFORE READING or WRITING

Intro:

- Read title. Discuss genre and their background knowledge.
- Decode first chapter title, "Childhood." Show how to use finger to look at each word part and blend all parts together to decode long words.
- Read Chapter 1 to find out facts about Abraham Lincoln's childhood.

DURING READING or WRITING

Prompts:

- *Use your finger to cover up the rest of the word and read it one part at a time.*
- *Move your finger across the word and read the parts in order.*

Notes: Arianna used finger to decode *cabin.*

AFTER READING or WRITING

Discuss:

- Facts learned about A. Lincoln's childhood.
- Long words they decoded and show how they figured them out.

REFLECTION

Keep working on this strategy of how to decode long words. Emphasize that these words must make sense and look right.

phonemes are the smallest units of speech sounds, individual sounds within words. For example, *horse* is made up of three phonemes or sounds—\h\or\s\. *Bat* also has three phonemes—\b\a\t\. For more information on phonemic awareness, please read Chapter 6. Phonemic awareness involves working with the *sounds* of letters, whereas phonics involves working with *print*—attaching sounds to letters and blending them to make words. Once children understand that words are made up of sounds (*phonemic awareness*) and that those sounds can be written down (*alphabetic principle*), they are ready to be taught *phonics*.

The English language is an alphabetic one, and somewhat complicated at that. Think about the words *dot, rote, love, boy, row, for, bought*. Each word has an *o*, and that letter makes a different sound in each word. Because English is alphabetic, it makes sense that children need to learn the sounds the letters make. Phonics has historically been used to teach reading, dating back to the early sixteenth century during the Protestant Reformation when there were widespread efforts to increase literacy rates (Parker 1894; Balmuth 1982).

Over the years, much debate has taken place about how to best teach reading. Most reading educators agree that all children need phonics to learn to read. Despite their agreement with the need for phonics, researchers have studied many different ideas on how to *best* teach phonics. In fact, at least five different ways of approaching phonics have been identified.

1. *Synthetic phonics* involves explicitly teaching children letter-sound relationships, and teaching kids to break written words apart, sound by sound. Students are first taught several letters and matching sounds. Then they learn to blend or "synthesize" the letter sounds into words. They read decodable books containing the letters and sounds taught.

2. *Analogy phonics* focuses on teaching about word families. Children use words they know how to read, and look for patterns in these words. They use those patterns to read new words. For example, if children know how to read and spell *cat*, they can also read and spell *hat, mat,* and *bat*. Children learn these patterns gradually and are not restricted to reading only books containing the taught patterns.

3. *Analytic phonics* relates to teaching children how to sort words and look at spelling patterns that make different sounds. For example, if students are learning about *r*-controlled

vowels, they might read word cards with *r*-controlled words on them and then sort these words into categories, depending on the vowel that *r* is combined with. They might sort words with *–ar* from words with *–or* patterns. They learn phonics rules and generalizations by examining these words and noticing patterns. Children read books using sight words, context, and prediction as they are learning the phonics rules.

4. *Phonics through spelling* involves children learning about phonics during writing experiences. They are taught to segment words into phonemes (individual sounds) and then select letters for those phonemes. This is often done during shared writing, where the class or a small group creates a story together. They record the sounds they hear as they write down words to capture their stories. For example, they might write, "We went on a feeld trip and sw the frm nmls" for "We went on a field trip and saw the farm animals." The teacher helps them match letters to the phonemes they hear. Their spelling is sometimes referred to as "temporary spelling" or "phonetic spelling."

5. *Imbedded phonics* is a method in which children are taught phonics through real reading experiences. This is a more implicit approach to teaching phonics. The teacher may highlight letters and sounds during shared reading of Big Books and poems. If the teacher notices that children are having difficulty learning the different sounds of long *e*, she may point out different words in the Big Book that use these various sounds. Or she may write a daily message to the children and have them find words with this sound.

No matter what approach is used, research support for *systematic* phonics is strong. The key to a systematic approach is that there is a planned, sequential set of phonics elements, and these are taught explicitly and methodically (National

Reading Panel 2000). In a systematic approach, you teach the letter sounds and relationships and then let children practice those on things that they're reading and writing.

Phonics Research at a Glance

As you can see, there are many ideas about how to teach phonics. I have briefly summarized several studies that I think will be useful to you as a teacher, in making decisions about and planning for phonics instruction in your classroom.

- Jean Chall (1967) concluded, after an extensive review of the reading research, that systematic phonics instruction introduced early in children's school experiences seemed to produce stronger reading achievement than instruction that began later and was less systematic.

- Marilyn Adams (1990) did a comprehensive review of decades of reading research and concluded that directly teaching the letter-sound system can speed up learning how to read. Struggling students need explicit phonics instruction, since many of them lack much exposure to reading and writing and have had fewer opportunities to figure out how our alphabetic language works.

    Adams also concluded that children, especially those who come to school with limited literacy knowledge, need a rich variety of reading and writing experiences that include, but are not limited to, phonics instruction.

- Anderson and colleagues (1985) show that, on average, children who are taught phonics get off to a better start in learning to read than children who are not taught phonics.

- Stanovich (1994) found that instruction in phonics facilitates early reading acquisition.

- The National Institute of Child Health and Human Development (National Reading Panel 2000) presented findings about phonics

instruction in the National Reading Panel report:

- Research shows that explicit, systematic phonics instruction produces significant benefits for students in kindergarten through sixth grade and for children having difficulty learning to read.

- Across all grade levels, systematic phonics instruction improves the ability of good readers to spell. For poor readers, the impact of phonics instruction on spelling was small.

- The effects of systematic early phonics instruction were greatest for children in kindergarten and first grade.

- No single approach to teaching phonics could be used for all children.

- Children who have already developed phonics skills and can apply them in the reading process do not require the same level and intensity of phonics instruction provided to children who don't have these skills.

- It is important to train teachers in the different kinds of approaches to teaching phonics and in how to tailor these approaches to particular groups of students.

- Systematic synthetic phonics instruction had a significant effect on the reading skills of struggling readers. This kind of phonics benefited students with learning disabilities, low-achieving students with no learning disabilities, and low SES (socioeconomic status) students.

- Systematic phonics instruction is only one component of a total reading program. It should not be the dominant component in a reading program, neither in the amount of time devoted to it nor in the significance attached.

- Teachers need to be flexible in their phonics instruction in order to adapt it to individual student needs.

- Systematic phonics instruction can be provided in an entertaining, vibrant, and creative way.

- Studies by Gough and Juel (1990) and Juel (1994) found that over five hundred different spelling-sound rules are needed to read, but that even the most comprehensive phonics programs rarely teach more than about ninety phonics rules.

- Juel and Minden-Cupp (1999) studied four demographically similar classrooms and found that children who entered first grade with few literacy skills benefited from a heavy dose of phonics instruction presented "first and fast." Other students, who entered first grade possessing middle-range literacy skills, did very well with a less-structured phonics curriculum.

- Using analogies to teach rimes in key words is not an effective instructional strategy until children have a good grasp of consonant and vowel sounds (Bruck and Treiman 1992; Ehri and Robbins 1992).

- Ed Henderson (1981) found that when children use invented spelling to write, the relationship between individual letters and sounds might be the most vivid (or transparent to the teacher).

Who Needs This Kind of Small Group?

All children can benefit from phonics instruction. It would be impossible to read an alphabetic language without some understanding of the sounds of that language. How you teach phonics is up to you, based on what you observe about your students and their understandings of how words work. The lessons in this book will give you a variety of ways to think about teaching phonics in small groups.

I have not included a prescribed sequence of which letters and sounds should be taught first, simply because there are so many different ideas on this. You might consult your school system's rec-

ommendations on a sequence for teaching letters and sounds. If none exist, examine the references for this chapter for more information on teaching phonics. Always be prepared to be flexible. Pay attention to your students' reading *and* writing. I have found that they will show us what they already know how to do independently. Our job is to take them where they need to go next.

Possible Focus for Lessons

I like to choose a focus for each phonics-oriented small-group lesson, but I remain flexible within my lessons and provide opportunities for comprehension and vocabulary development, too. Here are some possibilities you might choose from:

- *Initial letter sounds.* This is one of the first things you'll notice your children understanding and applying. Look for evidence of this in their writing in kindergarten and early first grade.

- *Final letter sounds.* You'll want your students to look through words from left to right. Again, final sounds will often start showing up in their writing. Once I see them do this, I *know* they can learn to apply these sounds in their reading, too.

- *Short vowel sounds.* When teaching kids about vowels, I like to highlight them in a different color, like red, so children pay attention to them. They should learn that every word has a vowel in it. They should also learn that some letters, like vowels, make more than one sound in English. Many phonics programs teach short vowels first, so kids can blend these into CVC words.

- *CVC patterns and blending sounds.* These are words made up of an initial and final consonant with a short vowel in between. Many kindergarten and early-first-grade programs focus on these words—words like *cat, hog, big, mop,* and *lap.* Once children know about ten letters and sounds, including at least one short vowel sound, they can begin to blend these sounds to read CVC words.

■ *Long vowel sounds.* Long vowel sounds are more complex, since there are multiple ways to represent these in English.

■ *Vowel plus* r *patterns.* Words containing *ar, er, ir, or, ur,* and *our* can be tricky. My experience with these is that they take practice, practice, and more practice.

■ *Funky chunks* (*oo, oy, oi, ow, ou, ough, augh*). Same as above.

■ *Reading long words.* Many students can benefit from explicit teaching of how to decode long words, breaking them apart syllable by syllable.

■ *Applying letters and sounds in writing.* I have worked in many Reading First schools across the United States and have noticed that many teachers are afraid to do writing during their reading instruction time. If you are teaching kids how to *apply* their phonics skills through writing a message related to something they've read, you are helping them with phonics. Reading and writing are reciprocal processes. You may be teaching kids *how* to write during writing time, but don't miss opportunities to teach phonics by writing simple responses to what they've read in small group. In these brief lessons, focus on the phonics patterns they're using.

Choosing Materials

Most teachers I know have a variety of materials to choose from when teaching with a phonics focus in small groups. You may want to have on hand some of the following for phonics warm-up activities you'll do at the start of each lesson:

■ sound charts (consonants, vowels, blends, rimes)

■ individual letter cards for making words and blending sounds

■ word sorting cards

■ dry erase boards and markers

■ magnetic letters (for building and manipulating words)

Sometimes I see teachers doing phonics worksheets with kids in small group. This is not exemplary phonics teaching. You'll want to help your students work with letters and sounds in hands-on ways, as demonstrated in the sample lessons in this chapter. I like to include a phonics warm-up activity where the children can manipulate letters and sounds, using magnetic letters or dry erase boards. Following the warm-up, I plan for reading or writing text as part of the lesson, so children understand that the reason they are learning phonics is to *use* it in their reading and writing.

There are different kinds of texts you might use with your students. Decodable books give kids the opportunity to directly apply just the letters and sounds you've been working with so far in their reading. I've found that these can help some children grasp how words work, but be careful in your choice of these books. Some of these books make little to no sense, and others are more meaningful, so choose wisely.

Figure 7.3 Kids work in small group making words with CVC patterns and blending those sounds.

You might have little books or leveled readers available that you can use with students in your phonics-focused lessons. I like to use these predictable books with beginning readers, too, so these children can *feel* like real readers. I encourage them to use the first sound of an unknown word along with the picture to be sure it makes sense. When children have more phonics skill, I move into having them read through the word, blending sounds on CVC words. I also use leveled readers with children in primary grades. These books are interesting and engaging and give children opportunities to apply their phonics skills on real text. They are usually not as difficult as trade books that have less controlled vocabulary.

When children have enough reading skill, I use short chapter books and informational text for practice with phonics, too. By the time children are able to read these types of books, they generally have learned many of the beginning phonics they need to decode. At this point, they are usually working on decoding multisyllabic words.

Occasionally, I might use phonics readers. These are stories built around a certain phonics element, such as the sound of *ar*. If I have a few students whom I notice are having trouble with this sound (often in both their reading *and* writing), I might spend a short time with them reading a book that has many words with this phonics pattern to reinforce it. I have them read other kinds of books, too, so they can transfer this knowledge.

The goal of my phonics lessons is not to have children read a particular *type* of book, but rather to enable them to read *any* kind of book. I want students to read fluently and with good comprehension. If they know how to use and apply their understandings of how letters and sounds work, they are on their way to being more fluent, thus freeing their brains for more thinking and better comprehension. I want phonics to be a tool to help them read words quickly and automatically. A child who labors on sounding each word out is not using letter-sound knowledge efficiently.

⠶ The Lessons ⠶

As you can see, there are many ways to approach phonics teaching. Begin with a system for how you will teach phonics whole group, and then plan your small-group lessons based upon your students' needs. The lessons in this section will give you many options for thinking about how to best meet the needs of every child in your classroom. The first lessons are for use with emergent readers. I've included adaptations in the Things to Think About lists before each lesson to help you extend the samples.

CVC Patterns and Blending Words (for Beginning Readers)

Things to Think About

- Use this kind of lesson once students have some knowledge of consonant letter sounds and you've introduced a short vowel sound or two.

- Allow children just learning how to read to use different kinds of books to practice their developing skills. Decodable books, such as the one used in this lesson, are one option. Consider books like *Cat in the Hat*, by Dr. Seuss, and other predictable little books for children at this stage of reading, too.

- Be sure to include comprehension as well as working on decoding in this kind of a lesson.

Before the Lesson

Mrs. Strickland has been teaching systematic phonics to her kindergartners for the past several years. This was hard for her at first, because when she began teaching kindergarten many years ago she taught just one letter a week. Her district uses a reading program that introduces the letters much faster than this. In fact, most of her five-year-olds are learning to read words and blend sounds by midyear.

As Mrs. Strickland looks at her class and decides which children to group together, she chooses five students who are learning how to take letter sounds they already know and blend them together to make words. These children are using some beginning and ending sounds in their writing and sometimes put a vowel in the middle of words as a placeholder. They know a sound goes in the middle, but they're not sure which one. Today she will work with them on blending sounds to read words and then have them practice this new skill in a decodable book that accompanies her core reading program.

During the Lesson

Mrs. Strickland gathers the five children around a small table and tells them that they are going to practice blending sounds today. She has been teaching this whole group, as well, so it is not a brand-new concept. It's just that these students need more hands-on practice with a bit of guidance. Mrs. Strickland pulls out a toy from Leap Frog called the Word Whammer. It is a colorful, six-by-eight-inch flat electronic game that teaches kids how to blend words. The children are instantly engaged.

She hands three of the students a magnetic letter that comes with this Fridge Phonics toy set, and asks them all to name the letter and its sound. The book they will read today centers around the short *o* sound, so she uses the letters *m*, *o*, and *p*. She turns the Word Whammer on (it is battery-operated) and has the children follow the audio directions for the "word builder" option. The toy says, "Professor Quigley here . . . time to build words." Then it instructs children to put three letters into the Word Whammer. The students follow the directions and the toy tells them the name of the letter; it even directs them to put a red letter in the middle space (vowels are red). Then it tells them to press each letter from left to right, names each, says the sound of each letter, blends the sounds, and reads the new word. Following this, it sings a little song and blends the sounds once more. They make the word *mop* with their letters.

The children love it and beg to make more words. This is phonics teaching at its best. Creative, vibrant, and fun! The kids take turns making several more short *o* words. They join in with naming the letters, blending the sounds, and singing the song. One time they put in letters that do not make a word. The Word Whammer names each letter, says each sound, and says, "Great sounds." Mrs. Strickland points out that just because they put three letters together, it doesn't mean this is a word.

After they have played with the Word Whammer and blended sounds to build CVC words for about ten minutes, Mrs. Strickland tells the children that now she wants them to try blending sounds to read words in their new book today. She gives them each a copy of the little book *The Spot* from her reading series. She helps them read the title; they blend the sounds to read *spot*. Then she asks them to look quickly through the book at the pictures and see if they can figure out what the spot might be. They laugh as they look through the pages and tell her that the dad spills a pot of something cooking in the kitchen and makes a big spot on the floor. She tells them to read and find out about the spot and how the family takes care of it. She reminds them to blend the sounds to read any words they get stuck on. She tells them they can check the pictures, too, to be sure it's making sense.

Figure 7.4 Kids manipulate special 3-D letters and hear their sounds as they blend sounds to make words with the Word Whammer by Leap Frog as part of a small-group lesson.

Figure 7.5 Lesson Plan for Blending and Reading CVC Words

⠶ Lesson Plan for Blending and Reading CVC Words ⠶

Group: Jen, Felipe, Carlos, Maria, Vi

Focus: PHONICS

☐ initial letters   ☐ final letters   ☐ short vowels   ☑ blending and CVC

☐ long vowels   ☐ vowel + r   ☐ funky chunks   ☐ long words

Warm-Up: 10 min. max!

■ Use Word Whammer to make and blend CVC words with short *o* sound.

■ *Make mop, cot, pot, top, hot, got, hop.*

■ *Make a nonsense word, too, and point out that it's just sounds, not a real word.*

Today's Book/Writing: *The Spot* decodable book   **Level:** end of kindergarten/early first grade/C

BEFORE READING or WRITING

Intro:

■ Read title. Blend *spot* using finger to slide under each sound.

■ Let kids look at pictures and think about what the spot might be from.

■ *Read to find out about the spot and how the family takes care of it.*

■ Remind kids to blend sounds to read words they get stuck on.

DURING READING or WRITING

Prompts:

■ *Blend the sounds. Put the sounds together fast.*

■ *Use your finger to blend the sounds.*

■ *Is that a real word? Does it make sense?*

Notes: Carlos had trouble with *mop*—got only first sound until I helped; did better then.

AFTER READING or WRITING

Discuss:

■ *What happened to the spot? Where did it come from? How did the family take care of it?*

■ Do quick retell.

■ Have kids show words they blended. Ask them to show how they did it.

■ Remind them to keep blending sounds into words.

REFLECTION

Kids loved the Word Whammer! Use it tomorrow with them. Keep blending CVC words. They're improving.

As the children read the book on their own at the table, Mrs. Strickland moves around and listens in to individuals. She is pleased at how they are tak-ing on the blending. She notices a few of them glancing at the Word Whammer, as if to remind them of how to blend sounds together. She encourages them to point to the words as they read and run their finger under the words to blend the sounds. Some of them finish reading before the others, and she tells them to read it again. Carlos gets stuck on *mop*. Mrs. Strickland reminds him that this is a word they made in the Word Whammer. She helps Carlos say each sound and blend the sounds fast to make the new word. She tells him to check the picture and see if it makes sense. He smiles and says it does.

After reading, the children talk about the book. They understood this simple text and do a quick retell of the story. Mrs. Strickland asks them what kind of family this is. The children say, "It's a helpful family. They all work together. My dad helps my mom, too. I don't have a dad, but I help my mom." They are making connections *and* applying their decoding skills. Mrs. Strickland asks them to show her words they blended, and Carlos quickly points to and reads *mop*. Others point to *spot, pats,* and *mops*. Their teacher reminds them that blending sounds can help them read new words. She tells them they can practice this during independent reading today. She'll have them practice rereading this book along with other familiar books that she's already taught with. These books are in baskets on their tables. They love to read and eagerly look forward to that time. She tells them they will use the Word Whammer again tomorrow.

After the Lesson

Mrs. Strickland jots down a quick note about her lesson. See her notes at the bottom of her lesson plan in Figure 7.5. The children loved this lesson! She'll meet with them again tomorrow and continue to work on blending. After school, she'll consult the teacher's guide for her reading series to see what's coming up in whole group and make appropriate plans for this group as well. She'll watch them closely during whole group tomorrow to see if they're transferring any of their learning between small and whole group and vice versa.

She'll use the Word Whammer with another small group that could also use help with blending. For a minute, she considers using this toy in whole group, but decides it would be best used in small group so everyone can easily have a turn. Besides, not everyone in her class needs this kind of work right now. Eventually, she might put this toy at an ABC station for practice, but she wants to teach with it for a while first.

Using Initial Letter Sounds in Reading—Day One (for Beginning Readers)

Things to Think About

■ Teach this kind of lesson to children who are just starting to understand initial sounds of consonants. They should also have learned a few sight words. In the following lesson, kids must know *I, like,* and *to* for success in reading this book.

■ It's okay to tell children to use the picture for checking on initial sounds. The picture is often their strongest known this early in their journey to become readers. You don't want them to rely totally on the picture, though; teach them to use it for *checking* to be sure their reading makes sense. And always have them check the first letter of the word to be sure it *looks right*. Your goal is to get children to use what they know to build new knowledge and understandings.

Before the Lesson

Mr. Slye is excited to help his young kindergartners start to read. Many of them are learning their beginning consonant sounds, and he wants them to learn how to apply these in their reading. The children in the group he will work with today know at least ten consonant sounds. They know a few sight words. Mr. Slye found a level B book, an emergent reader, in the school's literacy library. This is a book in which children may start to use some of their beginning-sound knowledge for figuring out new words. The pictures are very supportive, which will help.

As he plans his lesson, he thinks about what the children already know that he can build on. All the children in this group know *I*, *like*, *and*, *to*, and *my*. He chooses a book with some of these words as anchors for them to hold on to. The book *Playing* by Sarah Prince is about a girl who likes to do various things at a playground. It is very close to the children's experiences and contains the sight words *I*, *like*, *to*, and *my*, and the photos depict things his kids love to do—running, sliding, jumping. There will be lots of support to help them apply their letter-sound knowledge. He plans his phonics warm-up, a game, to get the children excited about reading; he reads through the book and jots down a few notes about how he will introduce it and questions he will ask after reading. He uses the chart in this book (Figure 7.13 and Appendix F) to help him think about the prompts he may use to help children do the reading work.

During the Lesson

Sarah, Kim, Nick, Mariel, and Jeff look at the management board for literacy work stations and see the Meet with Me icon beside their names. They happily join Mr. Slye at the reading table. He greets them and tells them they will be playing a game and reading a new book today. He starts his lesson by reminding them that they are doing a great job of learning their letters and sounds and tells them they are going to play a letter sound game called Guess My Sound. He has a paper bag with several magnetic letters in it. There are multiples of each letter—*b*, *c*, *h*, *j*, *l*, *m*, *r*, *s*, *t*. They take turns reaching into the bag, feeling a letter, trying to guess it by touch, pulling it out, and then saying its sound. If they get it right, they keep it. They love the game and do very well.

Mr. Slye hands them their new book, *Playing*, and tells them they will be able to read it on their own today. He reads the title to them and says,

"This little girl is playing on the playground. In this book, she tells us what she likes to do." Then he has them turn to page 2 and locate several known words. The children each point to *I*, *like*, and *to*. Then he asks them to find *run*. They eagerly point to the word. He asks them what the first sound says, and they reply, "\r\." He shows them how they can use the first sound and check the picture to be sure they are right. Then he invites them to read the book and find out what this girl likes to do.

As they read, Mr. Slye listens in to individuals, sometimes even two at a time, ready to lend a hand as needed. He notices that Jeff gets stuck on *hide*, so he points to the *h* in *hide* and asks Jeff what sound it makes. The child looks up at the ABC chart and says the correct sound. Mr. Slye tells him to try the sentence again, and Jeff reads, "I like to h-h-h." Mr. Slye tells him to look at the picture and think about what the girl is doing behind the tree. "Oh, she's hiding," says Jeff. He reads the sentence correctly this time. Mr. Slye repeats similar interactions with a few other children in the group, and is pleased overall with their attempts to read this book. They still need lots of practice, but they're starting to get the idea of how to use initial sounds. He has them reread if they finish early, and they gladly read the little book over and over, improving each time. When Kim says, "I can read it with my eyes shut," Mr. Slye knows they need to switch gears.

Finished with their reading, they talk briefly about what the little girl in the book liked to do. The children readily name her actions. They tell about some things they like to do at the playground, too. Then Mr. Slye asks them if they used the first sound of new words when they were reading. They show him how they did that, and he gives them each a high five, tells them to keep doing this when they read, and sends them off to their next work station to work independently.

After the Lesson

Mr. Slye quickly writes a note of reflection on his lesson plan, as shown in Figure 7.6. A few of

Figure 7.6 Lesson Plan for Using Initial Sounds in Reading: Day One

:: Lesson Plan for Using Initial Sounds in Reading: Day One ::

Group: Sarah, Kim, Nick, Mariel, Jeff

Focus: PHONICS

☑ initial letters   ☐ final letters   ☐ short vowels   ☐ blending and CVC
☐ long vowels   ☐ vowel + *r*   ☐ funky chunks   ☐ long words

Warm-Up:

■ Play Guess My Sound. They reach into bag of magnetic letters. Kid picks one and tries to guess it by feel. Then looks at it and says its sound. Use ABC sound chart for help as needed.

■ Include *b, c, h, j, l, m, r, s, t* (beginning sounds used in today's new book).

Today's Book/Writing: *Playing* by Sarah Prince   **Level:** mid-kindergarten/B

BEFORE READING or WRITING

Intro:

■ Read title to them. *This little girl is playing on the playground. She tells us what she likes to do. What do you think she might like to do on the playground?*

■ On page 2 have them find known words, *I, to, like,* and unknown word, *run. How did you know that was run?*

■ Tell them to use the first letter sound and picture to help figure out new words.

■ Ask them to read and find out what the little girl likes to do on the playground.

DURING READING or WRITING

Prompts:

■ *Look at the first letter. What sound does it make?*

■ *Get your mouth ready.*

■ *Check the picture and the first letter.*

Notes: Jeff—not using the first letter consistently.

AFTER READING or WRITING

Discuss:

■ *What did the girl in the book like to do?*

■ *What do you like to do best of all?*

■ *Did you use the first sound to help you? Show me how you did that.*

REFLECTION

Some are still not using first sound. Keep practicing. Review this in shared reading of Big Books tomorrow. Call on these kids to help. Do interactive writing next time with this group.

them are not consistently using the first sound to start the words. He decides to plan for a writing lesson tomorrow, since he has noticed that all the children in this group are using beginning sounds and sometimes ending sounds as they write.

Using Initial and Final Sounds in Writing—Day Two

Things to Think About

■ Giving students opportunities to share the pen with you can help them learn to apply what they know about phonics.

■ You might read a book one day and write about it the next to help children use the same words in both reading and writing.

■ You can teach a similar lesson with almost any phonics pattern under study. The key is to help children come up with something to write together that uses the phonics pattern being learned. For example, if you're working on vowel plus *r* with children who are much further ahead in their reading and phonetic understandings, you'll want to create a message together that will use lots of words with this pattern.

The Lesson

Yesterday, Mr. Slye worked with this group on using the first letter sound to figure out new words. He still wants to continue having the students practice this. See his lesson plan in Figure 7.8. He plays a quick phonics game to help the children warm up and get ready to apply their letter-sound knowledge. Then they do a reread of yesterday's book. He wants them to look carefully at the print and use what they know (some sight words and beginning sounds along with the pictures) to read this book. He tells them to pay attention to what they read, because today they'll make a list of what the little girl likes to do on the playground.

After reading, they begin their list. Mr. Slye uses a black water-based marker and a precut piece of six-by-eighteen-inch white construction paper, held the long way to look like a list. He labels it "What the Girl Likes to Do." Then he asks children to help him list what the girl in the book likes to do. The first response is *play*, so he has the children say the word once and then say it again slowly, segmenting the sounds and holding up a finger for each sound. He shares the pen with Nick, who says he hears \p\. Nick writes the letter *p*, and they segment the word again. This time, Sarah hears the *l*, so Nick hands her the pen and she writes this letter. They blend *pl* and say *play*. Kim says, "I know . . . *a*." She writes the *a*, and Mr. Slye says, "You heard all the sounds in order. Good writing! To make *play* look right we need one more letter." He writes the *y* to finish the word, and they read it together one more time.

They proceed in this way to write several more words on the list, naming an action, segmenting the sounds, and writing the letters they know. Mr. Slye fills in the unknown letters to keep the lesson moving quickly and keep student interest high. After they write a word together, they sometimes check it in the book (to connect the reading and the writing). Mr. Slye ends the lesson by telling the children that just like they used the sounds they know in writing today, they can use them in their reading, too. He reminds them to keep using the letters and sounds they know.

Figure 7.7 In this small group, children share the pen to interactively write a list in response to the reading they did.

Figure 7.8 Lesson Plan for Using Initial Sounds in Writing: Day Two

:: Lesson Plan for Using Initial Sounds in Writing: Day Two ::

Group: Sarah's Group

Focus: PHONICS

☑ initial letters   ☑ final letters   ☐ short vowels   ☐ blending and CVC

☐ long vowels   ☐ vowel + *r*   ☐ funky chunks   ☐ long words

Warm-Up:

■ Read sound chart (consonants and vowels).

■ Play game, Give Me a Word. Show a letter and kids take turns giving words starting with that sound. Use *b, c, d, h, j, l, p, r, s, t, w.*

Today's Book/Writing: Write a list   **Level:** mid–kindergarten/B

BEFORE READING or WRITING

Intro:

■ Reread yesterday's book, *Playing*. Remind kids to use the first letter to help them say the first sound if they don't know the word.

■ Tell them we'll write a list of what the girl in the book likes to do.

■ Make a list together, sharing the pen (might include *run, hide, jump, slide, swing, crawl, bathe*). Tell them they can write the parts they know, and I'll write the rest.

DURING READING or WRITING

Prompts:

■ *What sound does that letter make?* (reading)

■ *Use the sounds and think about what makes sense. The picture can help.* (reading)

■ *Think what letter makes that sound.* (writing)

■ *Think of how it looked in the book.* (writing)

Notes: Sarah—did well with writing first sounds on her own and is starting to hear some of the ending sounds, too; help her use this in her reading as well as her writing.

AFTER READING or WRITING

Discuss:

■ Show kids how they used the sounds they know in writing.

■ Tell them to use them in their reading and writing today.

REFLECTION

Some of the kids do better with using their sounds in writing than they do in reading. Try reading one day and writing the next, or vice versa.

Using Long-Vowel Patterns

Things to Think About

■ Once students know their short vowels, begin to compare and contrast these with long-vowel patterns. Most teachers begin with simple spellings of long vowels, such as the CVCe pattern, followed by other vowel combinations for that same long-vowel sound. For example, you might study long *a*, looking first at words like *cake*, *late*, and *page*. Then move into other spellings for long *a*, like those found in *rain*, *stay*, and *break*.

■ Word sorts, like those used in the phonics warm-up portion of this lesson, are good for any phonics pattern being studied. Just match up the type of sort to the phonics pattern kids need to practice. For example, if children are having difficulty with *oy*, *oi*, *ou*, and *ow*, do sorts with words containing these vowel combos.

■ In this lesson, the teacher prompts the kids to "try the other sound," if they say the short vowel sound instead of the long one. This technique works well for other letters, too. For instance, *c* and *g* both have two sounds. If a child reads *dank* for *dance*, say, "Flip it. Try the other sound of *c*." I've been amazed at how this helps some children.

The Lesson

Mrs. Lutz is working with four Title I reading students in Mrs. Nissley's second-grade class. She joins their class every day for about twenty minutes to work with a small group. In years past, Mrs. Lutz used to pull the children out to her room, but she finds that she is more effective by "pushing in" her services to the regular classroom. Mrs. Nissley enjoys having another teacher in the room, and it enables them to see two small groups at a time. In addition, Mrs. Nissley has learned a lot from overhearing the language Mrs. Lutz, a trained Reading Recovery teacher, uses when working with her boys and girls. Mrs. Lutz has just read about a new tech-

nique called "Flip It" in *The Reading Teacher*, the International Reading Association journal, and is eager to try it with her kids today.

Mrs. Lutz will focus on long-vowel patterns in her small-group lesson. In whole group, Mrs. Nissley is teaching vowel plus *r*, but this small group of children still has trouble reading long-vowel words. So Mrs. Lutz will work with them where they are in their phonics learning. She begins with a fun, engaging warm-up—a word sort using premade word cards from the book *All Sorts of Sorts* by Sheron Brown. The children love doing this and know the routine well. They read each word and sort it according to the vowel sound—short or long *e*. The goal is to sort quickly and accurately. They have a few moments of confusion, which Mrs. Lutz helps them with. She tells them to "Flip It" or try the other sound. For example, a student reads "*leet*" instead of *let*, so Mrs. Lutz directs her to try the other sound, and the child corrects her error. After about five or six minutes, they move from word sorting into reading today's book.

Mrs. Lutz introduces the new book *Can You Carry It, Harriet?* by Jane Buxton. She's chosen this text since it has several words with different long *e*

Figure 7.9 Students sort words according to their phonics pattern as a "phonics warm-up" before reading in this small-group lesson.

Figure 7.10 Lesson Plan for Using Long Vowels

⠿ Lesson Plan for Using Long Vowels ⠿

Group: Tyrone, Porsche, R. J., Abby

Focus: PHONICS

☐ initial letters ☐ final letters ☐ short vowels ☐ blending and CVC

☑ long vowels ☐ vowel + *r* ☐ funky chunks ☐ long words

Warm-Up:

■ Do word sort with long-vowel words (#42 in *All Sorts of Sorts* by Sheron Brown).

■ Sort words with short *e* from long *e*. Then sort long *e* words by spelling patterns (*ea, ee, ea, e*).

■ Read each sort. Then mix words up and sort again fast!

■ Refer to sound card for vowel patterns that say long *e*, too.

Today's Book/Writing: *Can You Carry It, Harriet?* by Jane Buxton   **Level:** mid–first grade/H

BEFORE READING or WRITING

Intro:

■ Read title. Find words that say long *e* (*carry, Harriet*).

■ *Today you'll read about some things Harriet finds that she can't carry. Find out how she solves her problem.*

■ *There are some words with long e. What letters might you see if the vowel says \ee\?*

■ *You might try the other sound of e if the word you say doesn't sound right or make sense. You can "flip it," or try the other sound.*

DURING READING or WRITING

Prompts:

■ *Flip it. Try the other sound.*

■ *You know that pattern. It's like _____ (show known word).*

■ *Look at the sound card for help.*

Notes: Porsche— <u>Her/SC</u>   <u>shos</u>   <u>here</u>   <u>?</u>   <u>pud-lee</u>   <u>neest/SC</u>
          Here   shoes   her   carefully   puddle   nest

AFTER READING or WRITING

Discuss:

■ Talk about what Harriet found and couldn't carry. *How did she solve her problem?*

■ *Did you figure out any hard words? Which ones? Show me words where you flipped the sound and tried the other one.*

■ Have kids practice long *e* sort at the Word Study Work Station.

REFLECTION

This will take some practice, but the "flip it" strategy worked pretty well. Sorts helped. Have them look for long *e* words in familiar books and add some of these words to the sorts.

spellings. It presents just the right amount of challenge, and students are able to try the Flip It strategy to figure out the correct vowel sound. She will definitely keep using this technique—with other groups experiencing confusion between letters that make more than one sound.

Using Funky Chunks

Things to Think About

- Some years ago, I began calling sounds for letter combinations like *ou, ough, oi, oy, au,* and *augh* the "funky chunks." My students liked the name and it made these challenging sounds seem less imposing.

- Learning these sounds takes *lots* of practice. Games, like the one in this lesson, can be great for reinforcement, but nothing beats real reading practice for children to learn these sounds. Use a gamelike format rather than flash cards to help students learn these sounds. It's more engaging.

The Lesson

In Ms. Andrews' third-grade classroom, there are six students who can benefit from some practice with tricky sounds—the "funky chunks" of *aw, au, ou,* and *ough*. The rest of the class is fairly good at decoding, and the whole-group phonics lessons Ms. Andrews teaches seem to be meeting their needs. So today she is working with Erin's group and focusing on the sounds of *aw, au, ou,* and *ough* in her lesson. The book she has chosen contains some words with these vowel patterns.

She begins her lesson with a quick warm-up by playing a Concentration game with words using the "funky chunks" she'll focus on in her lesson. She made the game with index cards by copying a word on each—words like *thought, outside, wouldn't, crawled, saw, August, caught,* and so on. Students will make matches by pairing cards with letters that make the same sound, such as *found* and *out* or *thought* and *brought*. Every time they turn over a

card, they must read the word aloud and listen *and* look at the word.

Then they read their new book, *When Foxes Came to Stay* by Janice Marriott. Ms. Andrews introduces the book, as noted in her lesson plan in Figure 7.11. As the children read silently, she listens in to individuals read a bit in a quiet voice. She pays attention to their decoding and talks with each student about what he or she read. In addition, she listens to their fluency. To end the lesson, Ms. Andrews talks with children about what they read and the tricky words they figured out. They look at words with the "funky chunks" that they were able to decode today.

How Do I Assess/Check on Phonics?

Assessing children's phonetic knowledge helps inform us about instruction for them in small group. There are several tools we might use to do this. Both the DIBELS and TPRI have components to help us know which students need help with decoding. As I take a running record on a child, I can look at a child's errors and determine patterns of letters and sounds a child is confusing. Sometimes I use Bear's Spelling Inventory from *Words Their Way* (Bear et al. 2000) to find a child's developmental spelling stage that can inform me about the kinds of phonics patterns that child needs next instructionally.

In addition to these more formal assessments, we might also pay attention to both children's reading and writing. Donald Bear, coauthor of *Words Their Way*, taught me to look for what students *use, but confuse;* it's often similar in both their reading and writing. For example, I found that some of the children in a second-grade classroom were *using, but confusing* long-vowel patterns. In their reading, they often used the short sound instead of the long vowel; and in their writing they would include one of the correct vowels in the long-vowel spelling, but the other one was often a

Figure 7.11 Lesson Plan for Using "Funky Chunks" in Reading

⠸ Lesson Plan for Using "Funky Chunks" in Reading ⠸

Group: Erin, Thom, Kelly, L. J., Stephan, Emma

Focus: PHONICS

☐ initial letters   ☐ final letters   ☐ short vowels   ☐ blending and CVC

☐ long vowels   ☐ vowel + *r*   ☑ funky chunks   ☐ long words

Warm-Up:

■ Play Concentration game with cards containing words with *aw, au, ought,* and *ou* (not too many words—about twenty cards).

■ Make a match if words have same spelling and make same sound.

■ Look at "funky chunks" chart and review these.

Today's Book/Writing: *When Foxes Came to Stay* by Janice Marriott   **Level:** early third grade/N

BEFORE READING or WRITING

Intro:

■ Read title—fiction or nonfiction?

■ *A girl becomes interested in foxes around her home. Read pages 2–7 to find out about the fox and how the girl discovered it.*

■ *There will be some words with funky chunks. Don't let them trick you!*

DURING READING or WRITING

Prompts:

■ *What sound could those letters make?*

Notes: Kelly

AFTER READING or WRITING

Discuss:

■ *What did Jenna and Kyle discover? How did this happen? What do you think might happen next?*

■ Discuss tricky words. Look at funky chunks in these words, too.

REFLECTION

Need to keep working on these. This is going to take time. Play game again tomorrow and continue reading this book. Start word study notebook. Have kids record new words with funky chunks by the phonics pattern (one pattern per page).

stab in the dark. These children might spell *boat* as *baot* or *bote* or even *boate*. In reading, they might read *float* as *flow-at* or *flot*. I've set up Figure 7.12 to give you some ideas of how you might take notes on kids' decoding (and spelling) to help inform your phonics instruction.

Figure 7.12 Aspects of decoding and what to look for when taking anecdotal notes.

Aspect of Decoding	What to Record/Look for	Sample Notes You Might Take
■ using letter sounds in reading	■ letter sounds miscued as kids read (including consonants at beginning or end of word; short or long vowels, funky chunks, etc.) ■ record what the child read on the top and what the text said on the bottom, divided by a line, as shown	■ _Dog_ _puppy_—child isn't using beginning sound, but is making it make sense ■ _bot_ _boat_—child is using, but confusing, vowels—is mixing up short and long sounds ■ _str_ _star_—child is having trouble with _ar_
■ using letter sounds in writing	■ letter sounds as represented by spelling patterns, showing confusion kids have ■ record what the child wrote on the top and what the conventional spelling looks like on the bottom, divided by a line, as shown	■ wrote _flp_ for _flip_—is not paying attention to short vowels in writing ■ wrote _cought_ for _caught_—is using, but confusing, _ough_ and _augh_
■ reading multisyllabic words	■ record what the child reads, noting the child's pronunciation on top and the actual word on the bottom, as shown	■ _been-olars_ _binoculars_ ■ _window_ _windowsill_ ■ _disapproved_ _disappeared_
■ writing multisyllabic words	■ record what the child writes, noting the child's spelling on top and the conventional spelling on the bottom, as shown	■ _growshree_ _grocery_ ■ _letovres_ _leftovers_

What to Look For and How to Take Notes on Phonics/Decoding

You will probably want to look at both students' reading and writing when making decisions about which phonics patterns to focus on in your small-group lessons. Figure 7.12 gives some sample notes to help you get started.

Some Prompts for Phonics/Decoding

As I listen to a student read, I've found it better to help that child problem-solve the word, rather than _my_ giving the child the word. My prompts to assist a child with decoding are designed to help the student think about what he already knows and _use_ this independently. Eventually, I want the child to

have this language in his head, almost as though he's thinking to himself, "That doesn't make sense. Flip it, and try the other sound. Hey, that worked. I'll keep trying that." Figure 7.13 shows some possible prompts for decoding that you might try in small-group instruction or when working with a child one-on-one.

Links to Whole-Group Instruction

I think it's important to teach phonics in whole group, so all students can be exposed to letter-sound patterns in on-grade-level text. There are many commercially produced programs to use while doing this, and many of them include sound charts. I often begin with a choral reading of a sound chart reinforcing a phonics element I'm teaching, especially in the lower grades. In addi-

Figure 7.13 Prompts for Phonics and Decoding

What Child Is Having Trouble With	Possible Teacher Prompts
Initial letter sounds	■ *Look at the first letter. What sound does it make?* ■ *Get your mouth ready.* ■ *Check the picture and the first letter.*
Final letter sounds	■ *Look through the word. Check the last letter, too.* ■ *Check it. What would you expect to see at the end of that word? Were you right?*
Short vowel sounds	■ *What sound does that letter make?* ■ *Use the vowel chart for help.* ■ *That's like in the word _____.* ■ *You know that sound. It's in this word, too.*
CVC patterns and blending sounds	■ *Say the sounds. Put them together fast.* ■ *Use your finger to blend the sounds.* ■ *Is that a real word? Does it make sense?*
Long vowel sounds	■ *Flip it. Try the other sound.* ■ *Use the vowel chart for help. Look at the long vowels.* ■ *Long e can be spelled many different ways. That's one way.*
Vowel + *r* patterns Funky chunks (*oo, oy, oi, ow, ou, ough, augh*)	■ *What sound could those letters make?* ■ *It's like in the word _____.* ■ *Use the (vowel + r or funky chunks) chart.*
Reading long words	■ *Read a part at a time. Put it all together.* ■ *Use your finger to cover up the rest of the word, and read it a part at a time. Move your finger across the word, and read the sounds in order.*
Applying letters and sounds in writing	■ *What letters make that sound?* ■ *Close your eyes. Think about what that word looks like in a book.* ■ *Say the sounds slowly. Write the sounds that you hear in order.* ■ *Clap the word parts. Write the sounds you hear.*

tion, I like to model how to use letters and their corresponding sounds to decode unfamiliar words and think aloud with kids the process I'm using to do this. For example, as I use shared reading to read a Big Book with students, we might come to the word *marching*. I may show kids the sounds I use to help me decode this word, pointing to the *m*, then *ar*, then *ch*, and then *ing*. I'll read each part and then blend the sounds together to read the word. If you use a core-reading program, your basal series will have many whole-group lessons for teaching phonics. The following section gives examples of a variety of ways you might teach phonics in whole group.

Using Initial or Final Sounds in Reading

■ Do word sorts with known words by initial or final sounds being studied (for example, contrast words that start with *b* with words that start with *m*; use kids' names and high-frequency words from word wall with beginning readers).

- Use sticky notes to mask words in a Big Book that children can figure out by starting with the first letter (cover up *puppy*, then have kids tell what letter they expect to see at the beginning or end of the word); then unmask the word, letter by letter, and have kids change their predictions as needed.

Using Short (or Long) Vowel Sounds in Writing

- Write a message together, using a vowel chart with pictures representing each short-vowel sound being studied (or long-vowel sound pattern) to help students choose the correct letter (see Appendix F for a sample whole-group lesson).

CVC Patterns and Blending Words in Reading

- Do Making Words lessons relating to letters and sounds being studied (see Patricia Cunningham's *Phonics They Use* [1999] for more information).
- Use pocket charts and letter cards to do word-family lessons (see Appendix F for a sample whole-group lesson).

Figure 7.14 Following several whole-group lessons on blending letters using cards in a pocket chart, the teacher does a similar lesson in small group with students needing extra help with this phonics skill.

Vowel Plus *r* Patterns in Writing

- Do word sorts, especially with words spelled with *ir*, *ur*, and *er*.
- Write together and use words with vowel plus *r*.

Reading Long Words

- Model how to decode longer words by pulling some of these words out of text, writing them on the board, circling known parts or syllables, and showing kids how to put the parts together. This can be done with words from a read-aloud text.
- Do shared reading of poems or nonfiction text on transparencies and think aloud how to decode longer words (see sample lesson in Appendix F).

Links to Literacy Work Stations Practice

After modeling phonics lessons in whole group and having children work with phonics in small groups, I recommend that they practice what you've taught at literacy work stations. Figure 7.15 shows some of the stations where your kids might practice what you've taught them about phonics.

Links to Standardized and State Testing

Being able to decode words automatically and accurately improves fluency and affects reading comprehension. Therefore, students who have difficulty with phonics patterns need help, often in small group, so they can learn to decode with increasing automaticity.

Of course, decoding alone won't improve reading scores because most state and standardized reading tests measure comprehension. But quality phonics instruction *will* help students learn to figure out what the words say. Remember, without adequate decoding skills, comprehension will be limited.

Figure 7.15 Work stations that support using phonics patterns (such as initial and final consonants, short and long vowels, funky chunks, etc.) or decoding long words.

Literacy Work Station	What Kids Do Here to Practice Phonics/Decoding	How This Station Supports Phonics
Word Study Work Station	■ Use hands-on materials to blend sounds to make words, using phonics patterns being studied (letter tiles, magnetic letters, letter cubes, etc.).	As you teach kids letter-sound correspondences in whole and small group, they practice with the materials here.
Big Book Work Station or Poetry Work Station	■ Make task cards students use to find words with the phonics element you are studying (i.e., vowel + r; oi, or oy; long o words, etc.).	Students return to familiar text to identify words with phonics elements being studied. Connecting phonics to real reading helps kids understand how to apply this knowledge in their reading.
Classroom Library	■ You might have a basket of decodable books or phonics readers in your library for use to help kids solidify a particular phonics pattern under study.	Reading some decodable books or phonics readers may help some students practice reading words with a letter-sound correspondence being studied, especially when they read many words with that same pattern.
Pocket Chart Work Station	■ Have kids sort words by phonics pattern in a pocket chart. They might sort by vowel pattern, initial sound, final sound, etc.	The brain is a pattern seeker. Having students sort words by phonics patterns can help them understand how words work.
Writing Work Station	■ Students use phonics patterns to spell words as they write messages. Display sound charts you're teaching with in this station and model for kids how to use these.	Spelling and phonics are closely related. Students' spelling provides a window into what they understand about how words work. When children write, they are often segmenting sounds.
Computer Work Station	■ Use computer programs related to phonics elements students are studying in whole or small group.	Many computer programs provide differentiated practice for phonics. The gamelike format of many of these provides immediate feedback to students.

Phonics Cautions

Phonics is an important part of learning to read, but it is not the goal. Children must learn that we read to understand, to enjoy, and to gain information from the printed page. When students can decode but have no idea what they just read, we need to look at our teaching. It is easy to become so excited that kids can finally decode that we keep pushing their reading levels, despite their limited compre-

hension. My antidote to that is to balance phonics instruction with good comprehension teaching. Certainly, many of the beginning little books that our kindergartners and first graders read don't offer much to comprehend. But we can and should simultaneously teach deeper comprehension through read-aloud and shared reading.

I like to focus some of my small-group teaching on phonics because it's a great place to differentiate. If I notice that some kids really understand what

Figure 7.16 Third graders make and record words using letter cards and a pocket chart at this word study station.

Figure 7.17 Students work with phonics patterns using magnetic letters on a file cabinet along with phonics charts and books.

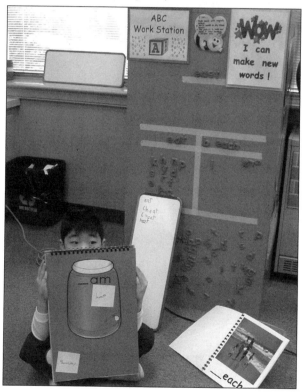

group, I usually backtrack and work with them on easier patterns.

Finally, I keep in mind that some kids are not phonetic readers. No matter how many phonics lessons and decodable books we give them, they never seem to "get it." My daughter, Jessica, was such a student, and I've met teachers who've had students like this, too. Jessica was a student with strong vocabulary and comprehension skills. She was an auditory learner who loved to listen to books on tape. By hearing stories and working with them contextually, she eventually learned to read well. She needed phonics, too, but she needed phonics instruction combined with meaningful text reading. Using phonics flash cards frustrated her. Children learn in different ways, but they all need phonics in the end. Observe your students carefully. Use phonics as one important tool in teaching your students to read, but not the only one.

Reflection Questions for Professional Conversations

1. How are you teaching phonics whole group? Is it systematic? What is the system? What do you teach first, next, etc.? How do the phonetic elements build upon each other? What could you do to make your phonics teaching more systematic?

2. What method(s) do you use for teaching phonics—synthetic phonics, analogy phonics, analytic phonics, phonics through spelling, imbedded phonics? What did you learn about these different types of phonics instruction from reading this chapter? What will you continue to do? What else might you try?

3. What does your small-group phonics teaching look like? How do you differentiate from one group to the next?

4. How do you use writing to help develop your students' phonetic understandings? Look at some of your children's writing to see how

I'm teaching in whole-group phonics instruction, I don't spend time repeating that in small group. Instead, I move on to higher levels of phonics and comprehension. Then if some students do not understand the phonics skills I'm teaching in small

their spellings show what they understand about how letters and sounds work. Use what you learned to plan some small-group instruction. Try some ideas from this book.

5. How are you collecting information on what your kids understand about phonics? How do you currently assess this? What else can you do? Share your ideas with a colleague.

6. Do you have students who decode well but don't comprehend? If so, read Chapter 4 on comprehension and plan to balance your instruction. What we model and focus most on is what students do.

7. Do you have children who have basic comprehension but don't decode well? If so, search through this chapter again and plan some more focused small-group phonics lessons. Share what you tried with another teacher.

For Further Information on Phonics Instruction

Bear, D. R., M. Invernizzi, S. Templeton, and F. Johnston. 2000. *Words Their Way: Word Study for Phonics, Vocabulary, and Spelling Instruction.* Upper Saddle River, NJ: Merrill.

Brown, Sheron. 2000. *All Sorts of Sorts: Word Sorts That Reinforce Spelling and Phonetic Patterns K–4.* San Diego, CA: Teaching Resource Center.

Cunningham, P. 1999. *Phonics They Use: Words for Reading and Writing.* Boston: Allyn & Bacon.

Stahl, S. A., A. M. Duffy-Hester, and K. A. Stahl, 1998. "Everything You Wanted to Know About Phonics (But Were Afraid to Ask)." *Reading Research Quarterly* 33: 338–355.

Vocabulary

Six first graders are sitting around a table with their teacher for a small-group reading lesson. They have been meeting and reading on-grade-level books for several months. These students are good decoders but have limited oral vocabulary and often don't stop to think about new words and what they mean. So the teacher has selected a few rich new words, *camouflage*, *trotted*, and *wriggle*, for teaching in this lesson. Although the children will not need to read the word *camouflage* in their new book, it is a term closely connected to the main idea of this traditional Navajo tale. The other new words are in the text. The teacher's lesson focus will be on new words.

They begin by reading the title, *How Lizard Lost His Colors*, retold by Jay Steele, and talking about the cover picture of a lizard and a cactus living in the desert. Their teacher tells them that the lizard is *camouflaged*. One of them has heard this word before and talks about the lizard matching the color of the rock he sits on. The teacher points out that *camouflage* helps to hide and protect Lizard. They discuss other examples of *camouflage*, using this word repeatedly. They discuss hunters and their

camouflage gear and baby deer *camouflaged* with spots. To deepen their understanding of this word, the teacher points out in each case that *camouflage* helps the creature blend in for protection.

She tells them they will read a story about how the lizard lost his colors, how he became *camouflaged*. She asks them to read and find out how this happened in the story. She tells them that they will find some new words today that they might not have heard before and asks them to jot down these new words on a sticky note on the page where they found them.

The children begin to read and the teacher listens in to Patrick read page 2 with ease. At the end of the page, she asks him what he learned about Lizard. Patrick says that Lizard was lazy. The teacher asks, "Was Lizard *camouflaged*?" Patrick says that the lizard was not. The teacher probes further, asking, "Why is he not *camouflaged*?" and Patrick replies that the lizard is colorful and can't hide on the rock. This child is gaining a deeper understanding of this new word. He continues to read on while the teacher listens to Gabrielle a bit. When she finishes reading the page, the teacher asks her what's happened so far, and through their discussion, she knows that Gabrielle has a good understanding of the text. As they talk, Gabrielle uses the word *camouflage* and her teacher gives her a high five for trying this new word.

As she listens to others read, she notes whether they've written any new words on their sticky notes. Some of them have written the words *Rock-the-Rock*, *trotted*, and *wriggle*. She makes note of which kids are paying attention to new words. (See her lesson plan and notes in Figure 8.1.)

When they've all finished reading the book, she talks with them about how Lizard became *camouflaged*. They discuss the game that Coyote and Lizard played—Rock-the-Rock—and she uses this opportunity to talk about how *rock* has more than one meaning. Here it means "to push" and also "a big stone."

Then they share their new words. They review the meaning of Rock-the-Rock and examine *trotted* and *wriggle* in context, creating kid-friendly definitions. The teacher challenges them to use these new words as they retell the story. With her help, they are successful: *There was a lizard that wasn't camouflaged, and Coyote was going to eat him. Coyote tried to trick Lizard with a game called Rock-the-Rock. That means he was going to move a big stone back and forth. Lizard trotted away and escaped. He made himself really skinny and wriggled under a rock. That's when he got camouflaged.* Finally, the teacher reminds them to be on the lookout for interesting new words, and asks them to *wriggle* out of their seats and quietly *trot* back to their desks.

This lesson was a successful one. The children paid attention to the new words and began to use them. They are on their way to developing a richer vocabulary. The teacher will ask them to share their words during sharing time after small groups today.

What Is Vocabulary?

Vocabulary refers to the words we know and use to communicate with others. It includes the words we understand and have meanings for. There are four kinds of vocabulary:

1. speaking (words we use in conversation);
2. listening (words we understand through hearing);
3. reading (words we read and comprehend); and
4. writing (words we can write to convey messages).

Sometimes speaking and listening vocabulary are referred to as *oral vocabulary*, and reading and writing vocabulary are referred to as *print vocabulary*.

There are also different levels of knowing words. For example, it is possible to know the meaning of a word when we hear it spoken but still not be able to read it in print. This is common for beginning readers, whose oral vocabulary is often larger than their print vocabulary. It is important for children to have large oral vocabularies, so they can understand the words they are reading. Their word knowledge combined with their knowledge of the topic helps comprehension. What does it mean to *know* a word? Dale and O'Rourke (1986) describe four levels of knowing words, including the following:

1. I never saw the word before.
2. I've heard of it, but I don't know what it means.
3. I recognize it in context, and I can tell you what it's related to.
4. I know the word well.

Our goal is for children to move through these levels of knowing. In order to help children grow in their word knowledge, you'll want to think about teaching lessons that include the following aspects of vocabulary learning:

Word Consciousness, or Being Interested in Words and Word Learning

A first step is to motivate children to learn new words and their meanings. Without this desire to

Figure 8.1 Lesson Plan for Paying Attention to New Words

∷ Lesson Plan for Paying Attention to New Words ∷

Group: Patrick, Gabrielle, Richard, Lauryn, Marianna, Amber

Focus: VOCABULARY

- ☑ new word recognition
- ☐ meaning from context
- ☐ multiple meanings
- ☐ using word parts
- ☐ NF text features
- ☐ using new words
- ☐ book language/idioms

Today's Book: *How Lizard Lost His Colors* retold by Jay Steele   **Level:** mid–first grade/G

BEFORE READING

New Words:

Tier II—*camouflage, trotted, wriggle*

Book Intro:

- ■ Read title and make predictions using the cover photo. Use *camouflaged*, and ask kids for examples.
- ■ Tell them this story tells how the lizard lost his colors and became camouflaged.
- ■ Ask them to read to find out how this happened.
- ■ Tell kids to pay attention to new words and jot these on sticky notes on the page where they found them.

DURING READING

Prompts:

- ■ *Do you know that word? What do you think that word means? How can you figure it out?*

Notes: Patrick decoded well; understood *camouflaged* with supportive questioning

AFTER READING

Discuss:

- ■ *How did the lizard become camouflaged?*

New Words:

Ask kids, "What were some of the new words you found while reading?" Look at their sticky notes and discuss new word meanings together. Use their new words to retell the story together. Tell them to look for new words every time they read.

REFLECTION

This lesson worked well. They liked the sticky notes and paid attention to new words. Have kids tell the class about new words they learned during sharing time after work stations and small group today.

"own" new words, vocabulary learning just won't stick. By modeling your own love of finding and using rich vocabulary, you can develop a classroom of word sleuths. Even young children love to use sophisticated language, like *enormous, famished,* and *royalty*. You can help kids develop *word consciousness*, an awareness and love of new words, through daily read-alouds of high-quality children's literature (fiction and nonfiction). Words learned in connection with a meaningful context, such as a favorite book, are more likely to be remembered and understood. Talking with, reading, and using rich language with your children in meaningful contexts are the best ways to develop word consciousness.

Learning Through Direct Teaching of New Words

Research suggests that it is possible to directly teach children between three hundred and five hundred words a year (eight to ten words per week). This is not enough to give all students a rich vocabulary, but it is a step in the right direction. I have never found much success with having children (or myself) copy dictionary definitions or memorize them for a test. Instead, I like to connect new words to context and encourage children to use them in their oral and print vocabularies. One method you might try is called Text Talk, described by Isabel Beck (2002) in her book *Bringing Words to Life*. The teacher chooses Tier II words (see below) before reading aloud a children's book and then uses the words in multiple ways with the class after reading. A sample lesson can be found in Appendix G. As you choose words for direct teaching of vocabulary, think about these three tiers of words, as identified by Beck:

- Tier I words are basic words, like *big*, *sleep*, and *today*, that are already in children's oral vocabulary, in their everyday speech. Students must simply learn to decode and recognize what these words look like in print. When students read these words, they easily know their meanings. Sight words or high-frequency words, like *the*, *to*, *my*, and *here*, are also Tier I words. (For more information on teaching high-frequency words, consult Chapter 5 on fluency. Remember that sight words help children develop automaticity, which leads to fluency.)

- Tier II words are words used frequently by people with mature speech, words such as *rummaging*, *dwelling*, and *immense*. But they're not just grown-up words. They must be useful across a wide variety of contexts and connect to concepts kids already know. For example, children might look for something or *rummage* in their desks; they live in an apartment, house, or trailer—a *dwelling*; and since they know what *big* means, they can readily learn the new word *immense*. Tier II words are the ones you'll want to choose for direct teaching to expand students' vocabulary during reading instruction.

- In contrast, Tier III words are very-low-frequency words and are often related to content-specific contexts. For example, *microscopy*, *fluorophones*, and *polarizer* are words my daughter is learning in her college-level cell biology class. You will want to teach Tier III words in social studies or science.

Word-Learning Strategies (for Indirect Learning)

Although we can teach some words directly, most new vocabulary will be learned indirectly. Before school begins, some children are read to and talked with every day, building a large oral vocabulary. In contrast, children who are not in language-enriched homes start school with limited vocabulary. They haven't learned to pay attention to new words, because they haven't been exposed to rich vocabulary.

Children should be taught word-learning strategies so they can add to their repertoire of vocabulary more rapidly. They must learn how to throw a red flag and say to themselves, "Stop! I don't know what that word means" when they come upon an unfamiliar word they hear (in read-aloud) or can decode but don't know the meaning of (in small group). Then they must have ways of figuring out the word's definition. Here are some strategies you can teach kids to try to determine the meaning of a new word or phrase:

- Use the picture.
- Look at other words before and after the new word for clues about its meaning.
- Substitute another word that makes sense there.
- Ask someone its meaning.
- Use a dictionary or glossary.

Trying Out the Word in New Contexts and in a Variety of Ways

Once children have learned about a new word, they need to be encouraged and given opportunities to use it in a variety of ways. In a small-group reading lesson, children may encounter new words before, during, or after the reading of the book. If you introduce new words *before* students read, you'll want them to be on the lookout for these words *during* the reading. You'll also want to encourage them to use the new words in their discussion *after* reading. If they come across a new word *during* the reading, again you'll want them to try it out in conversation and/or writing *after* they read. In order to really *know* a word, children need to use it over and over again.

Vocabulary Research at a Glance

What does the research say about the importance of vocabulary and how to teach it in school? A summary of some of the research you might find helpful when planning instruction follows:

Importance of Vocabulary

- Five-to-six-year-olds have a working vocabulary of 2,500 to 5,000 words according to Beck and McKeown (2001). By first grade, the vocabulary of a struggling student is half that of students who are successful in literacy.
- Stanovich (1986) found that the gap widens over time, according to what's been called The

Matthew Effect—where the rich get richer, and the poor get poorer. Those who know lots of words pick up new vocabulary while reading, and children with poor vocabulary lag further and further behind.

- Baker, Simmons, and Kameenui (1995) have found that vocabulary instruction is crucial to academic development. Nagy and Scott (2000) claim that children must understand the meanings of words they read if they are to learn from what they read.

How Vocabulary Develops

- Nagy and Anderson (1984) found that literacy and the volume of reading is highly correlated with vocabulary size. People who read a lot from a wide variety of text have much larger and richer vocabularies than people who do not.
- The average student learns about 3,000 words per year in the early school years, or about eight words a day, according to Baumann and Kameenui (1991).

How to Teach Vocabulary

- McKeown, Beck, Omanson, and Pople (1985) found that children need to encounter a word twelve or more times to know and understand it.
- Repeated readings can help young children's vocabulary growth, according to Senechal (1997).
- Kuhn and Stahl (1998) found that directly teaching children dictionary definitions for words did not enhance their comprehension of a passage of text containing those vocabulary words. They did not *know* the words deeply enough to affect their comprehension. Their study showed that the best approach to teaching vocabulary is to teach children some strategies for learning the meaning of words in context, and then encourage them to read widely and often.

- Reading aloud to students can help them learn unfamiliar words. Students with larger vocabularies benefit more from hearing stories read aloud, according to Robbins and Ehri (1994) and Nicholson and Whyte (1992).

- According to Biemiller (2004), teachers can significantly narrow, and in many instances close, the gap between lower- and middle-SES children's vocabulary knowledge by using new words in appropriate contexts; for example, reading aloud quality children's literature. Targeting several words related to the read-aloud by highlighting the word, defining it using words children know, discussing the word, and having children use the word can help children learn new vocabulary.

- Criteria from Graves, Juel, and Graves (1998) suggest considering the following when choosing vocabulary words to study: words students do not know; more important words; words students may not be able to figure out on their own; and words students will encounter frequently across a variety of text and settings.

- Words must be examined from a variety of perspectives, including comparing, contrasting, and discussing words according to Baumann and Kameenui (2004), Stahl (1999), and Templeton (1997).

Who Needs This Kind of Small Group?

All children can benefit from small-group instruction in vocabulary. Children who come to school with limited oral vocabulary may benefit most, since they have the most to gain from learning new words. Focusing on vocabulary in small groups will give students additional guided practice in learning to stop and notice new words as they read, so they can learn how to learn new words. This should be done in addition to teaching vocabulary during whole-group instruction.

Advanced students will benefit from lessons that help them pay attention to word etymology, or word origins and connections. They will enjoy seeing and making links between words like *flower*, *flora*, *floral*, and *flowering*.

Possible Focus for Lessons

Students at all reading levels can be taught how to figure out word meanings. They can benefit from learning to do things like searching the picture (at early reading levels), looking at the words before and after the new word for meaning clues (being a word detective), and using a glossary (when reading informational text). You will want to model these strategies during whole-group instruction and "coach" students to use them during small groups. Here are some possibilities of what you might focus on in a small-group lesson to build vocabulary. Choose one or two at a time, so you won't overwhelm your students (or yourself):

- *Recognizing new words.* As a reading specialist, I found it amazing that my struggling readers would just decode words and keep on going even if they didn't know what a word meant. It was as though they thought they *knew* the word since they could use their phonics skills to say it. One of my goals was to teach children to stop and say, "Hey, I don't know what that word means. Let me try to figure that out."

- *Getting meaning from context (pictures, other words).* There are multiple ways to figure out what a new word means. Young children can be taught to scan a picture for help. If the text says, "The dog ran behind the *shrubs*," and the picture has a dog running behind some bushes, the child can use the picture to figure out the meaning of this new word after decoding it. Of course, there is not always picture support for a new word, but often books for beginning readers have this type of scaffold.

Another way to determine a word's meaning is to use the context of other words surrounding it. You might teach children to *read before and after* the new word to find out what it means. Be aware, though, that not all text gives a supportive meaning directly in the words that precede or follow it.

- *Learning new definitions of multiple-meaning words.* Sometimes students will zip right past a word like *box* that they think they know, because they have one meaning for it. They read, "He practiced *boxing* at the gym" and keep on going, thinking that *box* means a container. They don't realize this word has another meaning. You'll want to teach kids to be on the lookout for old words with new meanings, or multiple-meaning words, as they're often called.

- *Using word parts to determine meaning.* Most second- and third-grade teachers teach children about prefixes and suffixes, but students often have trouble applying and transferring this isolated skill. Kids might be able to tell you that *re-* means "again," yet they don't use it to determine the meaning of a word like *reopen*. Your goal in this kind of a vocabulary-building lesson is to teach kids to stop and say, "Hey, that word starts with *re-* and that means 'again.' So *reopen* must mean 'to open again.'"

- *Thinking about book language and idioms.* Books written for children in mid-first-grade level and up begin to use book language, or figurative language, as well as idioms. These are more sophisticated language structures that can deeply affect meaning. I like to tell kids that writers sometimes use phrases, or groups of words that we wouldn't normally use in speaking. For example, an author may say, "The moon climbed higher in the sky" instead of the way we'd say it if telling a friend— "Look. The moon is way up in the sky."

  You'll want to alert students to idioms as well. Idioms consist of a group of words that

have little or nothing to do with the individual words. When we say, "Don't let the cat out of the bag," we aren't meaning to physically release a cat from a grocery sack. But some kids might picture this direct interpretation if they haven't been exposed to this idiom ahead of time.

- *Using text features like bold and italicized words in informational text.* Reading informational text presents its own vocabulary challenges, since most of the new words are content specific and are often Tier III words. To help readers pay attention to these new words, many writers of informational text for children use italics or boldface type to make these words stand out. I have found it helpful to show kids how to use these text features to figure out a word's meaning. If a bold or italicized word is followed by a dash or the word *or*, the definition will most definitely be the next thing they read. Informational texts often include a glossary or word bank to give students help with learning new words, too.

- *Using dictionaries and reference aids to learn word meanings and gain deeper knowledge of words.* Before choosing this as a focus for a small-group lesson, think about how often you use a dictionary to help you find the meaning of a new word. It is usually a last resort. Use this strategy carefully and in limited cases. I prefer to teach how to use a glossary while reading informational text, since this is a built-in reference tool.

- *Trying out the word in new contexts and a variety of ways.* You'll want to encourage students to use the words introduced before reading or found during reading as much as possible. Be enthusiastic in your discussion with them after reading; give them high fives and big smiles when they use the new words. Tell them to use these words during the school day and at home. Find ways to weave these new words into the day through talking, reading, and writing! You might even chart the words and have kids add tally marks to show each time they use a word correctly in their reading or their writing.

Choosing Materials

When choosing materials for teaching with a vocabulary focus, you'll want to think about the word-learning strategies you want your students to use in the lesson and be sure those kinds of opportunities exist in the book you select. For example, if you want students to pay attention to new words and think about what they mean, you'll want to be sure the new book has several new words—Tier II words that aren't already in their oral language. If you're focusing on using word parts like prefixes and suffixes to help kids unlock meaning, you'll want books that include several new words with prefixes and suffixes. If using context to determine word meaning is your focus, choose books with words that can be figured out by using the pictures or the words surrounding the new words.

Figure 8.2 As the teacher works with students in both whole group and small group, she reminds students to use "dollar words" by referring to this chart posted where all can see it. Words are attached to the chart with Velcro so they can be changed periodically.

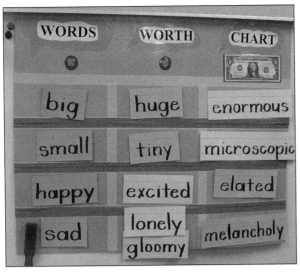

Choosing and Introducing New Vocabulary

Mostly you'll want to focus on Tier II words, like *hermit*, *frisky*, and *plodded*, words students don't already use while speaking and that are used in a wide variety of contexts so they can use them every day. Some teachers call these "million-dollar words," "wow words," or "lovely language." Once you've selected several words, you'll need to decide whether you'll teach them *directly* (giving a child-friendly definition) or *indirectly* (letting kids apply word-learning strategies to figure out the meanings). Here are some things to consider:

- *Directly* teach and introduce words *before* reading
  - if they are Tier II words that are needed to understand the main ideas of the text;
  - if the book has no Tier II words and you want to use some rich vocabulary related to the content;
  - by using the words in your book introduction several times so kids learn the meanings *before* reading and can better comprehend the text by learning these new words first.
- *Directly* teach vocabulary words *during* reading
  - if a child can't figure out the meaning, even with prompting (searching picture and reading words before and after the word);
  - by telling the child what the words mean.
- *Directly* teach vocabulary words *after* reading
  - if the students found new words but don't know their meanings.

- Use *indirect* methods of vocabulary learning *before* reading
  - by reviewing word-learning strategies you want students to practice today.
- Use *indirect* methods of vocabulary learning *during* and *after* reading

- by helping kids apply these word-learning strategies and asking them to show or tell how they figured out new meanings of words.

⠿ The Lessons ⠿

Now that you are thinking more deeply about how to include vocabulary learning in your small-group lessons, here are some examples that focus on helping children learn new words as they read. Remember to choose a focus and stick with it until it becomes more automatic for children in their reading. Then you'll want to expand to a new focus. You should soon start to see students paying attention to new words and inquiring about their meanings. A lesson-plan template for vocabulary is used for each of the following lessons. A reproducible copy of this form can be found in Appendix G if you'd like to use it to write your own vocabulary-focused small-group plans. Note that you can check the box by the specific vocabulary focus you choose for each lesson. There is also a "new word" space listed on the plan for jotting down a few new words you want to use before or after the reading of the book.

Direct Teaching of New Words Lesson

Things to Think About

- Choose words for direct teaching wisely. Use only a few new words at a time. The human brain can't remember more than five to seven new bits of information at once.
- You don't need to make a flash card for each new word. These are not high-frequency words, but are to be used to help develop meaning. You might write them on a dry erase board if kids can decode them. (Don't do this with emergent readers, since the words are usually too hard for them to decode.)
- When working with nonfiction text, be sure

students know many of the high-frequency words, so they can concentrate on thinking about the new vocabulary they are learning (if comprehension and vocabulary are your focus). If you want them to be learning new high-frequency words, choose a book with a limited number of Tier III or content-related words in the text. Or make the new words very familiar for them by using them multiple times in the book introduction, as in this lesson.

Before the Lesson

As a literacy coach, I'm working with Sarah's kindergarten class and have conferred with her about her kids and their needs. She wants to try more nonfiction but is unsure about how to handle the demands of all the unfamiliar new words for emergent readers. So we choose a book and plan a lesson together. This group is a reading level B text, according to the Fountas and Pinnell (1996) reading levels used by her school. We choose *Big Sea Animals* by Annette Smith, Jenny Giles, and Beverley Randall, since it has photos of ocean animals children will love. The book contains several high-frequency words this group is learning—*come, and, look, at, the, is*. Reading this book will reinforce the sight-word learning children are doing, as well as give us opportunities for the kids to learn some new vocabulary.

We talk about which new words to focus on and choose *come* as a sight word. It's not as familiar as the other high-frequency words, and reading this book will help children learn it. We also select *crocodile, dolphin, stingray, octopus,* and *sea lion*, since we think these will be new vocabulary for most of the children in this group. We write our lesson plan, as shown in Figure 8.3.

During the Lesson

I meet with the group while Sarah watches me work with her students and takes notes about what she sees. I hand a book to each child and read the title. I ask the group where they think this takes place.

Figure 8.3 Lesson Plan for Direct Teaching of New Words

⠿ Lesson Plan for Direct Teaching of New Words ⠿

Group: Shyanne, Audrey, Andrew, R. J.

Focus: VOCABULARY

☑ new word recognition   ☐ meaning from context   ☐ multiple meanings
☐ using word parts   ☐ NF text features   ☑ using new words
☐ book language/idioms

Today's Book: *Big Sea Animals* by Annette Smith, Jenny Giles,   **Level:** emergent readers in kindergarten/B
and Beverley Randall

BEFORE READING

New Words:

- sight word—*come*
- Tier II—*aquarium*
- Tier III—*crocodile, dolphin, stingray, octopus, sea lion*

Book Intro:

- Read title and talk about where kids are (aquarium). Discuss big sea animals they might see. Have students:
    - Look at each new animal and name it while touching its picture in the book.
    - Clap the word, then find it (long word).
    - Touch animal picture and name it again.
    - Use the new word in the sentence "*Come and look at the _____.*" (Pretend you're at the aquarium!)
    - Make and read *come* with magnetic letters. They write *come* 3 times on dry erase boards.
    - Tell them to point to each word as they read the book and use the picture to help them "read" the new words.

DURING READING

Prompts:

- *Use the picture to help you figure out that new word. That's a word you know.*

Notes: Shyanne figured out most of the new words. She loved this book and was motivated to read it several times. Looked at *come* to help her.

AFTER READING

Discuss:

- *What was your favorite big sea animal and why? Which of these have you seen and where?*

New Words: use them!

REFLECTION

Reading a nonfiction book of high interest gave the kids a chance to really practice reading high-frequency words. They had the extra benefit of learning some new vocabulary. They paid more attention to print, noticing that some words were big. They liked the big words!

They don't know, so I tell them it's in an *aquarium*, a place where sea animals live and people can come to visit them. I ask the children to repeat the new word. We talk about big sea animals we might see at an *aquarium*, and they name *fish*, *shark*, and *octopus*.

To directly teach the new content words, I have them look at page 4 with me. They say, "alligator," and I tell them this *aquarium* animal lives in the sea and is called a *crocodile*. I have them touch the picture and say, "crocodile" several times. Then I have them find the word on the page that they think says *crocodile*. We clap the syllables and realize it's a long word. They quickly find it and say *crocodile* again. I tell them that the little girl in the book is excited to see the *crocodile*, so she tells her family to *come and look at the crocodile*. They say it with me like she might say it. We repeat the process with pages 8 through 15, quickly looking at the pictures of the new animals, saying their names, and using each word several times.

Before reading, I build *come* with magnetic letters, showing them how this word looks and tell them it will be on every page in their books. They write the word quickly on a dry erase board three times, reading it each time by checking it with their finger. Then they start to read. The entire *before reading* segment takes only about seven to eight minutes. I keep the pace fast, so the children stay engaged.

Then they each read the book independently. Some of them begin reading it together chorally, so I stand between them and ask one to reread a page to me. This breaks them apart, and they try reading on their own. I've provided a very supportive book introduction, so most of them feel confident to try reading the book. I listen in to one child at a time and hear them successfully using most of the new words. One forgets *stingray*, and I show him the word. He knows the sound of *s*, and when I say it's a *stingray*, he says, "Oh, yeah. I forgot." He tries it on his own. When I check back later, he's rereading the book and remembers *stingray* the second time. I also notice that occasionally a child looks at the magnetic letters spelling *come* to help them remember this word. Most kids read the book twice while I move around and listen in to each of them read.

After reading, they tell me they liked this book and want to read it again. So we read it together (chorally) for extra practice. I ask them about their favorite animals, and many of them can tell me the names of these animals. We put the new book in their reading basket, so they can read it again during independent reading if they'd like.

After the Lesson

Sarah and I debrief about the lesson. She says she was really pleased to see how excited the kids were about reading nonfiction. Before this lesson, she wasn't sure about how to handle the new vocabulary, but now she thinks she'll just use the new words over and over again in conversation before the kids read, like she saw me do. This is a new idea for her; in the past, she simply went page by page, looked at each picture, and told them the new words. Sarah also comments on how fast the lesson moved and admits that her small-group lessons often take much longer, because she spends so much time talking. She noticed that I used a timer in my lesson and says she will try the same. That will help her keep an eye on how long she spends in her book introduction.

I jot down a quick reflection on my lesson-plan sheet and we discuss what she'll try in her next lesson with this group.

Using Word Parts to Determine Meaning Lesson

Things to Think About

- When teaching a lesson about prefixes and suffixes, be careful not to ask students to just read and find words with those parts. Your focus in this kind of lesson is to get them to *use* prefixes and suffixes to solve new words.

- When choosing a book for this kind of lesson, find one that has some words with prefixes and suffixes. You may be surprised at how seldom these word parts exist in the books your students are reading. *Re-, un-, dis-, in-, -ly, -ful,* and *-less* are the most frequently used and can be found mostly in texts written at a third-grade level or higher.

■ Realize that you'll be focusing on several aspects of vocabulary in this kind of lesson. You'll still want kids to pay attention to new words and use the new words. And, of course, you'll always want them to use context to check on meaning.

Before the Lesson

Mrs. Beasley has just formed a new group in her third-grade classroom. It consists of three of her advanced students and two reading on grade level. They notice new words as they read and are pretty good at figuring out what these words mean. However, their teacher has noticed that although she's taught lessons on prefixes and suffixes (as included in her state standards), she doesn't see the children applying them as they read. She has introduced prefixes and suffixes in whole-group lessons, so all children have been exposed to them. She has charted a list of a few common ones, so she can refer to these as she reads aloud to kids and can make students aware of how these word parts are used. (See Figure 8.4 for a photo of this chart.) But she still isn't seeing students apply these in their own reading, as she's noted while conferring with them in independent reading and during small groups. So she's decided to temporarily meet with these five children to help them focus in on how to use prefixes and suffixes.

She looks for a new book to read with them from her school's literacy library, a small room that houses a collection of leveled books. All the books are marked with a level along a continuum, and she finds one on DRA (Developmental Reading Assessment) level 38, or what kids should be reading by the end of third grade. It's a reading level she knows they can all comprehend and read with ade-

Figure 8.4 This prefix anchor chart was made during whole-group instruction with the class. It is used during small group to reinforce these word parts (and their meanings) and to help students figure out meanings of new words as they read.

quate fluency. She browses the books, looking for one that has some words with prefixes and suffixes so the children will be able to use these to determine the words' meanings. She decides on *Justin and the Best Biscuits in the World*, by Mildred Pitts Walter. It will interest the children in this group, and the word *rebound* is on the first page. She fills out her lesson plan, shown in Figure 8.5, and is ready to teach.

During the Lesson

Mrs. Beasley gives each child a copy of today's book. They read the titles of the book and first chapter and talk about the word *grounded*. They know two meanings for *ground*—dirt and not being allowed to do anything because you *misbehaved*. Mrs. Beasley takes advantage of the opportunity to use *misbehave* several times as she introduces this book. *Do you think Justin will misbehave? What kind of thing might he do to misbehave?* Then she writes the word on a dry erase board and has a child circle the prefix. This word wasn't on her original lesson plan, but it works! Louis circles *mis-* and says, "*Mis-* means 'not.' So *misbehave* means 'to not behave.'" Mrs.

Figure 8.5 Lesson Plan for Using Word Parts to Determine Meaning

⠿ Lesson Plan for Using Word Parts to Determine Meaning ⠿

Group: J. D., Sanitra, Jayda, Hassein, Louis

Focus: VOCABULARY

- ☑ new word recognition
- ☑ using word parts
- ☐ book language/idioms

- ☐ meaning from context
- ☐ NF text features

- ☐ multiple meanings
- ☑ using new words

Today's Book: *Justin and the Best Biscuits in the World* by Mildred Pitts Walter   **Level:** early fourth grade/P

BEFORE READING

New Words:

- ■ *grounded* (multiple meanings)

Book Intro:

- ■ Read titles of book and first chapter. Make predictions. Discuss new word. Point out that *ground* has more than one meaning. *Which one do you think it is here?*
- ■ Look at first picture together and notice the kids are playing basketball. Make quick predictions: basketball words that might be in this chapter. Tell them to be on the lookout for basketball words.
- ■ Tell students to read and find out what this new character, Justin, is like and why he's grounded.
- ■ Also tell them to pay attention to new words and what they might mean. Give them sticky notes. Jot down new word on each sticky note and page #. Remind them that some of the words may have prefixes and suffixes. Review, using anchor chart for prefixes and suffixes.
- ■ If anyone finishes early, they can go back and reread and look for words with prefixes and suffixes.

DURING READING

Prompts:

- ■ *You know this part. What does* re- *mean?*
- ■ *Look at our suffix chart. What does* –ful *mean? What could this word mean?*

Notes: Sanitra

AFTER READING

Discuss:

- ■ *What was Justin like? What happened to him in this chapter? Was he* grounded?
- ■ *What new words did you find? Which ones were "basketball words"? Which had prefixes and suffixes? What did the words mean? How did you figure out what they meant?*
- ■ Encourage students to use some of their new words in the discussion. Also remind them to use these in their talking and writing, whenever possible.

New Words:

basketball words

- ■ *rebounded*—p. 1
- ■ *one-on-one*—p. 1
- ■ *zigzagged*—p. 2
- ■ *dribbling*—p. 2

words with prefixes and suffixes

- ■ *rebounded*—p. 1
- ■ *untimed*—p. 2
- ■ *slowly*—p. 7

REFLECTION

It's hard to help kids apply prefixes and suffixes, because I don't want them to just read and find these. I want them to learn how to APPLY them. Keep working on this.

Beasley tells the group that one thing she wants them to do as readers today is to be on the lookout for words with prefixes and suffixes and to use these to solve new words' meanings just like they did with *misbehave*.

They all look at the first picture, which shows two boys and a basketball. The kids predict that Justin likes to play ball. Mrs. Beasley says, "Basketball must be important in this story, since the illustrator drew this picture. Let's predict some of the basketball vocabulary that might be in this book." The students give her a few words—*bounce*, *steal*, *shoot*, and *dribble*. Their teacher tells them to be word detectives and notice basketball words as well as words with prefixes and suffixes. She gives them each a sticky note and tells them to jot down new words and the matching page numbers. She reminds them to read Chapter 1 to find out what Justin is like and what he does to get grounded. If they finish reading early, they can go back and double-check for words with prefixes and suffixes. The children start to read immediately.

As the children read silently, Mrs. Beasley listens in to individuals. She begins with Sanitra, the child she will take notes on. (Systematically, she jots down notes on one student each day in small group so that by the end of two or three weeks, she's taken notes on every child. See Figure 8.6.) Sanitra reads the page she is on smoothly. Mrs. Beasley checks for comprehension by asking her a few questions. Then she asks about new words Sanitra found, and the child says there are none. Mrs. Beasley asks her about *rebound*, a word on this page. Sanitra says she thinks it means to catch the ball. "Reread it and check it again," says her teacher. Sanitra realizes this isn't right, so her teacher writes *rebound* on a dry erase board and asks Sanitra to look for a part she knows. Sanitra circles *re-* and says, "That means 'again.'" They look at *bound* together and think it's like *bounce*. "Bounce again?" asks Sanitra. She decides this is helping her understand the word's meaning—that the ball has bounced off the backboard and Justin

Figure 8.6 Teacher notes on Sanitra.

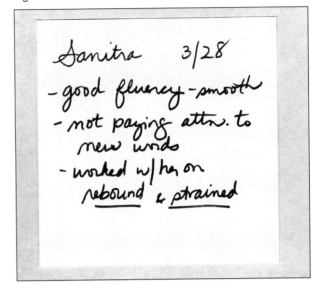

got the ball again. Sanitra writes *rebound—p. 1* on her sticky note.

Next, Mrs. Beasley moves to Jayda, who is reading on page 3. As Jayda reads aloud, she gets stuck on *strained*. She looks carefully and gets it right, but looks puzzled. "I don't know what that means," she tells her teacher. Mrs. Beasley asks Jayda what she can do to help herself, and Jayda rereads the sentence. "What do you picture?" asks Mrs. Beasley. "Somebody carrying lots of groceries," says Jayda. "What do you think *strained* might mean?" asks Mrs. Beasley. Jayda thinks it means "had trouble lifting the bags." She tries it again and smiles. She quickly jots *strained* on her sticky note and finishes reading the rest of the page easily. They talk briefly about the chapter, and Mrs. Beasley is satisfied with Jayda's comprehension.

Mrs. Beasley has time to listen in to one more child for a bit. She reminds the group they can go back and add new words or words with prefixes and suffixes to their sticky notes if they've finished, and a few do.

After reading, the group discusses the chapter they just read. They liked the book so far and want to read more. As they talk, Mrs. Beasley encourages them to use the new words on their sticky notes.

She notices that Sanitra uses *rebound* when talking about the boys playing basketball. Then they share new words they jotted down while reading. Some of the words are the ones Mrs. Beasley wrote on her original lesson plan. They group their sticky notes into three categories—basketball words, words with prefixes and suffixes, and other words, and discuss their meanings. They have mostly found basketball words, but the good news is that they are paying attention to new vocabulary.

After the Lesson

The children have asked if they can read the next chapter of their book, so Mrs. Beasley, satisfied with their comprehension, sends them back to their seats to continue to read. She arms them with extra sticky notes to be on the lookout for more new words. She reminds them to use prefixes and suffixes if they are in any of their new words. They can share their sticky notes next time the group meets, in two days.

Mrs. Beasley takes a minute to jot down a brief reflection about today's lesson. See her notes at the end of her lesson plan in Figure 8.5. She'll ask the group to discuss Chapter 2 and share their new words when she meets with them in two days. She wishes they'd had more opportunity to work with the prefixes and suffixes while reading, but is pleased that they are paying attention to new words and figuring out their meanings. She realizes it will take time until her students use this skill consistently. She'll continue to work on vocabulary with this group, using every opportunity to help them see how prefixes and suffixes can help them with word meaning. She'll also have them look for prefixes and suffixes in familiar books at the word study work station.

Getting Meaning from Context Lesson

Things to Think About

- Not all new words can easily be figured out from context. Choose books wisely when teaching this strategy. Be sure supportive clues are available in the text or pictures. Make this easy for kids by your book choice!

- I don't usually use the term *context clues* with struggling readers. When I'm trying to teach them how to find new word meanings, I tell them to "look at the words before and after the new word and think about what the word could mean here." This is much more explicit language than saying, "use your context clues," since that term is hard for some kids to understand.

The Lesson

Yesterday this group of second graders began *Henry and Mudge: The First Book,* by Cynthia Rylant. They are reading a bit below grade level, and are very excited to be in their first chapter book. Their teacher wants to increase their vocabulary skill, so she's working with them on attending to new words. As they reread Chapter 1 to warm up, she listens to one child read and takes notes on his reading. Then they describe Henry, using rich language they learned yesterday. The teacher jots down some of the words they use, as noted in the "during reading" part of her lesson plan. Today she asks the group to read the next chapter about Mudge and describe him. She gives each child an index card with a few pieces of highlighter tape on it and tells the kids to mark any new words they find that describe Henry's new pet. She uses explicit language to demonstrate how to find word meanings, as shown in the lesson plan in Figure 8.7.

Using Text Features Like Bold and Italicized Words in Informational Text

Things to Think About

- Many informational books have bold words in them, along with glossaries. Start by choosing books like this that are of high interest to your students and have related schema, so they can use their prior knowledge to figure out new words and add these to their vocabulary.

Figure 8.7 Lesson Plan for Getting Meaning from Context

⠿ Lesson Plan for Getting Meaning from Context ⠿

Group: Raul, Griffin, Larkyn, Mariel, Jack

Focus: VOCABULARY

- ☑ new word recognition
- ☐ using word parts
- ☐ book language/idioms
- ☑ meaning from context
- ☐ NF text features
- ☐ multiple meanings
- ☑ using new words

Warm-Up: Familiar Rereading   **Listen to:** Jack   **Title:** *Henry and Mudge* (Chap. 1)

Today's Book: *Henry and Mudge* by Cynthia Rylant (Chap. 2)   **Level:** end of first grade/J

BEFORE READING

New Words:

- ■ Tier II—(in book) *search*
- ■ Rich words describing Henry (not in book) (*friendless, lonesome, miserable*)

Book Intro:

Yesterday we read about Henry. How would you describe him?

DURING READING

Prompts:

- ■ *What's another word we could use here that makes sense? Use the picture to help you figure out what that word means.*

Notes: Jack used *lonesome* to describe Henry! *Floppy ears* to describe Mudge. Raul—*friendless* and *miserable*—WOW!

AFTER READING

Discuss:

- ■ *How would you describe Mudge? Use new words from the book.* (Chart these.) *Show how you figured out what each word means.*
- ■ *Use these words to write a short description of Mudge. Do this tomorrow.*

New Words:

floppy, drooled, slobbered, humongous

REFLECTION

These kids are really picking up new words and enjoying it! They remembered the new words we used yesterday and added to their vocab today. This focus is working. Next, work on deeper comprehension. The new vocab will help.

- ■ Some teachers chart features of nonfiction text to help kids pay attention to these and learn how to use them. This can be a helpful tool when teaching students how to use bold words and glossaries in their reading *and* their writing. See Figure 8.9 for a sample chart.

Figure 8.8 A student marks new vocabulary words with highlighter tape and talks with her teacher about these words as she reads in small group.

Figure 8.9 Throughout the year, the class makes a chart highlighting features of nonfiction text. They add new information as they learn more about nonfiction. The teacher refers to it to remind them that bold words signal new vocabulary.

The Lesson

This teacher's goal is to read more nonfiction in small group. In the past, she usually used stories because she was more comfortable with them. Today, she chooses an informational text about writing and mailing letters, since she knows kids will be familiar with this topic. They have been learning about how to read nonfiction in whole group and have made a chart of nonfiction text features and how to use them. They do a quick review of the chart before reading, and she reminds them there will be bold words, captions, diagrams, and a map in this book. They briefly discuss how to use each of these text features to help them comprehend. She points out a few bold words and reminds the children that these are important and tell the reader to pay attention—that's why the author made them dark. As they read, she guides them to use the text features to expand their knowledge about the postal system. She introduces just a few pages at a time, has the kids read, and then discusses them. You'll notice in Figure 8.10 that her lesson plan is divided into two parts for this one day, as noted by the dotted lines.

How Do I Assess/Check for Vocabulary Understanding?

In the lessons above, teachers used assessment to plan their lessons. They had to think about what their children already knew and make decisions about which vocabulary to focus on, based on the levels of language they heard students use in their classrooms.

When assessing vocabulary, I have found it useful to simply listen to the language children use across the day. Listen in to them during whole-group *and* small-group instruction. Eavesdrop during their independent practice at literacy work stations and when they're working in cooperative groups at other times in the day. Pay attention to which students are growing their vocabularies, and adjust your instruction accordingly. You might

Figure 8.10 Lesson Plan for Using Nonfiction Text Features

:: Lesson Plan for Using Nonfiction Text Features ::

Group: Lucia, Mindy, Ramon, Sharee

Focus: VOCABULARY

☐ new word recognition   ☐ meaning from context   ☐ multiple meanings

☐ using word parts   ☑ NF text features   ☐ using new words

☐ book language/idioms

Today's Book: *Letter to a Friend* by Lola M. Schaefer (pages 2–7)   **Level:** early second grade/K (20)

BEFORE READING

pages 2–5:

New Words:

pay attention to bold words, captions, and diagrams

Book Intro:

- Read title and make connections. Fiction or nonfiction (NF)? How can you tell?
- Read table of contents together quickly.
- Show bold words and discuss why important—they tell reader to pay attention.
- p. 2—Read heading (in bold). Tell them to use map and letter.
- p. 4—Look at bold word and diagram.
- Read to find out why Matt wrote Derek a letter.

pages 6–7:

- Point out bold words, *post office* and *clerk.* Read to find out what *postmarked* means.

DURING READING

Prompts:

- *When a writer uses bold words, she's showing you that those words are important. Good noticing.*

Notes: Mindy—good comprehension—reminded her to use graphics; *postmarked* was a new word for her

AFTER READING

Discuss:

pages 2–5:

- *Why did Matt write Derek a letter?*
- *How did he write and mail his letter?*
- *How did the bold words and diagram help you?*

New Words:

- in book: *stamp*—multiple meanings; *address*—noun and verb
- not in book: *stationery*

Discuss:

pages 6–7:

- *What happened to Matt's letter?*
- *What does* postmarked *mean?*
- *How did the bold words and captions help you?*

New Words:

- in book: *clerk, postmarked*
- not in book: *postal system*

REFLECTION

Lesson went well. Kids are paying attention to all features of NF text.

want to record some of the kinds of words you hear kids use during small group by taking anecdotal notes. See the examples in the section that follows. Your goal should be to close the gap between the "haves" and the "have-nots" in word ownership. You'll be giving kids a gift that keeps on giving. Vocabulary growth is contagious.

Note: Some schools are using DIBELS for assessment to gain information for working with their most struggling students. One subtest, called Word Usage Fluency, or WUF for short, gives children one minute to retell what they've read and gives them a point for each word they use. This is not really intended to measure use of rich words; rather it will tell you if children can speak fluently and generate related ideas. They don't get bonus points for using robust vocabulary. So be sure to pay attention to your children's vocabulary usage throughout the day in their oral and written language to know how they are progressing with vocabulary development.

What to Look For and How to Take Notes on Vocabulary

As you pay attention to your children's use of language, you'll find it very helpful to take a few notes on their vocabulary usage and development. Figure 8.11 describes some things you might look for.

Figure 8.11 Aspects of vocabulary and what to look for when taking anecdotal notes.

Aspect of Vocabulary	What to Record/Look For	Sample Notes You Might Take
■ Recognition of unknown words	■ If child stops to search and determine what a word means	■ *paused on* suburbs *and read on* ■ *stopped and asked what* lookout *means*
■ Using context to determine word meaning	■ Scanning or rereading behaviors ■ Uses pictures or points to other words in text that define a word ■ Tries another word that makes sense	■ *reread and self-corrected to make change* make sense *on page 6* ■ *checked picture to figure out* snail
■ Thinking about book language and idioms	■ Stops to reflect on phrases used in books that are not in our oral vocabulary	■ *noticed* off they went *and thought about what it meant* ■ off her rocker?
■ Using text features like bold or italicized words in informational text	■ Points out bold or italicized words and uses these to figure out word meaning	■ *noticed bold word and showed me the definition following it* ■ *showed me where text said* or *and gave the meaning in NF*
■ Learning new definitions of multiple-meaning words	■ Tells new meaning for a known word	■ *said* rock *has two meanings there*
■ Using word parts to determine word meanings	■ Notices prefixes and suffixes and uses them to figure out meaning of new word ■ Uses a root word and makes a connection	■ *saw* re *and said that means "again"* ■ *figured out meaning of* rebound *using* re *and* bounce
■ Trying out new words in oral and written vocabulary	■ Uses new vocabulary words in discussion after reading	■ *used* humongous *and* lonesome *in discussion after reading*

Some Prompts for Vocabulary

Remember that you'll want to give minimum support to kids *during* their reading. Here are some things you might say to help them solve their own problems and do their own work while learning new words and taking on vocabulary-learning strategies. You might match the focus of your lesson to the prompts in Figure 8.12.

Links to Whole-Group Instruction

You'll want to include plenty of vocabulary teaching in whole group preceding the small-group lessons mentioned in this chapter. This will give you an opportunity to "frontload" by modeling and showing students *how* to pay attention to and learn new words. You'll want to use explicit language as listed in the section above. Sample lesson plans for whole-

Figure 8.12 Prompts for Learning Vocabulary

What Child Is Having Trouble With	Possible Teacher Prompts
Recognition of unknown words	■ *You stopped. What can you do to figure out what that word means?* ■ *Do you know that word?* ■ *Asking about that word can help you learn what it means. _____ means _____.*
Using context to determine word meaning	■ *Use the picture to help you figure out what that word means.* ■ *Read on a bit. See if you can find clues to what that word means.* ■ *Which words give you a clue to the word's meaning?* ■ *What do you think it means? Why?* ■ *What's another word you could use here that makes sense?*
Thinking about book language and idioms	■ *What do you think off they went means?* ■ *The author said legs like sticks. What do you picture there?*
Using text features like bold or italicized words, dashes, and *or* in informational text to figure out what those words mean	■ *When a writer uses bold words, he's showing you that those words are important. Good noticing.* ■ *Look at this (point to dash or word or). It tells us the definition will follow!* ■ *It's written in italics. How can that help you?*
Learning new definitions of multiple-meaning words	■ *What does _____ usually mean? Does it mean that here? What do you think it means?* ■ *This word has more than one meaning. What could it mean here?*
Using word parts to determine word meanings	■ *You know this part. What does re- mean?* ■ *Look at our suffix chart. What does –ful mean? What could this word mean?* ■ *Find a part you know. What does that part mean?*
Trying out new words in oral and written vocabulary	■ *You sound so grown up when you use those "million-dollar words."* ■ *I love that new word! Use it at home to impress your family!* ■ *What a great word choice! I can really picture what you mean when you use that word.*

group vocabulary instruction are also included in Appendix G. A few examples are listed here:

Word Consciousness (Awareness of New Words)

- Read aloud and encourage kids to ask you about the meanings of the unfamiliar words they hear.
- Do shared reading of Big Books and poems that have a few Tier II words in them and mark new words with highlighter tape to make them stand out (see sample lesson plan in Appendix G).
- Display the new words kids discover on an Interesting Words chart (see Figure 8.13).

Direct Teaching of New Words

- Get kids to pay attention to sophisticated new words by listing five to seven of the words that will be found in a read-aloud on a chart before reading the book; have kids use a predetermined signal such as a thumbs-up each time they hear one of the words as you read aloud; then coconstruct the words' meanings after the read-aloud and add the kid-friendly definitions to the chart.
- Directly teach meanings of some new words after a read-aloud (see the "Text Talk" sample lesson in Appendix G).

Figure 8.13 An Interesting Words chart is generated during read-aloud to help students pay attention to and use new vocabulary.

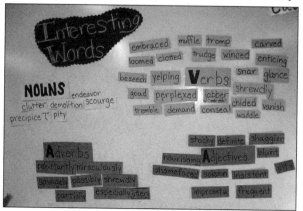

Word-Learning Strategies

- Do shared reading of Big Books and poems, modeling how to use context to determine the meanings of new words and using one color of highlighter tape to mark the word and another color to show what helped you figure out its definition (a picture or other words in the text).
- Use nonfiction Big Books to model (and think aloud about) how to use bold words, italics, and glossaries to figure out word meanings.
- Use colored transparencies of informational text (magazines and other types of news articles) on the overhead for shared reading, especially in grades two and up; model how to reread and figure out meanings of new words.

Trying Out New Words in New Contexts and a Variety of Ways

- Throughout the day, encourage kids to use their new words orally and in writing.
- Keep tally marks on a chart with the new words on it, and add a tally every time a new word is used correctly by a student.
- Model writing in front of the class and show how to use some of the new words; think aloud why you chose a particular word.

Links to Literacy Work Stations Practice

Once you've modeled for students how to think about and learn new words and their meanings, you'll want them to practice trying these strategies during both independent reading and literacy work stations time. Figure 8.14 describes some of the stations children might go to for vocabulary practice.

Links to Standardized and State Testing

Does vocabulary affect student achievement on standardized and state tests? Absolutely! Children

Figure 8.14 Work stations that develop vocabulary.

Literacy Work Station	What Kids Do Here to Practice Vocabulary Strategies	How This Station Supports Vocabulary
Listening Work Station	■ Listen to a recorded book that includes several Tier II words. ■ Stop the tape if they hear a word they don't know the meaning of, and jot down the word; then rewind slightly and listen again to find out what the new word might mean. ■ Draw a picture that represents a new word from the book.	As students listen to language and become aware of new words, they add to their oral vocabulary. This station can be especially beneficial for children who don't hear many books read aloud at home, since it gives them more opportunity to hear rich language.
Pocket Chart Work Station	■ Match vocabulary with kid-friendly definition and picture. ■ Match idiom with what it means. ■ Sort words that go together (synonyms, antonyms, or homonyms). ■ Do a prefix or suffix word sort.	This station gives kids a chance to practice working with new vocabulary by matching and sorting words. The more students work with words, the more they discover about how they work—especially when connected to explicit teaching.
Writing Work Station	■ Use new words from class-made chart to write more effectively. ■ Use a thesaurus to help with word choice (could be class-made). ■ Write a little book (nonfiction) that includes bold words and a glossary.	The more a student uses a word across a variety of contexts, the deeper the child's understanding of that word becomes. Here children apply their knowledge of new words by trying them out in their writing. They can experiment with word choice by using word charts and the thesaurus.
Word Study Work Station	■ Play vocabulary games related to synonyms, antonyms, homophones. ■ Play commercial vocabulary-building games, such as Pictionary Junior.	Working with different kinds of words may heighten students' awareness of many kinds of words. Word-building games make learning vocabulary fun.
Buddy Reading Work Station	■ Read fiction and nonfiction and be on the lookout for new words. ■ Jot down new words and what they think they mean on a chart or sticky notes.	As students pay attention to new words and talk with others about them, they learn how to learn new words.
Magazine Work Station	■ Pay attention to how authors use bold or italicized words. ■ Use these clues to figure out what new words mean. ■ Record new words found.	Reading in a variety of genres exposes children to new words across the curriculum and can also expand content-area vocabulary.
Science or Social Studies Work Stations	■ Use new vocabulary from content-area studies to create diagrams depicting units of study. ■ Add to chart of words related to that unit of study by reading other books about the topic. ■ Play Guess My Word by giving partner clues about a word on the content-area vocabulary chart.	See above.

Figure 8.15 New vocabulary work station. The teacher writes on the file cabinet with a dry erase pen to change the task every few weeks. Students review words using the Elements of Reading kit from Steck-Vaughn.

Figure 8.17 At the science station, students can read about a topic being studied. They can use related vocabulary in their conversations and their writing at this station. They can add new words to the posted list with sticky notes.

Figure 8.16 Word lists that relate to topics of study are brainstormed with the class. They are posted at this writing work station for students to use independently.

easily. Those with a larger, richer vocabulary don't have to guess at what words mean when they answer these types of questions. They often know the answers to the vocabulary questions without even reading the passage.

You'll want to include some direct teaching of new words to improve children's awareness of rich vocabulary, since these are the kinds of words they are tested on. In addition, you'll want to help students use word-learning strategies, like using prefixes and suffixes to tell what words mean. On the TAKS (Texas Assessment of Knowledge and Skills) test, third graders are asked the question, "On page 2, which words tell you what _____ means?" If they have been taught how to read before and after a word to figure out its contextual meaning, they will be able to answer this kind of question.

with limited vocabulary have more difficulty with comprehension, and comprehension is generally what's evaluated on state tests. Children who have learned how to attend to new words and their meanings answer vocabulary-type questions more

Vocabulary Cautions

Remember that research shows that looking up words in a dictionary and copying definitions is not an effective way to teach vocabulary. Teach new words throughout the day in meaningful contexts, both in large group and small group.

Vocabulary is such an important part of comprehension that you may want to include a bit of vocabulary learning in most of your lessons, in the form of either direct teaching of a few new words or learning to apply word-learning strategies to the text. When doing small-group teaching, avoid introducing the vocabulary for the book one day, working on comprehension the second, and practicing decoding skills on the third day. In your small-group lesson, the focus should always be on helping kids construct meaning from the first time they read a book. You'll want to read new text as often as possible to give kids opportunities to try the strategies you're teaching them. They may certainly revisit books you've worked with in small group, but they can do this independently of you.

When trying to help students pay attention to a certain aspect of vocabulary learning, be careful not to ask them to read a passage to find that kind of word. For example, if you are teaching prefixes and suffixes and tell them to find words with these parts, they'll simply be going on a word hunt, and this will take them away from thinking about the meaning of what they're reading. (Trust me, I've tried it and they don't comprehend at all!) *After* reading, they might do a word hunt and list words with prefixes and suffixes to help them see how these word parts work. Your goal is to help them understand how to *use* prefixes and suffixes *while* reading.

Remember to strike a balance between some direct teaching and some indirect learning of vocabulary in your classroom. We can't *give* kids all the vocabulary words they'll ever need, but we can teach them *some* of these words as well as teach them *how* to learn new words on their own.

Reflection Questions for Professional Conversations

1. What are the levels of vocabulary your students are using in their everyday language? Do they speak in sentences to express themselves? Which kids use rich language? Which ones don't? What can you do to encourage greater use of sophisticated vocabulary in your classroom?

2. How are you assessing vocabulary? You might begin by taking anecdotal notes on what you notice about several students' vocabulary use during whole-group and small-group instruction. Take notes now and then again in about six weeks on a few children with limited vocabulary. Plan to really target vocabulary instruction, especially with these kids. Share your ideas and results with a colleague.

3. How have you been choosing words to teach for vocabulary? What new ideas will you try after reading this chapter?

4. With some of your teammates, plan a reading lesson using Tier II vocabulary words. After teaching the lessons, discuss your observations with each other.

For Further Information on Vocabulary Instruction

Try some of the following for more information on teaching vocabulary:

Bear, D., M. Invernizzi, S. Templeton, and F. Johnston. 2000. *Words Their Way: Word Study for Phonics, Vocabulary, and Spelling Instruction.* Upper Saddle River, NJ: Merrill.

Beck, I. L., M. G. McKeown, and L. Kucan. 2002. *Bringing Words to Life.* New York: Guilford.

Brand, M. 2004. *Word Savvy: Integrating Vocabulary, Spelling, and Word Study, Grades 3–6.* Portland, ME: Stenhouse.

Stahl, S. 1999. *Vocabulary Development.* Cambridge, MA: Brookline Books.

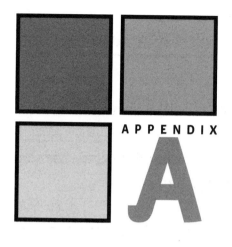

A

Organizing

Planning a Small-Group Lesson

1. Pick a group. Know the reading level.

2. Choose a focus. (Use your data and the reading level strips on the flexible groups folder for help.)

3. Pick a book. Find the LEVEL and match the FOCUS.

4. Plan the lesson.

5. Teach the lesson.

6. Reflect.

How to Choose a Lesson Focus

If You See This	Choose This Focus
■ low phonemic awareness scores ■ lack of response in whole-group lessons on phonemic awareness ■ inconsistency in phonemic awareness tasks ■ difficulty with segmenting sounds (oral task or when writing) ■ difficulty with blending sounds (oral task or when reading)	■ phonemic awareness
■ low letter-sound knowledge ■ decoding difficulties and reading miscues (pay attention to patterns of errors and focus on those phonics elements in small group) ■ spelling difficulties and writing miscues (pay attention to patterns of errors and focus on those phonics elements in small group)	■ phonics
■ low comprehension scores ■ good decoding but poor comprehension ■ basic understanding but could go deeper with comprehension ■ making errors and no self-correction with regard to meaning ■ difficulty with connecting to the text, visualizing, summarizing, or inferring	■ comprehension
■ low fluency scores ■ choppy or word-by-word reading ■ struggling over words ■ reading in a monotone voice with no intonation or expression ■ reading too quickly and not pausing for punctuation	■ fluency
■ low vocabulary scores ■ limited oral vocabulary (even if native English speaker) ■ little or no attention paid to new words while reading (or writing) ■ use of basic words and could use vocabulary expansion ■ lack of content-area word knowledge	■ vocabulary

Note: You may choose a focus and spend several lessons on the same focus. Work with it until you start to see students improving in this area. Then switch the focus to another area that will improve the reading of children in that group. Plan your lessons day by day, basing tomorrow's lesson on what you saw happening today. Small groups need to be flexible.

Suggested Small-Group Reading Lesson Sequence

BEFORE READING

Familiar Rereading	Kids get book bags. They choose familiar books to reread. They read quietly aloud. They read a book other than the running-record book. While kids read other books on their own, take a running record with one child from the book the group read the last time they met. Make a teaching point about what the child did well or needs to do in his or her reading today. Be sure to analyze running records and use this information to plan for prompting during reading in future lessons.
Fluent Writing (for Beginning Readers)	Particularly at early levels, have kids practice writing a few words fast on a dry erase board. These are words you are trying to bring to fluency in reading and writing. They should be high-frequency words. You might use a one-minute egg timer. Ask students, How many times can you write it in one minute?
New Book Introduction *Note:* Consider the students and the demands of text at this level as you plan your book introduction.	Read the title to or with the kids and tell them briefly what the new text will be about. Talk with kids about what they know and what they think the book will be about. Tell children anything they will need to know to understand how the text in this book works. Discuss unfamiliar concepts and words with which they may have no background knowledge. Have kids locate a familiar word or two and an unfamiliar word, especially at early levels. Set purpose for reading. Read to find out . . . (give specifics). Highlight reading strategies you want kids to use today.

DURING READING

Kids Read New Book Independently/Teacher Listens in on the Reading and Gives Prompts	Each student quietly reads the text on his or her own. Observe each child's reading by "listening in" on the child. Prompt when the child gets stuck, but not to fix every error. Take the opportunity to make a teaching point as it arises. Note accuracy, fluency, and comprehension. If possible, record what you noticed. Early finishers may reread for fluency or do some related writing.

AFTER READING

Discuss the Book	Talk with the kids about what they read. Relate back to the purpose set before reading and check for comprehension by having students retell and answer questions. Discuss any tricky words and how students solved them. Have them tell you about questions they had, too. Kids may read aloud favorite parts. Or you may reread for fluency practice.
Teaching Point(s)	Tell the children what you noticed that they did well today in their reading (or have them share). Use your notes and the running record to help you show them specific examples, if possible. Remind children to do that in their reading today.
Word Work (might do as follow-up the next day, depending on your observation of student needs)	Demonstrate principle(s) needed at this level. Have students help solve new words. They may or may not come from today's book. Consider what types of word work best suit the level of the reader. Tell kids how to use this understanding in books they read.
Writing (might do as follow-up the next day, depending on your observation of student needs; or could be done as independent practice)	You might write a summary of the book together. You could scribe or you could do interactive writing of one or two sentences or students could write independently. You might do some kind of follow-up writing, such as listing characters or making a graphic organizer that will aid understanding of the text.

Making the Most of Small Groups: Differentiation for All by Debbie Diller. www.debbiediller.com. Copyright © 2007. Stenhouse Publishers.

Group: _____ Date: _____

Focus/Goal: _____

Title: _____ Level: _____

BEFORE READING

Running Record with: _____ Title: _____

Book Intro:

DURING READING

Prompts:

Notes:

AFTER READING

Discuss:

REFLECTION

When Do I Move a Student into a Different Small Group?

- Use the "Reading Levels and What to Focus on in Lessons" chart in Appendix B.
  - Does the child have all those reading behaviors in place?
  - Consistently?
  - Across a variety of books?
- Use running records. Look at:
  - Fluency (Has rate, phrasing, expression, intonation, and pacing on a variety of texts)
  - Comprehension (Can retell with details on a variety of texts)
- Decoding (Reads consistently with 95 percent accuracy or above.)
- Observe student during the small-group lesson.
  - Does the child finish faster than others?
  - Does the child have better comprehension than others?
  - Is the student having an easier time (working more independently) than the rest of the group?
- Listen in to the child's reading during independent reading. Observe his or her accuracy, fluency, and comprehension and take notes.
- Look at testing data to determine skill improvement or mastery.

Recommendations When Moving Students Up a Level
- Try easier books or tasks at the next level to start.
- Be flexible. Don't be afraid to move the student down again if needed.
- Beware of making a big ceremony of moving up the levels (just in case you have to move down again).

APPENDIX

B

Grouping

Flexible Small Groups Folder

Making the Most of Small Groups: Differentiation for All by Debbie Diller. www.debbiediller.com. Copyright © 2007. Stenhouse Publishers.

Reading Levels and What to Focus on in Lessons

Level	Phonological Awareness	Phonemic Awareness	Concepts About Print	Letter ID	Oral Language	Phonics	Vocabulary	Comprehension	Fluency
PreK/early Kdg.—Pre-Level A	• rhyming • sentence segmenting • syllable blending and segmenting • onset-rime: blending and segmenting	• phoneme segmenting and blending • phoneme substitution and manipulation	• left-to-right movement • return sweep • print matching • paying attention to print (print carries message)	• letter sounds • letter names • letter formation	• is easily understood • speaks in expanding sentences • connects ideas • expands oral vocabulary				
Kdg.—Levels A and B		• phoneme segmenting and blending • phoneme substitution and manipulation	• left-to-right movement • return sweep • 1-1 matching • pays attention to print • begins to self-correct 1-1 matching			• starts to use beginning consonant sounds • may start to use ending consonants, too	• remembers and uses language patterns • acquires sight words • predicts words that might be in the book	• uses pictures to check on words • makes connections	
Kdg./Early first grade—Level C		• phoneme segmenting and blending • phoneme substitution and manipulation	• has left-to-right and return sweep controls 1-1 matching, even on longer words • rereads to self-correct			• decodes CVC words • uses beginning and ending sounds to figure out new words	• uses known words as anchors • acquires high-frequency words	• uses pictures and words to predict meaning • can retell • self-corrects to make sense	
Early first grade—Level D		• phoneme segmenting and blending • phoneme substitution and manipulation				• uses consonants and blends to decode words • uses parts of words (chunks) to predict and check meaning • knows and uses most short vowels	• is acquiring high-frequency (sight) words • uses vocabulary of the book for retelling	• makes predictions and checks on them • uses pictures and words to predict and check meaning • retells • rereads to confirm or problem-solve	• moves away from finger pointing • learning to read in phrases when rereading

continued

Reading Levels and What to Focus on in Lessons

	Phonics	Vocabulary	Comprehension	Fluency
Early first grade—Level E	■ decodes slightly longer words ■ uses long vowel sounds, including two-letter vowels (*ay, ea, ai,* etc.) ■ reads compound words	■ continues to acquire high-frequency words ■ uses new vocabulary, especially when reading nonfiction	■ makes predictions and checks on them ■ using words more than pictures ■ makes connections across texts ■ rereads to check meaning ■ retells and remembers	■ finger-points only on hard words ■ starting to read in phrases ■ sounds more fluent, especially while rereading
First grade—Level F	■ uses short and long vowel sounds more flexibly ■ decoding more two- and three-syllable words ■ begins to use vowel + *r* combinations	■ notices new words and figures out meanings, using the picture for support ■ learns new words, especially when reading nonfiction	■ makes and checks predictions ■ using words more than pictures ■ makes connections across texts ■ rereads ■ retells and remembers ■ needs to infer at times	■ notices punctuation and uses for phrasing ■ beginning to use more intonation ■ moves more quickly through text
First grade—Levels G and H	■ uses short and long vowel sounds more flexibly ■ learns and uses more complex vowel patterns (funky chunks) ■ decoding more two- and three-syllable words ■ vowel + *r* work	■ pays attention to new vocabulary while reading ■ uses new words in retelling and conversation ■ rereads to get meaning of new words	■ deeper understanding of characters ■ text-to-text connections ■ retells with more detail ■ determines importance	■ pays attention to a wider variety of punctuation and uses for phrasing ■ uses more intonation and expression ■ moves more quickly through longer text
End of first grade—Level I	■ decodes most one- and two-syllable words easily ■ growing grasp of "funky chunks" (*ough, eigh, au, oi,* etc.) ■ decodes silent letters like *kn, wr, gn*	■ pays more attention to new words and tries to figure out their meaning ■ discovers specialized vocabulary in nonfiction	■ begins to learn how to build schema on less familiar topics ■ retells with increasing detail using graphic organizers ■ connects to characters and topics	■ reads in a more fluent, phrased way ■ uses character voices ■ reads with intonation and expression ■ begins to transition to silent reading

continued

Making the Most of Small Groups: Differentiation for All by Debbie Diller. www.debbiediller.com. Copyright © 2007. Stenhouse Publishers.

Reading Levels and What to Focus on in Lessons

	Phonics	Vocabulary	Comprehension	Fluency
Early–mid-second grade— Levels J and K	■ decodes longer words (two–three syllables) ■ decodes two–four vowel combinations (*ou, igh, ough,* etc.) more easily on longer words ■ decodes silent letters on longer words (*kn, wr, gn,* etc.) ■ may use pronunciation guide in nonfiction	■ pays attention to new words and uses context of words and pictures to determine meaning ■ starting to read and understand idioms and figurative language ■ understands meanings of homophones and homographs ■ uses prefixes and suffixes to determine word meanings	■ moves more flexibly from fiction to nonfiction ■ summarizes and extends text ■ comprehends text read over several days ■ infers, predicts, and analyzes characters ■ uses text features to aid comprehension in nonfiction	■ processes the text more smoothly ■ reads in phrases and with expression over longer text ■ reads silently most of the time
Mid-second grade—Level L	■ decodes more multisyllabic words and many words with two–four vowel combinations within those longer words (*eigh, augh,* etc.) ■ decodes words with chunks like *tion, ance, cial,* etc. ■ decodes more quickly, which aids fluency	■ understands more difficult vocabulary ■ understands idioms and figurative language in text ■ prefixes and suffixes used to figure out word meanings	■ figures out who's talking when reading more complex dialogue ■ deeper understanding of multiple characters ■ comprehends longer chapters ■ greater range of genre understood ■ uses text features and structures	■ sustains fluency while reading longer sentences and longer texts ■ reads more rapidly with phrasing and limited self-correcting ■ reads character voices with greater intonation
End of second grade—Level M	■ decodes longer words with more complex phonics patterns ■ can decode most two–three-syllable words ■ uses letter sounds flexibly and fluently (sounds of *c, g,* and vowels, etc.)	■ understand more sophisticated vocabulary and more complex language structures ■ prefixes and suffixes used for determining meaning ■ reads and understands many new vocabulary words, especially in nonfiction	■ understands subtlety of plot and humor ■ builds schema for unfamiliar topics when reading ■ infers, reads critically, makes more connections ■ deeper understanding of multiple characters ■ expands reading in a variety of genres ■ visualizes as pictures are included less	■ sustains fluency while reading longer sentences and longer text ■ reads more rapidly with phrasing and limited self-correcting ■ reads character voices smoothly and with greater intonation ■ varies reading rate depending on the type of text read

continued

Reading Levels and What to Focus on in Lessons

Third grade—
Levels N, O, P

Phonics

■ decodes most two–four-syllable words
■ uses letter sounds flexibly and fluently
■ may miscue simple words (like *a* and *the*) when reading more fluently—words that don't change the meaning

Vocabulary

■ understands more sophisticated vocabulary and more complex language structures in longer text
■ wider range of prefixes and suffixes used to determine meaning of new words
■ is exposed to many new words in both fiction and nonfiction and determines meaning

Comprehension

■ infers, reads critically, makes deeper connections
■ asks more questions as reading
■ answers higher-level questions with increasing depth
■ reads across a wider variety of genres
■ visualizes most of the time

Fluency

■ sustains fluency on longer texts with more complex sentences and wider range of punctuation and text nuances
■ reads more rapidly with phrasing and limited self-correcting on longer text
■ uses intonation and expression to match mood, characters, type of text, etc. (interpretive reading)

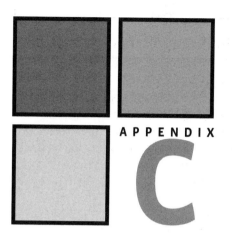

C

Comprehension

Possible Focuses for Comprehension Lessons

Understanding text structure	Use in fiction and nonfiction Teach students how to think about characters, setting, problem, solution, and beginning/middle/end of a story before and during their reading, as well as after. Teach how to identify nonfiction text structures, such as cause and effect, description, question and answer, and time order or sequence.
Asking questions	Teach kids how to generate and ask inferential questions. Use sticky notes to have them jot down questions they have as they read. They can move notes to show where questions were answered in the text, too.
Answering questions	Have students answer questions about the details and inferences of the text Ask more *thick* questions that require deeper thinking and have potentially layered responses rather than *thin* questions that require only one-word answers.
Summarizing	Kids must first demonstrate basic comprehension and also determine which ideas are most important in order to summarize. Focus on helping readers learn to identify and remember the main ideas or events from the text read.
Using schema/making use of prior knowledge	Help kids use their personal experience and schema (background knowledge) to help them understand what they are reading. Have them do this before reading as they preview the text as well as during their reading.
Visualizing (using mental imagery)	Readers with strong comprehension form vivid mental pictures. They often see, hear, taste, smell, and feel what's going on in the book. Quick sketching helps some kids learn to visualize while reading.
Monitoring	Help kids learn to stop and reread when their mind wanders or when meaning breaks down. Successful readers think about their thinking and are aware when it's not working so well.
Inference	Teach students to think by modeling and expecting that they can and will infer. Build on their background knowledge and insist that they use the text as well. Help kids connect what they know to what the text says, and they can begin to infer.
Graphic organizers	Use these as tools for thinking while kids read, especially when they have trouble comprehending. Graphic organizers can be used as reminders and recording devices for what a reader is thinking.
Deeper meaning	This includes higher-level thinking, including generalizing, determining importance, synthesizing, and analyzing what was read. Use of quality questioning will help push kids' thinking deeper.

Group: _____ **Date:** _____

Focus: COMPREHENSION

☐ monitoring ☐ schema ☐ asking ?s ☐ visualizing ☐ inference
☐ summarizing ☐ text structure ☐ graphic organizers ☐ deeper meaning

Warm-Up: Familiar Reading   **Listen to:** _____ **Title:** _____

Today's Book: _____ **Level:** _____

BEFORE READING

Book Intro:

Genre:

Set purpose for reading:

Read to find out:

DURING READING

Prompts:

Notes:

AFTER READING

Discuss:

REFLECTION

Prompts for Comprehension

What Child Is Having Trouble With	Possible Teacher Prompts
■ monitoring	■ *You stopped. Is it making sense?* ■ *What have you read about so far?* ■ *Rereading is smart. When you don't understand what you've read, go back and read it again.*
■ using schema/making connections	■ *What does that make you think about/remind you of? How does that help you understand what you're reading?* ■ *What do you already know about ___? How can that help you?*
■ asking questions	■ *What are you wondering about as you read?* ■ *What questions do you have?* ■ *Did the author answer any of your questions? Where?* ■ *What questions do you still have?*
■ visualizing	■ *What are you picturing? What do you see/hear/smell/feel as you read this?* ■ *Which part helped you see something more clearly?*
■ inference	■ *What might happen next? What else might you find out?* ■ *Why do you think . . . ?* ■ *Join together what you know with what the words say. What are you thinking now?* ■ *What does the author mean? How did you figure that out?*
■ summarizing	■ *If you wanted to tell a friend about what you just read, what would you say? Don't give away the whole thing. Just tell what it was mostly about.* ■ *What are the most important parts?*
■ using text structure	■ *What kind of structure did this author use? question/answer . . . problem/solution . . . compare and contrast . . . time order* ■ *How can that help you understand what you're reading?*
■ using graphic organizers	■ *What kind of graphic organizer might help you better understand what you're reading? How could that help you?* ■ *Try a graphic organizer that might help you think about what you're reading and help to organize your thoughts.*
■ deeper meaning	■ *Why? What else are you thinking?* ■ *How could that have happened?* ■ *Tell me more.*

Whole-Group Lesson for COMPREHENSION

Focus: using schema (prior knowledge)

Method to maximize student engagement: jotting down their ideas on sticky notes, dry erase boards, or clipboards

Materials: book relating to topic of interest to students—things for which they have background knowledge (to begin); large sticky notes and pencils or dry erase boards for you and students

Model: making connections (text-to-self or text-to-text)

Explicit language:

■ *That reminds me of . . . and helps me better understand . . .*

■ *That's a text-to-self connection. It's like something from my life.*

■ *That's a text-to-text connection. It's like another book I read . . .*

Lesson:

NOTE: This lesson works best if you've modeled *your* thinking about using your schema several times prior to this lesson.

1. Tell students that today they'll learn about using *schema* or what they already know to help them better understand what they read.

2. Give each child something to write on (sticky notes, dry erase materials, or clipboards) and tell them you want them to think about what the book reminds them of during your read-aloud.

3. Model by using your sticky note or dry erase board to model what the book reminds you of before you read. Use the title and pictures from the cover.

4. As you read aloud, have them jot down connections they are making. Pause at selected points and give them time to talk or write. You might use a two-column entry—My Connections; How It Helps Me Understand. (In kindergarten or early first grade, have kids talk to a partner about their connections and how those help them understand, instead of writing.)

5. After reading, have kids share their connections with partners. Then have several share with the class. Help them to see that their connections should help them better comprehend.

Small-group connection: Use books kids can easily connect to for starters. Have them jot down their connections on sticky notes and share how these helped them comprehend.

Whole-Group Lesson for COMPREHENSION

Focus: visualizing

Method to maximize student engagement: sketching on blank paper on clipboards; sharing with a partner

Materials: poem (or other short text) of interest to students, printed so all can see on a chart , a transparency, or in a PowerPoint; paper and pencils for students; chart paper and markers

Model: think about what you're picturing in your mind as you read

Explicit language:

- *I see . . . in my mind; I hear. . . I can almost taste . . . It smells like . . . I can almost feel . . .*
- *Those words made me picture . . .*

Lesson:

1. Choose a poem that creates a strong visual image. Look for one with strong verbs and vivid adjectives. Copy it onto a chart, a transparency, or into PowerPoint.
2. Read the poem to them once for enjoyment. Then read it again with them a line or a stanza at a time, asking them to sketch what they see in their minds as you read.
3. Start with the title. Read it and give them a minute to draw what they're picturing in their minds—it's a sketch. Do your own, too. Let them share briefly with a partner.
4. Then read a few lines, pause, and have them sketch what they are picturing now in their minds. Again, join them.
5. Continue in this way until finished.
6. After reading, talk about the pictures and how they changed as the poem continued. Help them see that they may have slightly different pictures depending on their schema. But they should be creating pictures in their minds as they read.

Small-group connection: Read a poem or other short text in small group that creates a strong visual image. Remind students to think about what they are visualizing. They might even do a quick sketch of what they see in their minds, just like they did in the whole-group lesson. Have them share words that created particularly strong pictures in their minds as they read.

NOTE: It's best to do this with texts with fewer pictures. If the books have lots of pictures, kids don't need to visualize as much.

Whole-Group Lesson for COMPREHENSION

Focus: summarizing

Method to maximize student engagement: choice of an interesting text; showing your thinking and writing it down; buddy talk (talking to a partner near them); shared writing of a summary

Materials: short, high-interest text (picture book, news article, opening paragraphs, or a short chapter); chart paper and markers

Model: how to choose and use new words in writing about something you know and care about

Explicit language:

- *If you wanted to tell a friend about what you just read, what would you say? Don't give away the whole thing. Just tell what it was mostly about.*
- *Summarize—say it in just a few sentences.*
- *What was most important?*

Lesson:

1. Choose an interesting text that kids will find easy to summarize. Tell students that summarizing can help them understand what they read. They'll have to think about what was most important in the text, since they'll have to say it in just a sentence or two.
2. Read the beginning, stop, and think aloud about what was most important. Jot it down by the word *Beginning*. It might be useful in your summary.
3. Continue this procedure with the middle and end of the text, labeling them also. You might have kids join in and talk with a buddy to summarize the section you just read, depending on their readiness. They can compare their ideas to yours.
4. When finished reading, come up with a summary together. You can do it orally or in writing. If you write it, have kids tell you what to write (shared writing).

Small-group connection: You might have students place a sticky note on preselected pages at the end of the beginning, middle, and end of a short book. Have them jot down what they think was most important in each section. Then work together after reading to tell summaries. If they get good at this, they might write a summary.

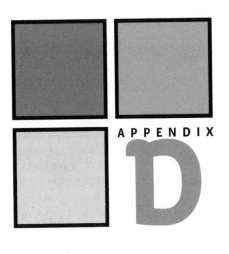

D

Fluency

Possible Focuses for Fluency Lessons

Decoding words effortlessly and automatically	Students who are able to easily decode words will be able to give more attention to phrasing and expressive reading. Focus on strategies that help students "chunk" words by reading parts of words rather than decoding letter by letter. Record decoding errors using a running record or a miscue analysis and look for patterns of words misread.
High-frequency-word work	Practicing with sight words or words that appear often in text will often help students achieve greater fluency.
Reading the punctuation	Help students see the purpose of punctuation. The author put it there intentionally to give meaning to the text. Teach students to pause at commas, stop at periods, read excitedly with exclamation marks, and sound like the character when the words are in quotations.
Reading in phrases	Teach kids how to move their eyes more quickly across the line to the end of a phrase. Help them to read in phrases so it sounds like speech (rather than reading word by word). Discourage finger pointing to each word when working on reading fluency.
Reading with intonation and expression	Teach students to vary their voices by changing pitch, dialect, and even speed as they portray events and information. Tell students to "read so it sounds interesting."
Reading dialogue	Show students how to change their voices when different characters speak. By doing so, they have to think about each character and what he or she is really like.
Regulating the speed of reading	Teach students how to vary the rate at which they read. While reading, they should speed up their reading when the action is exciting and slow down their reading when they want to illustrate that something is suspenseful.

Group: _____ **Date:** _____

Focus: FLUENCY

☐ fast decoding ☐ HF words ☐ punctuation ☐ phrases

☐ intonation and expression ☐ dialogue ☐ adjusting rate

Warm-Up: Familiar Reading **Listen to:** _____ **Title:** _____

Today's Book: _____ **Level:** _____

BEFORE READING

Book Intro:

Set purpose for reading:

Read to find out:

DURING READING

Prompts:

Notes:

AFTER READING

Discuss:

REFLECTION

Fluency Score Rubric

Name: _____ Date: _____

1. choppy reading; no stops at . , ?

2. mostly choppy reading with a little bit of reading so it sounds interesting; some stops at . , ?

3. some choppy reading, but mostly reading so it sounds interesting; stops at . , ?

4. reading so it sounds interesting; stops at . , ?

Fluency Score Rubric

Name: _____ Date: _____

1. choppy reading; no stops at . , ?

2. mostly choppy reading with a little bit of reading so it sounds interesting; some stops at . , ?

3. some choppy reading, but mostly reading so it sounds interesting; stops at . , ?

4. reading so it sounds interesting; stops at . , ?

Prompts for Fluency

What Child Is Having Trouble With	Possible Teacher Prompts
Decoding words effortlessly and automatically	■ *Read through the word quickly and think about what makes sense.* ■ *Use the parts you know and read it fast.*
High-frequency-word work	■ *That's a word you know.* ■ *It's a word-wall word.* ■ *It's a spelling word.*
Reading the punctuation	■ *Stop at the periods.* ■ *Make your voice go up at the end of a question.* ■ *Read it with excitement.* ■ *Someone's talking. Sound like that character.*
Reading in phrases	■ *Think about where you'd pause if you were talking.* ■ *Read to the punctuation and stop.* ■ *Read it in phrases.*
Reading dialogue	■ *Who's talking here?* ■ *Read it like the character would say it.*
Reading with intonation and expression	■ *Make it sound interesting.* ■ *Make your voice go up at the end when there's a question mark.* ■ *Read it with excitement when you see an exclamation point.* ■ *Your reading helps me know how that character feels.*
Regulating the speed of reading	■ *Speed up the exciting parts.* ■ *Use pauses to build anticipation.*

Making the Most of Small Groups: Differentiation for All by Debbie Diller. www.debbiediller.com. Copyright © 2007. Stenhouse Publishers.

Sources of Easy-to-Read Plays and Reader's Theater

Note: Make enough copies of reader's theater texts for each child in the group to have one.

Internet Sources for Reader's Theater

www.readinglady.com

http://raven.jmu.edu/~ramseyil/redhen.htm

www.stemnet.nf.ca/CITE/langrt.htm

http://raven.jmu.edu/~ramseyil/billygoat.htm

www.aaronshep.com/rt/RTE.html

http://falcon.jmu.edu/~ramseyil/readersmine.htm

Sources for Short, Easy-to-Read Plays

Bany-Winters, Lisa. 1997. *On Stage: Theater Games and Activities for Kids*. Chicago: Chicago Review Press.

———. 2000. *Show Time: Music, Dance, and Drama Activities for Kids*. Chicago: Chicago Review Press.

Barchers, Suzanne. 1993. *Reader's Theater for Beginning Readers*. Greenwood Village, CO: Teacher Ideas Press.

Blau, Lisa. 1997. *Fall Is Fabulous! Reader's Theatre Scripts and Extended Activities*. Bellevue, WA: One from the Heart.

———. 1997. *Favorite Folktales and Fabulous Fables: Multicultural Plays with Extended Activities*. Bellevue, WA: One from the Heart.

———. 1997. *Super Science! Readers Theatre Scripts and Extended Activities*. Bellevue, WA: One from the Heart.

Crawford, Sheryl Ann, and Nancy I. Sanders. 2001. *Fifteen Easy-to-Read Holiday and Seasonal Mini-Book Plays*. New York: Scholastic.

———. 2001. *Fifteen Easy-to-Read Mini-Book Plays*. New York: Scholastic.

———. 2003. *Fifteen Easy-to-Read Neighborhod and Community Mini-Book Plays*. New York: Scholastic.

———. 1999. *Fifteen Irresistible Mini-Plays for Teaching Math*. New York: Scholastic Professional Books.

———. 2001. *Just Right Plays: Twenty-Five Science Plays for Emergent Readers*. New York: Scholastic Professional Books.

Cullum, Albert, and Janet Skiles. 1993. *Aesop's Fables: Plays for Young Children*. Parsippany, NJ: Fearon Teacher Aids.

Laughlin, Mildred, et al. 1991. *Social Studies Readers Theater for Children: Scripts and Script Development*. Englewood, CO: Libraries Unlimited.

Martin, Justin McCory. 2002. *Twelve Fabulously Funny Fairy Tale Plays*. New York: Scholastic Professional Books.

Pugliano-Martin, Carol. 2002. *Fifteen Plays About Famous Americans for Emergent Readers*. New York: Scholastic Professional Books.

———. 1999. *Twenty-Five Emergent Reader Plays Around the Year*. New York: Scholastic Professional Books.

———. 1999. *Twenty-Five Just-Right Plays for Emergent Readers*. New York: Scholastic Professional Books.

———. 1999. *Twenty-Five Spanish Plays for Emergent Readers*. New York: Scholastic Professional Books.

———. 1998. *Just-Right Plays: Twenty-Five Science Plays for Emergent Readers*. New York: Scholastic Professional Books.

Pugliano, Carol, and Carolyn Croll. 1999. *Easy-to-Read Folk and Fairy Plays*. New York: Scholastic Professional Books.

Schafer, Liza, and Nancy I. Shafer. 1999. *Fifteen Easy-to-Read Mini-Books Plays*. New York: Scholastic Professional Books.

West, Tracy. 2000. *Big Book of Thematic Plays*. New York: Scholastic Professional Books.

Little Books for Reader's Theater

Leveled books for reader's theater are available from the following sources.

Reader's Theater series. Pelham, NY: Benchmark Education.

Rigby PM Collection Orange Tales and Plays. Barrington, IL: Rigby.

Inside Stories series. DeSoto, TX: Wright Group.

Whole-Group Lesson for FLUENCY

Focus: improving automaticity/reading in phrases

Method to maximize student engagement: echo reading (or choral reading) with all students reading together

Materials: poems on charts or short pieces of text written in phrases; pointer

Model: reading smoothly in phrases

Explicit language:
- *Move your eyes across the page quickly.*
- *Read it in phrases.*

Lesson:
1. State lesson purpose: to read in phrases so it sounds like talking and will help you better understand what you read.
2. Look at poem together. Point out how the words are written in phrases.
3. Read it to the class, using a pointer to show how to glide across the words and read to the end of the line.
4. Remind children to move their eyes quickly across the page to the end of the line. Tell them this is called reading in phrases and that it helps the reading sound more like talking.
5. Then have them read it chorally with you or echo read it (read each line after you read it to them).
6. Discuss the poem you just read. Be sure kids comprehend it. Talk about interesting words in the poem, too.
7. You might have students read the poem several times, noting how their fluency improves each time they read it.
8. You might give each child a copy of the poem to be kept in a poetry folder. Kids can reread it during independent reading time for fluency practice.

Small-group connection: Have students read text written in phrases to practice . . . remind them to move their eyes quickly across the page just like they did when reading in phrases in the whole-group lesson.

Making the Most of Small Groups: Differentiation for All by Debbie Diller. www.debbiediller.com. Copyright © 2007. Stenhouse Publishers.

Whole-Group Lesson for FLUENCY

Focus: building accurate decoding

Method to maximize student engagement: shared reading with all students reading together

Materials: Big Book with onomatopoeia or some nonsense words, such as *The Jumbaroo* by Joy Cowley; colored sticky notes

Model: fast, accurate decoding

Explicit language:

- *Blend the sounds fast.*
- *When you come to a new word, look for parts you know.*

Lesson:

1. Choose a book with large print, so kids can easily read along with you. Ahead of time, mask some of the nonsense words with colored sticky notes.
2. Read the title and make predictions. Help kids look for parts they know to decode the title (*Jum- bar- oo*)
3. Tell them that this book will have some nonsense or fun, made-up words in it. They will have to blend the sounds and look for parts they know to read the new words. They will also have to think about what these new words might mean.
4. Begin reading the book and have kids take guesses at the covered-up words. For example, cover up the word *woggly* and have kids guess that it means "stomach," based upon the picture and what would make sense there. Then unmask the word, one part at a time, and have kids decode it. Blend it together fast.
5. Be sure to talk about meaning as you read the book and figure out the nonsense words and what they mean.
6. After reading, repeat the reading again several days in a row, reminding your class to read it so it sounds interesting.

Small-group connection: Read a short text with nonsense words or onomatopoeia (or just new words) . . . no more than about three to four new words per 100 words of text. Remind students how to blend sounds and/or look for parts they know just like they did in the whole-group lesson.

Whole-Group Lesson for FLUENCY

Focus: developing interpretive and meaningful reading

Method to maximize student engagement: reader's theater or read a play with the whole class

Materials: reader's theater script (on chart paper or transparency) or individual copies for each child (Scholastic has many great resources); colored pens

Model: reading with different character voices in a dramatic way

Explicit language:

■ *Read it so it sounds like the character.*

■ *Make it sound interesting.*

Lesson:

1. State lesson purpose: to read like the character voices would sound to make it interesting and to help you understand better.

2. Show the script to the class. Use a transparency or chart so everyone can see it. Look at the different format used. Point out the box with character names listed and why that is used. Look at how each character's name is written in bold letters followed by a colon to show what each says.

3. Read the title and make predictions about what the play will be about. Then read it all together, using different voices for each part. You might circle each different part with a different-colored pen to show different voices. For example, circle the police officer's lines in blue, the firefighter's in red, the teacher's in green, the librarian's in brown, etc.

4. After reading through the whole script, read it again, assigning different parts to different groups of students. Be sure each child is in a group!

5. Read the script several days in a row, reminding the class to read so it sounds like the character and to make it sound interesting. You might even add simple student-made props, such as character hats made from sentence strip and construction paper, on the final day of reading to enhance comprehension.

Small-group connection: Have a small group read the same or another reader's theater or play while you serve as the "director." Help them read using expression just like what was modeled in the whole-group lesson.

Making the Most of Small Groups: Differentiation for All by Debbie Diller. www.debbiediller.com. Copyright © 2007. Stenhouse Publishers.

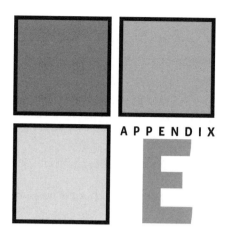

APPENDIX

E

Phonemic Awareness

Possible Focuses for Phonological Awareness Lessons

Rhyming	Look at students' stages of rhyming development. Teach rhyming by playing with language while using nursery rhymes, poems, songs, objects, pictures, and rhyming books.
Alliteration	Help children listen for words that start with the same letter. Use books, nursery rhymes, objects, pictures, and songs to do this.
Sentence segmenting	Have kids hold up a finger for each word in a sentence as you're thinking of a message to write together. Ask students to push counters or blocks for each word said in a sentence. Again, play with language.
Syllable blending and segmenting	Begin with children's names or book titles. For segmenting, have them clap the parts of their names, like *Thom-as*. To blend syllables, call students by their names, such as *Bri-an-na* and have children say, "Brianna" while that child stands up or children point to her picture on a chart.

Possible Focuses for Phonemic Awareness Lessons

Onset/rime segmenting and blending	Play games with words, helping students isolate the first part of a word from the rest of it. For example, point to your *leg* and say \l\eg\. Onset is the part before the vowel, and rime is the part including and after the vowel. In *leg*, \l\ is the onset and \eg\ is the rime. Use one-syllable words for onset and rime.
Sound matching	Kids match sounds that are the same. They might tell which word doesn't belong, based on the beginning sounds, or they might generate words that start with that sound. Kids don't need to know alphabet letters to be successful here. They are focusing on the sounds. Sorting objects and pictures works well.
Counting phonemes in a word	Use objects or pictures or just say a word aloud. Have children hold up a finger for each sound as they say the word slowly.
Blending phonemes to make a word	Give children individual speech sounds and have them try to guess the word. For example, "I'm thinking of a word. I'll say it slowly and you guess it. \M\ou\se\." Kids say, "Mouse."
Isolating the beginning phoneme in a word	Have students isolate just the first sound of a word. To do this, kids enjoy repeating the first sound several times, such as in *c-c-c-car*.
Isolating the final phoneme in a word	This is similar to the preceding task, except now the emphasis is on the last sound in a word. You might help them do "echo talk" and have them repeat the last sound in a word. For example, my name is *Deb-b-b-b*.
Isolating the medial phoneme in a word	This is the hardest of all for most kids to do since it involves listening to the sound in the middle. Use words with only three phonemes for this, such as *light, bag, hat, meal, soup, net, hug, feel,* and *name*. Have kids tell the sound they hear in the middle of the word. Focus on the sound, not the letter.
Segmenting phonemes in a word	Again, play with the sounds of words. This is one of the more difficult phonemic awareness tasks, but if kids have been successful at the preceding tasks, this will be much easier. Here they must take a word and break it into parts. It's easiest to begin with two-phoneme words such as *bee* and *two*. Use picture cards and objects to play with this task, then move to three-phoneme words, and then to four. You might have kids add body motions to help, having them touch their head while saying the first sound, touch their shoulders during the medial sound, and touch their waist as they say the final sound.
Substituting one phoneme for another	This is fun to do with songs or with kids' names. Take a familiar song such as "Mary Had a Little Lamb," and sing it with a new sound at the start of each word, such as \w\. You'd sing, "Wary wad a wittle wamb, wittle wamb, wittle wamb. Wary wad a wittle wamb. Wits weece was white was whoa." This will work only if the kids really know the original version.
Deleting phonemes from words	This is much easier to do once you've attached some print to the sounds. For example, if you tell kids to say *plop* without the *l*, that's much easier to do if you can see the print. This is not the goal of phonemic awareness. Most of the research points to phonemic segmentation, not phoneme deletion, as being key to children learning to read.

Group: _____   Date: _____

Focus: PHONOLOGICAL AWARENESS

☐ rhyming   ☐ alliteration   ☐ sentence segmenting

☐ syllable blending and segmenting ☐ onset and rime blending and segmenting

Activity 1:

Activity 2:

Prompts:

Notes:

REFLECTION

Making the Most of Small Groups: Differentiation for All by Debbie Diller. www.debbiediller.com. Copyright © 2007. Stenhouse Publishers.

Group: _____ Date: _____

Focus: PHONEMIC AWARENESS

☐ sound matching   ☐ initial sound isolation   ☐ final sound isolation

☐ medial sound isolation   ☐ sound blending   ☐ sound segmenting

☐ sound addition, deletion, or substitution

Activity 1:

Activity 2:

Activity 3:

Prompts:

Notes:

REFLECTION

Rhyming Groups Folder

can't hear/can't produce rhymes

can hear but can't produce rhymes

can hear/can produce some rhymes

can hear and produce rhymes consistently

syllable blending and
segmenting
cat/nip

sentence segmentation
The/cat/is/furry.

rhyming and alliteration
cat/hat
cat/cup

Less Complex Tasks

More Complex Tasks

individual phonemes, including blending and segmenting
\c\a\t\

onset and rime blending and segmenting
\c\at\

Begin phonemic awareness activities here.

Phonological Awareness Groups Folder

Prompts for Phonemic Awareness

What Child Is Having Trouble With	Possible Teacher Prompts
Rhyming	■ *What rhymes with _____?* ■ *It sounds the same at the end.* ■ *_____, _____. Hear how they're the same at the end.* ■ *(Jill), (/b/) _____. (Give first sound to scaffold rhyming.)*
Alliteration	■ *_____, _____ sound the same at the beginning.* ■ *What else starts like _____ _____?*
Sentence segmenting	■ *Listen for each word in the sentence.* ■ *Push the block for each word you hear.* ■ *Clap each word with me.* ■ *_____ is just one word, not two.*
Syllable blending and segmenting	■ *Put the parts together. Say the word.* ■ *Break the word into parts. Clap it with me.*
Onset-rime blending and segmenting	■ *Put the sounds together. Say the word fast.* ■ *Say the parts. I'll start and you finish. (cat . . . \c\ . . .)*
Counting phonemes in a word*	■ *Push a counter each time you hear a sound.*
Phoneme isolation (initial, final, medial)*	■ *Listen for _____. Where do you hear_____? At the beginning, the middle, or the end of the word?* ■ *Look at my mouth. Make your mouth look like this when you say _____.*
Blending phonemes*	■ *Put the sounds together. Blend them to say the word.* ■ *Say the sounds fast. Say the word.*
Segmenting phonemes*	■ *Say the word slowly.* ■ *Say it sound by sound.*
Adding, deleting, or substituting phonemes*	■ *Add _____ to _____. What's the new word?* ■ *Take away _____. What word do you hear now?*

Whole-Group Lesson for PHONOLOGICAL AWARENESS

Focus: syllable blending and segmenting

Method to maximize student engagement: chanting, clapping, and playing with the sounds of children's names

Materials: photos of your students

Model: how to blend or segment syllables

Explicit language:
- *Put the parts together to say the name.*
- *Clap the parts of _____'s name.*
- *How many parts does _____'s name have?*

Lesson:
1. Tell the kids they will play a Name Game. There is a mystery child and they have to figure out who it is. You'll say the parts of this person's name and they have to say the name and point to this child. (Say the name syllable by syllable, like *Bri-an*.)
2. Repeat with lots of names. Have kids clap the syllables with you and say the name again. Tell how many parts in the name, too.
3. To segment, have kids lead the game. They think of a name and segment it, and others guess the name.

Small-group connection: You can play a similar game in small group with kids who need extra support with this phonological skill. Use it as one brief activity, so kids don't tire of it. Vary the game by using picture cards, or by naming objects in a photo.

Whole-Group Lesson for PHONEMIC AWARENESS

Focus: phoneme segmentation

Method to maximize student engagement: chorally saying sounds slowly and touching head, shoulders, and waist in order to represent speech sounds (using voice and body)

Materials: overhead projector; sound boxes drawn on transparency; picture cards to use on overhead; plastic counters

Model: how to say a word slowly, segmenting each phoneme (smallest speech sound)

Explicit language:

- *Say the word slowly.*
- *Push a counter into the next box each time you hear a new sound.*

Lesson:

1. Show a picture on the overhead. Have kids say the word and then say it slowly, sound by sound. Begin with two-phoneme words, like *toe* and *bee*. Then progress to three-phoneme words.
2. Have a child come to the overhead and demonstrate how to push a plastic counter into each box on the overhead as he says each speech sound in order.
3. The rest of the kids touch their heads on the first phoneme, their shoulders on the next phoneme, and their waists on the final sound as they say the sounds in order. This physical movement can help them cement this in their brains.
4. Repeat with other pictures until many kids have had a turn at the overhead.

Small-group connection: Do a similar lesson with kids in small group. Focus on two-phoneme words with kids having difficulty. Then move to three- and four-phoneme words. Kids can do this independently at work stations, too, after they've practiced with you in small group and are starting to show signs of success.

Whole-Group Lesson for PHONEMIC AWARENESS

Focus: medial sound isolation

Method to maximize student engagement: manipulating letter cards in a pocket chart game

Materials: picture cards (of three-phoneme objects); letter cards that fit in pocket chart (vowel cards); pocket chart with Wikki Stix dividing it into number of sounds in a word in one pocket

Model: how to say words slowly and think about the sound in the middle

Explicit language:
- *Say the word slowly and think about the middle sound.*
- *What sound do you hear in the middle?*
- *Where do you hear the sound _____?*

Lesson:

1. Play Sound in the Middle. Use a pocket chart with one pocket divided into the number of sounds in the words you'll use. Use Wikki Stix to "draw" lines on one pocket to show where each sound goes.

2. Show a picture of something with three phonemes, like a pig. Have kids say *pig* with you and tell them to say it slowly, sound by sound with you, \p\i\g\. Tell them to do it again and listen for the middle sound. Have them use their right hand to touch their shoulder as they say the first sound, inside their elbow as they say the second sound, and their wrist as they say the final sound. Ask them to say the sound in the middle (\i\).

3. After kids do this, one child puts the *i* card in the middle part of the pocket to show where this letter goes.

4. Repeat with other words, like *log, map, pot, tub, dog, cat, pen.*

Small-group connection: Repeat in a similar way in small group. Give each kid sound cards and lowercase vowel cards. Use only vowels they know. Review vowel sounds first and have a vowel sound chart handy to help kids use these. NOTE: If it's too hard for kids to match the correct letter, abandon the letters and just focus on kids hearing which sound is in the middle. Or hand the child the vowel card to put in the middle to help him apply the alphabetic principle.

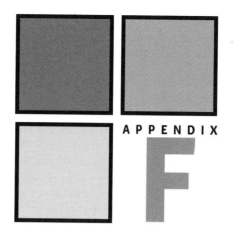

F

Phonics

Possible Focuses for Phonics Lessons

Initial letter sounds	Teach kids how to identify and apply the first letter sound of words. They can do this in reading and writing.
Final letter sounds	Teach students to read through words from left to right. Look for final sounds to show up in the writing of beginning readers. Once you see them do this, you'll know they can learn to apply these sounds in their reading, too.
Short vowel sounds	When teaching kids about vowels, I like to highlight them in a different color, such as red, so children pay attention to them. They should learn that every word has a vowel in it. They should also learn that some letters, including vowels, make more than one sound in English. Many phonics programs teach short vowels first, so kids can blend these into CVC words.
CVC patterns and blending sounds	CVC words are made up of an initial and final consonant with a short vowel in between (consonant-vowel-consonant pattern). Many kindergarten and early first-grade programs focus on these words—words like *cat, hog, big, mop,* and *lap.* Once children know approximately ten letters and sounds, including at least one short vowel sound, they can begin to blend these sounds to read CVC words.
Long vowel sounds	Long vowel sounds are more complex, because there are multiple ways to represent these in English.
Vowel + *r* patterns	These are words containing *ar, er, ir, or, ur,* and *our.* Kids need lots of practice with these patterns in one-syllable words at first, and over time in longer words.
Funky chunks	These patterns found in English words have multiple sounds. They are often referred to as diphthongs and digraphs and are combinations such as *oo, oy, oi, ow, ou, ough, augh.* I call them "funky chunks" to help kids have fun learning them.
Reading long words	Many students can benefit from explicit teaching of how to decode long words, breaking them apart syllable by syllable.
Applying letters and sounds in writing	Teach kids how to *apply* their phonics skills through writing a message related to something they've read. You are helping them with phonics. Reading and writing are reciprocal processes.

Group: _____ Date: _____

Focus: PHONICS

☐ initial letters ☐ final letters ☐ short vowels ☐ blending and CVC
☐ long vowels ☐ vowel + *r* ☐ funky chunks ☐ long words

Warm-Up:

Today's Book/Writing: _____ **Level:** _____

BEFORE READING or WRITING
Book Intro:

DURING READING or WRITING
Prompts:

Notes:

AFTER READING or WRITING
Discuss:

REFLECTION

Phonics Warm-Ups for Small-Group Lessons

- Phonics Bingo—use short-vowel words, words that begin or end with a certain sound, long-vowel words . . . teacher calls out B . . . *cup* . . . and then kids search the B column and mark that word, if they have it.
- Roll the Letter Dice—kids take turns rolling the dice and make words and read them. Be sure to include the vowel dice.
- Word Chain—give kids small strips with a letter on each to make a word and put vowels in a different color; or give kids strips and have them write a word on each with the same phonetic pattern and glue these together to make a chain.
- Word Hunt—have kids find words with the phonics element being studied and write this on a grid. These words can be cut apart and used in sorts also.
- Word Sort—prepare word sort cards, using *All Sorts of Sorts* as a source. *Note:* Have kids tell how sounds of *c* and *g* (and short to long vowels) change based on pattern. Always have kids read the words after sorting! Can choose between different kinds of sorts:
  - closed sort—you tell kids how to sort the words
  - open sort—kids sort however they'd like, and then tell how they sorted their words
  - speed sort—kids sort and try to beat the clock
  - write the sort—kids set up columns labeled with the phonics patterns they will sort for; teacher tells word and kids write it in the appropriate column; teacher holds up word and kids check it.

a	e
cat	peg
Pam	

Note: Always have kids read the sort after they sort the words.

- Phonics Chart—with kids, make an anchor chart about the phonics element being studied. Post it and use it with small groups and review it daily or as needed.
- Guess My Sound—put magnetic letters representing sounds being studied into a paper bag. Kids take turns choosing a letter, identifying it by touch, saying its sound, and pulling it out of the bag. All take turns giving words that have that sound in it. Have kids use the word in a sentence if you need to. Write words they're confusing on a whiteboard as needed.
- Phonics Tic-Tac-Toe—see Lakeshore game for ideas.
- Give Me a Word—show a letter card and have kids take turns giving words that start with that sound. Decide on initial, final, or medial sound.
- Roll the Cube—same as above with letter dice.
- Phonics Concentration—play Concentration game with cards containing words with phonics element being studied. Make a match if the phonics element matches (same

initial letter or sound; same vowel sound; short vowel to long vowel, etc.). Be sure to have kids read word cards each time they turn them over.
- Word Whammer—buy from Leap Frog. Good for blending CVC words.
- Pick It Up—each kid has several word (or letter) cards in front of him or her; each kid has same words (or letters); teacher tells kids which word (or letter) to pick up or can name sound and tell kids to pick up word with that sound.
- Flip It—lay out three stacks of letter cards with consonants at beginning and end; vowels in the middle. Kids take turns flipping over cards to make words and decode them. Have them tell if it's a real word or nonsense word.
- Making Words—give kids letter cards, like *a, t, c, p, e* and have them make certain words with these. Use two letters to make *at*. Add a letter to make it say *cat*, etc. Use Patricia Cunningham's *Making Words* book.
- Try the Other Sound—have letter cards with CVC words that can be changed to long-vowel words: *cap, can, hat, pet, rat, sit, mad, man, pan, pin, mop, rip, tap, kit*. Have kids read word and then "try the other sound" and make that word by changing letters. Also, have them come up with CVC words and "try the other sound." Look at how to change short vowels to long-vowel patterns.
- Chunk the Word—write long word on dry erase board. Kids take turns circling chunks they know and then read through the word. Also teach them to use their finger to find parts they know and then read through it. *Note:* Don't use hard words from the book. Use words with similar phonics patterns. Might use Wiley Blevins book.

Materials Needed:

For Phonics Warm-Ups
- magnetic letters
- letter dice
- sound charts
- letter cards
- Word Whammer by Leap Frog
- *All Sorts of Sorts* by Sheron Brown
- *Making Words* by Patricia Cunningham
- little dry erase boards and markers with built-in erasers
- bingo cards
- word sort cards
- Phonics Tic-Tac-Toe from Lakeshore
- Concentration cards

For Phonics Reading and Writing
- www.readinga-z.com subscription for little leveled books
- desktop file folders to help kids with writing and spelling
- sound charts from *Words Their Way*

Prompts for Phonics

What Child Is Having Trouble With	Possible Teacher Prompts
Initial letter sounds	■ *Look at the first letter. What sound does it make?* ■ *Get your mouth ready.* ■ *Check the picture and the first letter.*
Final letter sounds	■ *Look through the word. Check the last letter, too.* ■ *Check it. What would you expect to see at the end of that word? Were you right?*
Short vowel sounds	■ *What sound does that letter make?* ■ *Use the vowel chart for help.* ■ *That's like in the word _____.* ■ *You know that sound. It's in this word, too.*
CVC patterns and blending sounds	■ *Say the sounds. Put them together fast.* ■ *Use your finger to blend the sounds.* ■ *Is that a real word? Does it make sense?*
Long vowel sounds	■ *Flip it. Try the other sound.* ■ *Use the vowel chart for help. Look at the long vowels.* ■ *Long e can be spelled many different ways. That's one way.*
Vowel + *r* patterns Funky chunks (*oo, oy, oi, ow, ou, ough, augh*)	■ *What sound could those letters make?* ■ *It's like in the word _____.* ■ *Use the (vowel + r or funky chunks) chart.*
Reading long words	■ *Read a part at a time. Put it all together.* ■ *Use your finger to cover up the rest of the word, and read it a part at a time. Move your finger across the word, and read the sounds in order.*
Applying letters and sounds in writing	■ *What letters make that sound?* ■ *Close your eyes. Think about what that word looks like in a book.* ■ *Say the sounds slowly. Write the sounds that you hear in order.* ■ *Clap the word parts. Write the sounds you hear.*

Whole-Group Lesson for PHONICS

Focus: using short vowel sounds in writing

Method to maximize student engagement: shared writing, with students helping to write a message and the teacher being the scribe

Materials: chart paper, black marker, short vowel sound chart with pictures, six-line white correction tape (for covering up errors)

Model: thinking about which short vowel represents the sound needed to write a word

Explicit language:

■ *What letter makes that sound?*

■ *Use the vowel chart for help.*

Lesson:

1. Gather the class near you and decide on a short message with your students. It could be a note to your principal or a request for the custodian or cafeteria.

2. Together decide what you want to say, one sentence at a time. Have kids help you spell words with short vowel sounds. Refer to the chart and help them decide upon the correct vowel.

3. After you write a sentence, go back and reread it. Then add the next sentence. Write a message that's a bit more advanced than you'd expect students to write independently.

4. When you're finished writing the message, have students come up to the chart paper and circle or highlight words with short vowel sounds. Have them read these words together.

Small-group connection: Review the short vowel sound chart before reading a new book that has lots of short-vowel words. Remind students that they know these sounds and that when they see words with these vowels, they can use the sounds to help them figure out the new words. During the lesson, praise students for using the chart if needed and for reading the correct short vowel sound to problem-solve on new words. After reading, students might go on a word hunt in their new book for short-vowel words to reinforce these patterns. Do writing in response to what they read also. You might share the pen and write together in small group.

Note: This same type of lesson could be done with long vowel sounds. Focus on a particular long vowel or two, though.

Whole-Group Lesson for PHONICS

Focus: decoding CVC words and blending sounds

Method to maximize student engagement: word sorting

Materials: pocket chart, large letter cards, word cards (three-by-five-inch)

Model: how to blend known sounds to read words; how to change the first letter to make a new word

Explicit language:

- *Say the sounds. Put them together fast.*
- *Use your finger to blend the sounds.*
- *Is that a real word? Does it make sense?*

Lesson:

1. Seat the children around a large pocket chart. Tell them they are going to help you make words with letters they know.

2. Start with letters they know. Hand each child a letter card. Then say a word, and have those kids bring their letters up to the chart (in order). For example, for *mat*, the children with *m*, *a*, and *t* come up and place their letters in the pocket chart. Then blend the sounds together to read the word. Place a word card that says *mat* beside the letters and have the class read it with you again.

3. Then take away the *m* and ask for the letter that will make this word say *hat*. Have the child holding *h* come up to the chart and place the *h* in front of *at*. Blend the sounds together and repeat as above.

4. Continue making words, including *mat, cat, hat, sat, that, fat, rat, bat, flat, splat*. Then make another family of words, such as *jam, yam, bam, slam, ram, wham, swam*.

5. Put a word card like *cat* on the top left of the pocket chart and read it together. Put a word card from the other word family, like *jam*, on the top right of the pocket chart. Hold up the cards, one at a time; have kids read each with you and point to the side it goes with. Sort the words by word family and read them.

Small-group connection: Give kids magnetic letters or letter cards and have them build several CVC words with you before reading a book with CVC words in it. Remind them that they know how to blend and to do this as they read today.

Whole-Group Lesson for PHONICS

Focus: decoding long words

Method to maximize student engagement: shared reading of a poem or nonfiction text

Materials: transparency or PowerPoint of a poem or nonfiction text with several multisyllabic words that students might not recognize instantly

Model: how to break a word into parts, read each syllable, and blend them together

Explicit language:

■ *Read a part at a time. Put it all together.*

■ *Use your finger to cover up the rest of the word, and read it a part at a time. Move your finger across the word, and read the sounds in order.*

Lesson:

1. Project a poem or short piece of nonfiction text onto the board.
2. Read it with the students. Pause when you get to a long word, such as *permission*. Show kids how to look at one part of the word at a time, syllable by syllable, read each part, and then blend them together. Then go back and reread the phrase or sentence to be sure it makes sense.
3. Repeat several times, reiterating the process of how to decode a long word.

Small-group connection: Review this process by writing several long words on a dry erase board. Have kids take turns circling parts they know, and then blending the sounds together. Remind students to do this as they read by using their finger to look across the word and blending together the parts in order to decode the new word. Also tell them to go back and reread if they've forgotten what the sentence was about.

Making the Most of Small Groups: Differentiation for All by Debbie Diller. www.debbiediller.com. Copyright © 2007. Stenhouse Publishers.

G

Vocabulary

Possible Focuses for Vocabulary Lessons

Recognizing new words	My goal is to teach children to stop and say, "Hey, I don't know what that word means. Let me try to figure that out."
Getting meaning from context (pictures, other words)	Teach students several ways to figure out what a new word means. Young children can be taught to scan a picture for help. Also teach kids to use the context of other words surrounding it. You might teach children to *read before and after* the new word to find out what it means. Be aware, though, that not all text gives a supportive meaning directly in the words that precede or follow it.
Learning new definitions of multiple-meaning words	Teach students to be on the lookout for old words with new meanings, or multiple-meaning words, as they're often called.
Using word parts to determine meaning	Teach kids to stop and say, "Hey, that word starts with *re* and that means 'again.' So *reopen* must mean 'to open again.'" Move beyond having kids just learn that *re* means "again."
Thinking about book language and idioms	Book language is the way writers sometimes use phrases or groups of words that we wouldn't normally use in speaking, such as, "The moon climbed higher in the sky" instead of, "Look. The moon is way up in the sky." Teach students the meaning of idioms. Idioms consist of a group of words that have little or nothing to do with the individual words, such as, "Don't let the cat out of the bag."
Using text features like bold and italicized words in informational text	Most of the new words in nonfiction are content-specific and are often Tier III words. Show kids how to use these text features (such as bold and italicized words) to figure out a word's meaning. If a bold or italicized word is followed by a dash or the word *or*, the definition will most definitely be the next thing they read. Also teach kids how to use a glossary or word bank in nonfiction.
Using dictionaries and reference aids to learn word meanings and gain deeper knowledge of words	Teach the use of a dictionary to find out word meanings with care, and don't overuse it. I prefer to teach how to use a glossary while reading informational text, since this is a built-in reference tool.
Trying out the word in new contexts and a variety of ways	Encourage students to use the words introduced before reading or found during reading as much as possible. Have them use these words during the school day and at home. You might even chart the words and have kids add tally marks to show each time they use a word correctly in their reading or writing.

Group: _____ **Date:** _____

Focus: VOCABULARY

- ☐ new word recognition
- ☐ using word parts
- ☐ book language/idioms

- ☐ meaning from context
- ☐ NF text features

- ☐ multiple meanings
- ☐ using new words

Warm-Up: Familiar Rereading   **Listen to:** _____ **Title:** _____

Today's Book: _____ **Level:** _____

BEFORE READING

New Words:

Book Intro:

DURING READING

Prompts:

Notes:

AFTER READING

Discuss:

New Words:

REFLECTION

Prompts for Vocabulary

What Child Is Having Trouble With	Possible Teacher Prompts
Recognition of unknown words	■ *You stopped. What can you do to figure out what that word means?* ■ *Do you know that word?* ■ *Asking about that word can help you learn what it means. _____ means _____.*
Using context to determine word meaning	■ *Use the picture to help you figure out what that word means.* ■ *Read on a bit. See if you can find clues to what that word means.* ■ *Which words give you a clue to the word's meaning?* ■ *What do you think it means? Why?* ■ *What's another word you could use here that makes sense?*
Thinking about book language and idioms	■ *What do you think* off they went *means?* ■ *The author said* legs like sticks. *What do you picture there?*
Using text features like bold or italicized words, dashes, and *or* in informational text to figure out what those words mean	■ *When a writer uses bold words, he's showing you that those words are important. Good noticing.* ■ *Look at this (point to dash or word* or*). It tells us the definition will follow!* ■ *It's written in italics. How can that help you?*
Learning new definitions of multiple-meaning words	■ *What does _____ usually mean? Does it mean that here? What do you think it means?* ■ *This word has more than one meaning. What could it mean here?*
Using word parts to determine word meanings	■ *You know this part. What's* re- *mean?* ■ *Look at our suffix chart. What's* -ful *mean? What could this word mean?* ■ *Find a part you know. What does that part mean?*
Trying out new words in oral and written vocabulary	■ *You sound so grown up when you use those "million-dollar words."* ■ *I love that new word! Use it at home to impress your family!* ■ *What a great word choice! I can really picture what you mean when you use that word.*

Whole-Group Lesson for VOCABULARY

Focus: awareness of new words and getting meaning from context

Method to maximize student engagement: shared reading with all students reading together

Materials: poem on a chart or Big Book that contains a few Tier II words; highlighter tape cut into pieces the length of words it will cover

Model: stopping and paying attention to new words, and then trying to figure out what they mean

Explicit language:

- *Asking about that word will help you learn what it means. Good noticing! _____ means _____.*
- *Yes, that is a new word. What do you think it means?*

Lesson:

1. Choose a poem or Big Book that has a few Tier II words, such as *befriended*, *stranded*, and *wary*.
2. If using a poem, copy it in large print onto a chart. Precut several pieces of highlighter tape the length of individual new words. Put them on an index card so they'll be handy.
3. Gather the class near you and read the Big Book or poem to them. Then read it with them. As you read it a second time, ask them to tell you if they hear any new words. Place highlighter tape over each new word. Tell children they should stop and think, "That's a new word" when they come across a new word in their reading. That's how they'll start to learn new words.
4. Figure out what the words mean together. Relate the new words to things your students already know about. For example, "If you do not feel safe about something and don't really trust it, you might say you are *wary*. I am *wary* of climbing up on that rock, because I'm afraid I might fall and hurt myself. You should be *wary* of taking a spelling test if you haven't studied. Can you think of something you're *wary* of?

Small-group connection: Precut highlighter tape the size of individual words in the little book they'll read. Give each child an index card with several pieces of tape on it. Have them use the highlighter tape to mark new words as they read. Share and discuss the words and their meanings.

Whole-Group Lesson for VOCABULARY

Focus: direct teaching of new vocabulary, using context of a story to help kids connect and remember the new words

Method to maximize student engagement: "Text Talk" by reading aloud a book with several Tier II words in it

Materials: trade book with several Tier II words pre-selected; chart paper for recording new words

Model: formulating kid-friendly definitions; using the new words multiple times in a variety of ways

Explicit language:
- *This new word, _____, means _____.*
- *Show me how you might look if you _____.*

Lesson:
1. Choose three Tier II words from a book you'll read aloud.
2. Read aloud the book. After reading, share each new word and relate its meaning to the book. *Jeremy felt panicked, or really nervous, when his enemy ate the Enemy Pie because he thought it had poison in it.*
3. Kids repeat the new word, *panicked*. Explain its meaning and give a few quick examples of the word in other contexts.
4. Then have kids give examples of when they felt *panicked*.
5. Have them repeat the new word.
6. Repeat the procedure with other new words from the book, such as *relieved*, *squinted*, and *ingredients*.
7. Close by having the children tell you how they would look if they were *relieved*, when they might *squint*, and where they could find *ingredients* for a cake.
8. You might add these new words to a wall display labeled "Wow Words." Use these words whenever possible, and encourage children to do the same.

Small-group connection: Introduce Tier II words that are essential to the comprehension of a new book before reading in small group in a similar way. Read the title first and look at the cover; then connect the new words to what kids already know. Help them use the new words.

Whole-Group Lesson for VOCABULARY

Focus: trying out new words in new contexts and a variety of ways

Method to maximize student engagement: modeled writing or writing and thinking aloud in front of the class

Materials: chart paper and markers; new words posted on a chart or board or pocket chart (words gathered during read-aloud or other whole-group reading teaching)

Model: how to choose and use new words in writing about something you know and care about

Explicit language:

- ◼ *What a great word choice! That word will really help others picture what we're trying to say.*
- ◼ *That's a "million-dollar word." It makes our writing sound so much richer.*

Lesson:

1. Tell students that good writers think about the words they choose as they write messages. Tell them that today as you write, you are going to be thinking about using the best words you can to help the reader picture your message.

2. Choose a topic to write about—something the kids can relate to, like a time you were sad or excited. Be sure you can use a few of the words on your word chart to enhance your writing.

3. Write your story on the chart paper and think aloud about the words you choose. Ask the children for their input. Model how to cross out a word and choose a better word. Praise them for the rich words they help you select.

4. As you write, periodically stop and reread what you've written. Show the kids how you ponder your word choices to see if your message is the best it can be, or if a different word would paint a clearer picture for the reader. Have kids join in with you as you read, and ask them what they think.

Small-group connection: As you read and write with students in small groups, help them be aware of and use rich words. Encourage them to use these meaningfully and across a variety of contexts.

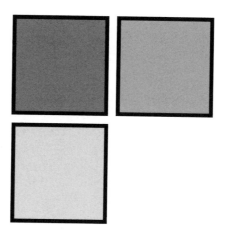

References

Adams, M. 1990. *Beginning to Read: Thinking and Learning About Print.* Cambridge, MA: MIT Press.

Allington, R. L. 1983. "The Reading Instruction Provided Readers of Differing Reading Abilities." *Elementary School Journal* 83 (5): 548–559.

———. 2005. *What Really Matters for Struggling Readers: Designing Research-Based Programs,* 2nd edition. Boston: Allyn and Bacon.

Anderson, R. C., E. H. Hiebert, J. A. Scott, and I. A. G. Wilkinson. 1985. *Becoming a Nation of Readers: The Report of the Commission on Reading.* Champaign, IL: Center for the Study of Reading.

Armbruster, B. B., T. H. Anderson, and J. L. Meyer. 1991. "Improving Content-Area Reading Using Instructional Graphics." *Reading Research Quarterly* 26: 393–416.

Baker, L., and A. L. Brown. 1984. "Metacognitive Skills and Reading." In *Handbook of Reading Research,* ed. P. Pearson, R. Barr, M. L. Kamil, and P. Mosenthal. White Plains, NY: Longman.

Baker, S., D. Simmons, and E. Kameenui. 1995. *Vocabulary Acquisition: Synthesis of the Research.* National Center to Improve the Tools of Education. Available online through the University of Oregon at http://idea.uoregon.edu/~ncite/documents/techrep/tech13.

Ball, D., and B. Blachman. 1988a. "Does Phoneme Awareness Training in Kindergarten Make a Difference in Early Word Recognition and Developmental Spelling?" *Reading Research Quarterly* 26: 49–66.

Ball, E. W., and B. A. Blachman. 1988b. "Phoneme Segmentation Training: Effect on Reading Readiness." *Annals of Dyslexia* 38: 220–225.

Balmuth, M. 1982. The *Roots of Phonics: A Historical Introduction.* New York: McGraw-Hill.

Baumann, J., and E. Kameenui. 1991. "Research on Vocabulary Instruction: Ode to Voltaire." In *Handbook of Research on Teaching the English Language Arts,* ed. J. Flood, J. M. Jensen, D. Lapp, and J. R. Squire. New York: MacMillan.

———. 2004. *Vocabulary Instruction: Research to Practice.* New York: Guilford.

Beck, I. 2002. *Bringing Words to Life: Robust Vocabulary Instruction.* New York: Guilford.

———. 2006. *Making Sense of Phonics: The Hows and Whys.* New York: Guilford.

Beck, I., and M. McKeown. 2001. "Text Talk: Capturing the Benefits of Read-Aloud Experiences for Young Children." *Reading Teacher* 55 (1): 10–20.

Bentin, S., and H. Leshem. 1993. "On the Interaction Between Phonological Awareness and Reading Acquisition: It's a Two-Way Street." *Annals of Dyslexia* 43: 125–148.

Bereiter, C., and M. Bird. 1985. "Use of Thinking Aloud in Identification and Teaching of Reading Comprehension Strategies." *Cognition and Instruction* 2: 131–156.

Biemiller, A. 1977–78. "Relationships Between Oral Reading Rates for Letters, Words, and Simple Text in the Development of Reading Achievement." *Reading Research Quarterly* 13: 223–253.

———. 2004. "Teaching Vocabulary in the Primary Grades." In *Vocabulary Instruction: Research to Practice*, ed. J. F. Baumann and E. J. Kameenui. New York: Guilford.

Blevins, W. 1998. *Phonics from A-Z: A Practical Guide.* New York: Scholastic.

Blum, I., P. Koskinen, N. Tennant, E. Parker, M. Straub, and C. Curry. 1995. "Using Audiotaped Books to Extend Classroom Literacy Instruction into the Homes of Second-Language Learners." *Journal of Reading Behavior* 27 (4): 535–563.

Brown, R. 2002. "Straddling Two Worlds: Self-Directed Comprehension Instruction for Middle Schoolers." In *Comprehension Instruction: Research-Based Best Practices*, ed. C. C. Block and M. Pressley. New York: Guilford.

Bruck, M., and R. Treiman. 1992. "Learning to Pronounce Words: The Limitations of Analogies." *Reading Research Quarterly* 27: 374–388.

Chall, J. 1967. *Learning to Read: The Great Debate.* New York: McGraw-Hill.

Clay, M. 2000. *Running Records for Classroom Teachers.* Portsmouth, NH: Heinemann.

Cunningham, A. 1990. "Explicit Versus Implicit Instruction in Phonemic Awareness." *Journal of Experimental Child Psychology* 50 (3): 429–444.

Dale, E., and J. O'Rourke. 1986. *Vocabulary Building.* Columbus, OH: Zaner-Bloser.

Davey, B., and S. McBride. 1986. "Effects of question generating training on reading comprehension." *Journal of Educational Psychology* 78 (4): 256–262.

Diller, D. 2003. *Literacy Work Stations: Making Centers Work.* Portland, ME: Stenhouse.

———. 2005. *Practice with Purpose: Literacy Work Stations for Grades 3–6.* Portland, ME: Stenhouse.

Ehri, L. 1984. "How Orthography Alters Spoken Language Competencies in Children Learning to Read and Spell." In *Language Awareness and Learning to Read*, ed. J. Downing and R. Valtin. Mahwah, NJ: Erlbaum.

Ehri, L., and L. Wilce. 1987. "Does Learning to Spell Help Beginners Learn to Read Words?" *Reading Research Quarterly* 22 (1): 48–65.

Ehri, L., and C. Robbins. 1992. "Beginners Need Some Decoding Skill to Read Words by Analogy." *Reading Research Quarterly* 27: 13–26.

Fountas, I. C., and G. S. Pinnell. 1996. *Guided Reading: Good First Teaching for All Children.* Portsmouth, NH: Heinemann.

Gough, P., and C. Juel. 1990. "Does Phonics Teach the Cipher?" Paper presented at the annual meeting of the American Educational Research Association, Boston, MA.

Graves, M., C. Juel, and B. Graves. 1998. *Teaching Reading in the Twenty-First Century.* Boston: Allyn and Bacon.

Hasbrouck, J. E., C. Ihnot, and G. H. Rogers. 1999. "'Read Naturally': A Strategy to Increase Oral Reading Fluency." *Reading Research and Instruction* 39 (1): 27–38.

Henderson, E. 1981. *Learning to Read and Spell.* DeKalb, IL: Northern Illinois Press.

Hurford, D. P., J. D. Schauf, L. Bunce, T. Blaich, and K. Moore. 1994. "Early Identification of Children at Risk for Reading Disabilities." *Journal of Learning Disabilities* 27: 371–382.

Johns, J., and R. Berglund. 2002. *Fluency: Questions, Answers, Evidence-Based Strategies.* Dubuque, IA: Kendall/Hunt.

Johnson, F. 2001. "The Utility of Phonics Generalizations: Let's Take Another Look at Clymer's Conclusions." *The Reading Teacher* 55: 132–143.

Juel, C. 1994. *Learning to Read and Write in One Elementary School.* New York: Springer-Verlag.

Juel, C., and C. Minden-Cupp. 1999. *Learning to Read Words: Linguistic Units and Strategies.* Ann Arbor, MI: University of Michigan Center for the Improvement of Early Reading Achievement.

Klingner, J., S. Vaughn, and J. Schumm. 1998. "Collaborative Strategic Reading During Social Studies in Heterogeneous Fourth-Grade Classrooms." *Elementary School Journal* 99 (1): 3–22.

Kuhn, M., and S. Stahl. 1998. "Teaching Children to Learn Word Meanings from Context: A Synthesis and Some Questions." *Journal of Literacy Research* 30 (1): 119–138.

LaBerge, D., and S. J. Samuels. 1974. "Toward a Theory of Automatic Information Processing in Reading." *Cognitive Psychology* 6: 293–323.

Liberman, I. Y., and D. Shankweiler. 1979. "Speech, the Alphabet, and Teaching to Read." In *Theory and Practice of Early Reading, Vol. 2*, ed. L. B. Resnik and P. A. Weaver. Hillsdale, NJ: Erlbaum.

Lundberg, I., J. Frost, and O. Petersen. 1988. "Effects of an Extensive Program for Stimulating Phonological Awareness in Preschool Children." *Reading Research Quarterly* 23 (3): 263–284.

McKeown, M., I. Beck, R. Omanson, and M. Pople. 1985. "Some Effects of the Nature and Frequency of Vocabulary Instruction on the Knowledge and Use of Words." *Reading Research Quarterly* 20 (5): 522–535.

Nagy, W., and R. Anderson. 1984. "How Many Words Are There in Printed School English?" *Reading Research Quarterly* 19: 304–330.

Nagy, W., and J. Scott. 2000. "Vocabulary Processes." In *Handbook of Reading Research, Vol. 3,* ed. M. Kamil, P. Mosenthal, P. Pearson, and R. Barr. Mahwah, NJ: Erlbaum.

National Reading Panel. 2000. *Teaching Children to Read: An Evidence-Based Assessment of the Scientific Research Literature on Reading and Its Implications for Reading Instruction.* Bethesda, MD: National Institute of Child Health and Human Development. Available online at http://www.nichd.nih.gov/publications/nrp/upload/smallbook_pdf.pdf.

Nicholson, T., and B. Whyte. 1992. "Matthew Effects in Learning New Words While Listening to Stories." In *Literacy Research, Theory, and Practice: Views from Many Perspectives: Forty-First Yearbook of the National Reading Conference,* ed. C. Kinzer and D. Leu. Chicago: National Reading Conference.

Parker, F. W. 1894. *Talks on Pedagogics.* New York: E. L. Kellogg.

Pearson, P., R. Barr, M. L. Kamil, and P. Mosenthal, eds. 1984. *Handbook of Reading Research.* White Plains, NY: Longman.

Pinnell, G. S., J. J. Pikulski, K. K. Wixson, J. R. Campbell, P. B. Gough, and A. S. Beatty. 1995. *Listening to Children Read Aloud: Data from NAEP's Integrated Reading Performance Record at Grade 4.* Washington, DC: National Center for Education Statistics, U.S. Department of Education.

Pressley, M., and V. Woloshyn, eds. 1995. *Cognitive Strategy Instruction That Really Improves Children's Academic Performance, 2nd ed.* Cambridge, MA: Brookline.

Pressley, M., P. El-Dinary, and R. Brown. 1992. "Skilled and Not-So Skilled Reading: Good Information Processing and Not-So-Good Information Processing." In *Promoting Academic Competence and Literacy in School,* ed. M. Pressley, K. Harris, and J. Guthrie. San Diego: Academic Press.

Rasinski, T. 1990. "Investigating Measures of Reading Fluency." *Educational Research Quarterly* 14 (3): 34–44.

Robbins, C., and L. Ehri. 1994. "Reading Storybooks to Kindergartners Helps Them Learn New Vocabulary Words." *Journal of Educational Psychology* 86 (1): 54–64.

Rosenblatt, L. M. 1978. *The Reader, the Text, the Poem: The Transactional Theory of the Literary Work.* Carbondale, IL: Southern Illinois University Press.

Samuels, S. 2002. "Reading Fluency: Its Development and Assessment." In *What Research Has to Say About Reading Instruction,* ed. A. Farstrup and S. Samuels. Newark, DE: International Reading Association.

Schulman, M. B., and C. D. Payne. 2000. *Guided Reading: Making It Work.* New York: Scholastic.

Senechal, M. 1997. "The Differential Effect of Storybook Reading on Preschoolers' Acquisition of Expressive and Receptive Vocabulary." *Journal of Child Language* 24 (1): 123–138.

Shany, M., and A. Biemiller. 1995. "Assisted Reading Practice: Effects on Performance for Poor Readers in Grades 3 and 4." *Reading Research Quarterly* 30 (3): 382–395.

Smith, J., and W. Elley. 1997. *How Children Learn to Read.* Katonah, NY: Richard C. Owen.

Stahl, S. 1999. *Vocabulary Development.* Cambridge, MA: Brookline.

Stallings, J. 1980. "Allocated Academic Learning Time Revisited, or Beyond Time on Task." *Educational Researcher* 8 (11): 11–16.

Stanovich, K. 1986. "Matthew Effects in Reading: Some Consequences of Individual Differences in the Development of Reading Fluency." *Reading Research Quarterly* 21: 360–406.

———. 1994. "Romance Versus Reality." *Reading Teacher* 47 (4): 280–291.

Taylor, N., M. Wade, and F. Yekovich. 1985. "The Effects of Text Manipulation and Multiple Reading Strategies on the Reading Performance of Good and Poor Readers." *Reading Research Quarterly* 20 (5): 566–574.

Templeton, S. 1997. *Teaching the Integrated Language Arts, 2nd ed.* Boston: Houghton Mifflin.

Torgesen, J., S. T. Morgan, and C. Davis. 1992. "Effects of Two Types of Phonological Awareness Training on Word Learning in Kindergarten Children." *Journal of Educational Psychology* 84 (3): 364–370.

Uhry, J. K., and M. J. Shepherd. 1993. "Segmentation and Spelling Instruction as Part of a First-Grade Reading Program: Effects on Several Measures of Reading." *Reading Research Quarterly* 28: 219–233.

van den Broek, P., and K. Kremer, 2000. "The Mind in Action: What It Means to Comprehend During Reading." In *Reading for Meaning: Fostering Comprehension in the Middle Grades,* ed. B. Taylor, M. Graves, and P. van den Broek. New York: Teachers College Press.

Yopp, H. 1992. "Developing Phonemic Awareness in Young Children." *The Reading Teacher* 45: 696–703.

Children's Literature Cited

Alexander, D. 1998. *Pignocchio.* Austin, TX: Steck-Vaughn. (Pair-It Books series.)

Buxton, J. 1989. *Can You Carry It, Harriet?* Auckland, New Zealand: Shortland Publications. (Literacy 2000 series from Rigby in the U.S.)

Galdone, P. 2006. *The Three Little Pigs.* New York: Clarion.

George, J. C. 1996. *One Day in the Alpine Tundra.* New York: HarperTrophy.

Ginsburg, M. 1988. *The Chick and the Duckling.* New York: Aladdin.

Marriott, J. 2002. *When Foxes Came to Stay.* Huntington Beach, CA: Pacific Learning. (Double Takes series.)

Marshall, E. 1994. *Four on the Shore.* New York: Puffin.

Martin, A. T. 2006. *Ten Kids, No Pets.* New York: Scholastic.

Opie, R. 2002. *Five Senses.* Vernon Hills, IL: ETA/Cuisinaire. (Sun Sprouts series.)

Osborne, M. P. 1992. *Dinosaurs Before Dark.* New York: Random House. (Magic Tree House series.)

———. 1994. *Pirates Past Noon.* New York: Random House. (Magic Tree House series.)

Prince, S. 1999. *Playing.* Littleton, MA: Sundance Publishing. (Alpha Kids series.)

Rylant, C. 1996. *Henry and Mudge: The First Book.* New York: Aladdin.

Schaefer, L. M. 1999. *Abraham Lincoln.* Mankato, MN: Capstone Press. (Pebble Books series.)

———. 2001a. *How Did This City Grow?* Pelham, NY: Benchmark Education.

———. 2001b. *Letter to a Friend.* Pelham, NY: Benchmark Education. (Early Connections series.)

Seuss, Dr. 1957. *Cat in the Hat.* New York: Random House.

Smith, A., J. Giles, and B. Randall. 2000. *Big Sea Animals.* Crystal Lake, IL: Rigby. (Rigby PM Plus series.)

Steele, J. 1997. *How Lizard Lost His Colors.* Auckland, New Zealand: Shortland Publications. (Literacy Tree series from Rigby in the U.S.)

Walter, M. P. 1990. *Justin and the Best Biscuits in the World.* New York: Yearling.

Williams, R. L. 1991. *Who's Hiding?* New York: Little Simon.

Wiseman, B. 1983. *Morris Goes to School.* New York: HarperTrophy.

———. 1989. *Morris the Moose.* New York: HarperCollins.

Woodland Mysteries series. De Soto, TX: The Wright Group.